PROUD TO BE

KELLY FLINN

PROUD TO BE

RANDOM HOUSE NEW YORK

Library of Congress Cataloging-in-Publication Data

Flinn, Kelly.
Proud to be / Kelly Flinn.
p.   cm.
ISBN 0-375-50109-8 (alk. paper)
1. Flinn, Kelly.   2. Women air pilots—United States—Biography.
3. United States.   Air Force—Biography.   4. B-2 bomber.   I. Title.
UG626.2.F59A3   1997
358.4'0092–dc21
[B]   97-41542

All photographs courtesy of the author.

Random House website address: www.randomhouse.com

Printed in the United States of America on acid-free paper

24689753

FIRST EDITION

Book design by Carole Lowenstein

I dedicate this book to my entire family.
Without their unconditional love and support,
I would never have made it this far.
Thank you for generating the wind
to keep my wings aloft.

Stretch.
Anyone can be good,
but only those who stretch
can be brilliant.

—Frank Belatti, soccer coach

AUTHOR'S NOTE

The following are pseudonyms, to protect the identity of those still on active duty, and others: Scott, Kevin, Veronica, Elizabeth, Captain Brian Green, "The Doc," Tom, Allison, Lazarus, Jane, and Ellen.

CONTENTS

PROLOGUE

One year ago, I was a B-52 bomber pilot. I flew highly classified missions and was trained to carry nuclear weapons. I was entrusted with defending the most powerful nation on earth. I loved defending that nation. I was committed to protecting it from its enemies, abroad and at home.

Six months ago, I was called a threat to national security. I was sent to court-martial. The Air Force, the institution I loved—my home, my base, my identity—now considered me its enemy. I was considered unfit to defend my country.

All because I loved the wrong man.

I was twenty-five years old. I'd never been in love before. I didn't know how to tell a true friend from a liar. This was, in large measure, a failure of my education. The Air Force had taught me to operate some of the most complicated machinery in the world. I could fly a Stratofortress. I could drop weapons of mass destruction. I could evade capture and survive in the wilderness by eating bugs and drinking mud. But I had no knowledge of the workings of the human heart. I had never read a manual that could tell me how to love and be loved.

My story should have ended when the relationship did—as it would have, inevitably, once the lies came to the surface. And then, like so many other twenty-five-year-olds, I would have been simply a fool for love. I would have suffered, recovered, and moved on with my life. But too many forces were weighing in against me, judging me, scrutinizing me, waiting for me to slip up. And so, instead of simply being another woman who loved the wrong man, I am the woman who made history. I was once the First Female Bomber Pilot. I am now the First Female Bomber Pilot to Have Been Forced Out of the Air Force. I am a celebrity. I am a lightning rod for debate—to advocates of women's rights, a poster girl; to others, a symbol of all that is wrong with having women in the military.

I never wanted to be any of these things. I never wanted to be a poster girl of any kind. I just wanted to be a pilot—the best pilot I could be. Not a "woman pilot." Not a first. Not an icon. But, because the Air Force needed me to be a poster girl, I couldn't just fly. And because I was a poster girl, I couldn't just be a fool for love in private. My case touched a nerve, which resonated all the way up and down the Air Force chain of command. It couldn't be swept under a rug, and handled quietly, as every consensual-sex case I'd seen before had been. It took on a life of its own. It became a national issue.

I am not writing this book with an eye to proving my innocence or guilt. The story is far too complicated for that. I have made errors of judgment, errors that I will regret for the rest of my life. I did not believe that the Air Force could actually care about my love life. I thought if I held my breath long enough and closed my eyes, I could make a bad situation go away. I was wrong. I was arrogant, perhaps. I was foolish and in love. I am writing because, despite the reams of newsprint that have been devoted to my case, despite all the photo spreads, cover stories, talk show hours, and testimony, the real story has never been captured, nor have I been able to speak freely and fully.

For some, my life story is an emblem of the barriers that still exist to women's achievement and to the full integration of women into the armed forces. For them, I am a heroine who was used and abused by a cynical and sexist military. For others, my life story is a cautionary tale about what happens when the military lets down its guard and discipline falls apart. As they see it, I have not been punished enough. I don't expect this book to resolve that debate. But I do expect it to allow me to get on with the business of being a person, not an icon. The Air Force trained me for many things, but did not teach me how to be a human being. That was touch-and-go all the way, a kind of apprenticeship by fire. And in this past year of living in the media spotlight, my human side fell casualty to the demands of the news of the day. I have been handled and packaged, represented and advised, and never given a chance to speak openly for myself. I swallowed my pride and my protests and took the noncriminal punishment of a general discharge (under honorable conditions) from the Air Force. In doing so, I was saved from the indignities of court-martial and a possible jail term and gained a kind of negotiated peace. But it was, as far as I am concerned, a peace without honor. A peace without understanding or resolution. Now is my chance to set the record straight and say my piece.

This is my day in court.

PROUD TO BE

CHAPTER 1

Playing to Win

No one can predict to what heights you can soar, even you will not know until you spread your wings.

—FROM A POSTER ENTITLED "GOALS"

ANYONE WHO SAYS THAT WOMEN AREN'T MEANT TO BE WAR-riors doesn't know much about little girls. Little girls are intense, stubborn, and passionate. Some, of course, put their intensity into pushing baby buggies and dressing up their dolls. But others are simply wildcats. They're the fastest kids in the class. They're the terrors of the jungle gym and swings. They play competitive sports to win. They don't mind getting down and dirty in the mud. And they're no less girlish for it.

I was that kind of little girl. I was the baby of my family, with four much older brothers and sisters. (Another older brother, Kevin, died of spina bifida after only one month of life.) For the first years of my life, my role in the family was to be cute. At my Catholic school, St. Monica's, I tried to give the impression of being a perfect student. I sat quietly, day in and day out, in my red-and-black-plaid jumper, trying to please the sisters. But I wore red athletic shorts under my jumper, and the moment I was out of the classroom, there was no stopping me.

I was the terror of the playground: fast, furious, competitive. When I was five, I joined my first soccer league. I played on a boys' team—there wasn't a girls' team in Creve Coeur, Missouri, then. When the boys ran around the field trying to kiss me, I'd run the other way. I was there to play—and to win. I was training to beat my brother Don, who'd taught me to play by kicking a soccer ball around the yard with me when he came home from college. Never mind that he was fourteen years older and a varsity athlete. With daily practice, I believed, I could take him on.

I *had* to be combative, with two older brothers. Getting what I wanted, holding my own, was often a matter of hand-to-hand combat. My brother Tim, for example, used to fight me every afternoon over my choice of TV programs. I could watch whatever I wanted—provided I could get past him to the TV set to change channels. He was eight years older than I, so this wasn't easy, particularly since he had a trick: he'd pick me up by my feet, hold me upside down, and scream: "It's the pile driver!" That usually put an end to the fight, left me screaming and laughing while my father yelled, "Knock it off!" from upstairs. The next day, we would start up again. It was like trench warfare: little progress, many casualties. Tim also used to practice his hockey skills with me in the basement. I'd don a goalie mask and a baseball mitt and grab a hockey stick; then he'd move a few paces back and take slap shots at me with a tennis ball. Every once in a while, he'd body-slam me against our rec room walls. I defended myself pretty well, considering that he was sixteen and I was only eight. It honed the reflexes I'd need for soccer playing. And my survival skills.

Things were different, of course, with my sisters, Patti and Gail. Unfortunately, since they were ten and eleven years older than I, we weren't very close while I was a child. I glimpsed their teenage lives from a distance: clothes, makeup, hair worries, and dates were all part of a mysterious world just out of my reach. Gail was a cheerleader who knew how to have a good time; Patti, who is deaf, was a top swimmer and basketball player. I admired them enormously, but I couldn't really be like them. I tried to play with the dolls they'd handed down to me, but I couldn't figure out how. The dolls seemed like such lifeless things. They were boring. One of them, Chatty Cathy, actually frightened me. I'd inherited her from a neighboring family after their daughter, a good friend of Gail's, committed suicide. The doll was eighteen inches long, with brown hair and a slot in her back for a two-inch record. You would insert the record into the slot and pull a string on her back and she'd repeat, "I'm Chatty Cathy," over and over again. I used to have nightmares about Chatty Cathy. The thought of her still spooks me today.

Patti and Gail's Barbie dolls simply stumped me. I just didn't know how to play with them. I'd take two of the dolls by their skinny plastic legs and hold them opposite each other, pretending that they were having a conversation; I'd shake them up and down, move them around, try to create some action. But nothing ever happened. So I'd throw them aside and end up reaching for the yellow Tonka trucks or Hot Wheels cars I'd inherited from my brothers. I'd rush out of my bedroom and into the backyard, climb onto the dirt pile, and toss the trucks to the ground, filling them with dirt, battling with ants and worms, throwing spiders into the back of the cement truck and taking them for a ride. My parents tried to spur my interest in dolls by buying me Barbie's airplane set. I loved the plane: I pictured myself flying around the world, solving mysteries, having adventures. Barbie and friends just tagged along for the ride.

Had there been some little girls in my neighborhood, they might have been able to show me how to play with dolls. But there were just little boys. My best friend was a boy named Tommy who lived next door. He had all the orange plastic tracks for the Hot Wheels car set and was always up for a race or for building a fort in his living room. Or, if we felt like going outside, we'd hike off to our nearby creek, where we'd chase frogs, catch tadpoles and turtles, and cover ourselves head to toe in mud.

Being a tomboy wasn't anything I ever thought about as a child. With no girls in the neighborhood, I had no one to compare myself with, and my parents didn't pressure me to be a "real" girl. My mother did try, it's true, to interest me in ballet and tap dancing. But she let those go pretty easily, once it became clear that I wasn't having any of them. She'd learned, early on, that it was virtually impossible to get me to do something I didn't want to do. I never wanted, for example, to wear skirts or dresses. I felt they cramped my style. They kept me from scrambling up jungle gyms and from running as fast as I could in races, beating all the boys. This wasn't much of a problem on school days—I wore shorts under my jumper. But it led to a major conflict when I was seven and first-communion time came around. The ceremony was extremely important to my mother. We were practicing Catholics; we went to mass every Sunday and on devotional days. My mother insisted I dress correctly: white dress, white veil, no shorts. We battled over this for weeks. My mother—as I came to realize when the Air Force turned our lives into a circus—is every bit as strong-willed as I am. So I gave in. I dressed; she inspected me, making sure I didn't have on shorts, and then she went to the ceremony. Little did she know I had hidden a pair of red gym shorts in the car. I balled them up in my hands, took them with me into the school assembly room, ran to the back, hid behind the coats, and discreetly put my shorts on under my dress. Then I donned my white gloves and fell in line for the procession with a big smile on my face.

Puberty changed everything. When you're a little girl, you can basically get away with doing and being whatever you want, provided you have the support and encouragement to do so. But once you start maturing, it's as though you have to make a choice. You have to be a "real" girl, or be an outsider. I was afraid of losing the freedom and fun I'd always known as a child. When I turned eleven and we moved to Georgia, I immediately signed up for all the teams and sporting activities I could. I was scared of becoming a teenager, of the mixed-up world of boys and sex and experimentation of all kinds that lay ahead. I saw the girls around me developing and heard how people snickered at them, commenting on their bras and their breasts. I was mortified at the thought that I could be like those girls. I was terrified of getting my period. I played as much soccer and tennis as I could, thinking that with so much activity, I could stave off my period for a while. And I prayed that my body would not develop. I just didn't want to stand out for being a girl. I wanted to continue to blend in with the boys and get on with my life as I knew it.

Things changed, however, once I reached high school. I was attracted to boys; I wanted them to be attracted to me. I'd always had a romantic, even melodramatic side. By the end of junior high school I'd filled notebooks with my poetry—tearful odes to love and loss, neither of which I'd ever experienced. The great event at the end of my ninth-grade year was my first date. It was on a Saturday afternoon. My "boyfriend" and I went to see *St. Elmo's Fire.* My mom had to drive us, of course. In the dark, furtively, he leaned over and kissed me. The earth didn't move. But I came out of the theater feeling much more knowledgeable about the ways of men. At last I could at least keep my head up when the talk at the lunch table turned to boys and sex. But mostly, I just continued to listen. I had so much to learn.

No one in my family had ever talked to me about the birds and the bees, or even about dating. Or, for that matter, about anything emotional at all. We didn't have the kind of family life that you see on TV shows like *The Brady Bunch*, where the kids come down before dinner and sit on Dad's lap and hug and talk. My relationship with my parents was much more formal: it was based on love, for sure, and on pride and admiration, but not on sharing deep feelings. For one thing, they were quite a bit older than most parents of kids my age. For another, my father was very rarely home. He was an executive with IBM and traveled all the time, while my mother stayed at home with the kids. So she was incredibly busy during the week, and the few days when he was home were precious. I would ride my bicycle and watch my father while he worked on the house, painting the shutters, fixing the porch, or just watering the flowers.

All week I looked forward to Friday evenings, when my mother and I would go to the airport to collect him and bring him home from his latest trip. We would always come hours early so that my mother could watch the planes for a while. She'd take a seat near a window and gaze at their takeoffs and landings, totally captivated by their speed and their grace. I quickly caught the same flying bug and soon was sitting, craning my neck up against the glass, holding my face as close as possible to the windowpanes, mesmerized by the mysterious white objects lifting off into the sky. I'd noisily try to guess which plane had my daddy on it. My mother would just sit quietly, staring off into the distance. Becoming a pilot was not a dream she could have entertained as a girl. But I could. And I did.

My mother had been a pioneer as a young woman. She was the first person in her family to attend college. Her mother, Mary (Ikey, to me), had grown up in the Irish slums of Yonkers, New York. She'd left school in sixth grade to get a job to support her nine brothers and sisters and perpetually drunk father. My grandfather, Pop, had been born poor, too. But together they moved up in the world, struggling for success. They gave my mother an iron will and a strong sense that education was the most important thing in the world. She graduated in the top of her class from Mount St. Vincent College, where she studied mathematics and also learned how to properly hold a wineglass and choose a fork. Armed with this knowledge, she became an engineer—one of the first female engineers at M. W. Kellogg, a crude-oil processing company.

She met my father there. He'd grown up only a few miles away from my mother, but in an entirely different world. His family was prosperous and lived in a much larger house. My paternal grandfather had fought in the American army in the trenches of World War I and knew all the horror and terror of that very bloody war; he'd been wounded in the Meuse-Argonne Offensive. First Lieutenant Flinn couldn't have dreamt that his granddaughter would one day learn to dig trenches and do battle with a bayonet. The thought would probably not have made him happy.

In our family, independence, self-reliance, and strength were valued above all. After we moved to Georgia, I realized that my father had been traveling so much for so many years simply because his work had shifted and he hadn't wanted to uproot us while so many kids were still at home. He'd done it stoically, without complaining. That was our way. If we had problems, we worked them out on our own. This characteristic served me poorly when I found myself in trouble with the Air Force.

High school was the first time in my life that I felt somewhat isolated. It wasn't easy finding a place for myself in high school. I had my crowd—dubbed the Donut Club because we brought Dunkin' Donuts with us to class—and I had sports. But when it came to socializing I always felt a bit as if I were on the outside looking in. Lassiter High was a typical American school—though on a grand scale: 4,000 students mostly well-off, from the fast-growing upper-middle-class residential suburbs of Atlanta. Being part of the in crowd, the East Cobb Snobs, meant being a cheerleader, dating a football player, driving one of the brand-new BMWs and Mercedeses that dotted the parking lot. I played my own sports; I didn't cheer from the sidelines. I drove an old Toyota Corolla. I had a boyfriend for a while, but I didn't sleep with him. I had promised myself that I wouldn't have sex until I was married. All in all, I wasn't particularly cool.

I was out of step, holding my breath through days of class, cafeteria, and soccer until something better came along. And then, like magic, it did. In the Atlanta *Journal-Constitution*, my father happened upon an ad for something called Space Camp. It was a simulated space program for teenagers, located four hours away at the Space and Rocket Center in Huntsville, Alabama. I begged and pleaded to go. I'd been obsessed with space ever since fifth grade, when my teacher had interrupted our school day to show us the televised takeoff of a space shuttle. The sight of the magnificent white winged object leaving the earth and blasting off to worlds unknown had stirred my soul. I saw red and orange plumes of smoke and fire, heard the rumble of engines, watched as the shuttle cleared its holding tower and shot off into the sky. Destination: Space. The unknown. Sheer freedom. I wanted to be there, too. I swore to myself that one day I'd get there. I'd dreamt, ever since, of being an astronaut. Space Camp gave me a chance to try that dream out.

For ten days, sixty other teenagers and I heard lectures by NASA astronauts and scientists. We suited up in real space gear and trained for reality-based missions. We learned to use the kind of equipment and deal with the kinds of emergencies that real astronauts encounter on space shuttles. In "Mission Control," we dealt with engine failures and rocket boosters that would not light. We learned to outsmart bad weather. On the simulated space station we ran medical tests to check the effects of vertigo and gravity. We floated in space, hanging from trapezelike harnesses and propelling ourselves carefully along cords: if we pushed too hard in any direction and forgot to secure ourselves, we risked being lost in space. We built rockets. And we learned about creative engineering. In one exercise, for example, we had to create a container to protect an egg from breaking during a two-story fall. My partner and I grabbed the last scraps from the supply table: a plastic container, some Ivory shampoo, and some foam cushioning. We made it work. During my second visit to camp, as we grew more advanced, we were able to work sometimes with real astronauts. I learned to scuba dive and worked with a Japanese astronaut who was training for his scheduled mission in 1992, helping him retrieve any tools he dropped as he practiced his duties weightlessly underwater.

This was nothing like high school. It was challenging, exciting, meaningful. And I was in good company. The other campers were every bit as obsessed with space as I was. We worked in teams, controlling one another's movements with remote controls. We depended on one another. If we messed up, we knew, we were lost in space.

After Space Camp I knew who I was and what I had to do. I also knew how to do it. I'd had trouble imagining myself getting into NASA through the academic route. I couldn't imagine putting in the time to get a Ph.D. in engineering. But a fellow camper had told me that there was a more active route: you could go to the Air Force Academy and learn how to fly! That was it, I decided. The Academy was my future. My best friend, Scott, was a Space Camp veteran, too. Now *he* was obsessed with getting into the Air Force Academy. It was all we could talk about, all we could think about. We sat together in class and passed notes incessantly about it. We drove out to the school playing fields at night and sat outside, gazing up at the stars and dreaming.

High school now had a purpose: it was a proving ground that would give me all the credits and credentials I needed to get into the Academy. I took all the advanced-placement courses I could. I joined student council, the Beta Club (an academic group), the French club, the academic bowl team, and the model United Nations. I worked odd jobs on the weekends, earning some spending money but also, more important, adding another box or two to check off on my Air Force Academy application. My life became a nonstop rush of studying, soccer practice, more studying, and work. And then the application process began.

Choosing the Air Force Academy is easier than making sure the Air Force will choose you. The application process was so long that you had to get started junior year. You had to have SAT scores of at least 1200, unless you were an intercollegiate athlete; then 1000 would do. You had to make sure your grades were in order and that you were taking the right kinds of courses, and you had to begin seeking nominations from your senators and representatives. I wrote an earnest 200-word essay on "guiding this nation into an uncharted and uncertain future" and sent it to Senators Wyche Fowler and Sam Nunn and Representative George "Buddy" Darden. Senior year, I agonized as I prepared for the interviews. Each member of Congress could nominate only two candidates, I knew, and they took the selection process very seriously. Plus, in order to attend an academy, you had to have both the congressional nomination and an appointment from the academy. For Senators Fowler and Nunn, I had to meet with a panel of three people who batted questions at me rapid-fire. Buddy Darden gave me a one-on-one interview. He ended up nominating me for the Air Force Academy, while Senator Nunn nominated me for the Naval Academy, my second-choice school. In truth, Annapolis was said to be even harder to get into than USAFA. But I didn't really want to go there. To be a Navy pilot in those days, you had to have uncorrected 20 / 20 vision, which I didn't. And the Navy's treatment of women was said to leave a lot to be desired. Plus, just about the last thing I wanted was to be stuck on a boat. I wanted to soar, not cruise. To please my parents, I also applied to the University of Georgia, the University of Virginia, and various other universities as backups.

Once the congressional interviews were done, I figured the hardest part of the application process was over. I was dead wrong. To my great surprise, I failed the Air Force physical fitness test. I did just fine on the sprints—the "shuttle run"—the sit-ups, and the push-ups. But I'd never done a pull-up before, and couldn't manage a single one. My dad took care of that in a hurry. He put up a bar in our basement. I practiced—and the next time around I aced the test.

The Department of Defense medical examination was another unexpected ordeal. The doctors, let's say, left no stone unturned. They inspected every crevice and cavity. They brought out the plastic gloves and the petroleum jelly. They checked out my eyes, ears, nose, and throat, did an EKG, even had me read a paragraph to see if I had any speech pathology. They ran neurological tests, checked my reflexes and balance, and took so many vials of blood that I felt faint. But worst of all was the urine test. To guarantee the authenticity of your sample, the Air Force doctors made you pee in a cup before a witness. At least it was someone of the same sex. But that didn't make things easier for a lot of the candidates; when push came to shove, they just couldn't produce. Scott, for one, took half the day to fill his little plastic cup. He sat next to the water fountain, drinking and drinking and filling up his bladder, and the more anxious he became, the more difficult it became for him to go. He kept pacing, mumbling to himself, "I'm not going to make it into the Air Force Academy because I can't pee in a cup in front of someone." Tough though it was, the urine test was a pretty good form of hazing. It gave us a pretty accurate picture of the total lack of privacy we'd have once we were in basic training.

Applying to the Academy had made the first half of my senior year rush by in a wave of frantic activity and anxiety. Waiting for a response afterward was sheer torture. Scott and I grew even closer. We spent all our time together, partners in our obsession. We'd helped each other apply; now we swore that if we got into the Academy, we'd help each other get through.

People joked that once Scott and I hit eighteen we'd get married. Even if we wanted to, we could not have been married at the Academy, but there was nothing romantic between us anyway. We were just the closest of friends, like two sides of the same person.

Scott learned in early spring that he had been accepted, but I still did not know. The next month was sheer agony as I waited for my acceptance call. My call finally came one afternoon in late spring while I returned home from soccer practice. Holding a tall glass of milk in one hand, I listened as Buddy Darden said "Congratulations!" I immediately called Scott. He was ecstatic, and we were both beside ourselves with joy and relief. We had made it. It turned out that my brother Don had received a promotion at work that day, as well. The stars were on our side; my family went out to a local steak house to celebrate.

Then, a few weeks later, the other shoe fell. I received a letter from the Academy telling me I wasn't qualified to be a pilot because of my poor vision, 20/25. I felt as if I'd been sent to hell after a quick taste of paradise; this was almost worse, I felt, than simply having been rejected. I drove to the track to see Scott and ran up to him, crying. I buried my face in his shoulder and just kept asking "Why?" over and over again. He didn't have any answers. When I finally calmed down, I decided to do some research. I called the Academy and asked to speak with a doctor, who set me straight. It turned out that you only needed 20/70 vision, correctable to 20/20, but to fly with that vision required a waiver, and the waiver was granted only once you were a cadet. Never trust the Air Force to tell you anything straight out.

At some point as the calm weeks of my last semester drew to a close, I realized that high school had largely passed me by. I'd been so obsessed with my future that I'd barely taken the time to notice the present. And along the way, I'd ended up with hardly any friends. Prom night approached, and I had no date. I had no prospects for a date, either. My friends had grown sick of me and my obsession with the Academy. They'd let me drop, and I was spending most of my time with some of the younger players from the men's soccer team. There was no one there to ask to take me to the prom. I no longer had a boyfriend; he'd gone to college and had sex as soon as he could. As for Scott, he was taking a girl he'd met during his visit to the Academy. In the end, I asked my pen pal from Space Camp to fly down and be my escort. We had a wonderful time together. But it wasn't easy. I watched my friends arrive in groups in their rented limousines. I watched them leave in groups to go to the after-prom parties. My pen pal and I just observed, then climbed into my Dad's Honda and went home.

Graduation day left me feeling strangely empty, too. I had won several awards, including the Congressional Award for Academic Excellence and the Georgia Certificate of Merit. I hoped that my classmates would elect me "Most Likely to Succeed." Instead, I was named Miss Lassiter High, the female student who best embodied the school's values. (Scott was the male counterpart.) It was a strange honor, given that I'd always felt so at odds with high school. And it was an award given by the school's teachers. My peers, I knew, wouldn't have honored me.

I was very successful, and very alone. Success and popularity, I was learning, don't necessarily go hand in hand. It was a sign of things to come.

CHAPTER 2

Proud to Be

The discipline which makes the soldiers of a free country reliable in battle is not to be gained by harsh or tyrannical treatment. On the contrary, such treatment is far more likely to destroy than to make an army. It is possible to impart instruction and give commands in such a manner and such a tone of voice as to inspire in the soldier no feeling but an intense desire to obey, while the opposite manner and tone of voice cannot fail to excite strong resentment and a desire to disobey.
The one mode or the other of dealing with subordinates springs from a corresponding spirit in the breast of the commander. He who feels the respect which is due to others cannot fail to inspire in them respect for himself while he who feels, and hence manifests disrespect toward others, especially his subordinates, cannot fail to inspire hatred against himself.

—MAJOR GENERAL JOHN M. SCHOFIELD
Address to the West Point Class of 1879

"Get off the bus!"

The voice boomed like a shock wave through the rows of gangly teenagers half-asleep in their seats on the Air Force Academy bus. We shot up, startled, looking around, blinking fast. We'd been lulled into a forgetful calm by the hour-long bus ride that had brought us to the United States Air Force Academy from the Colorado Springs airport. I, for one, was exhausted. It had been a very long day. My family, as usual, had arrived at the Atlanta airport hours in advance for my flight to Denver. Then, the connecting flight from Denver to Colorado Springs had been delayed. Every delay, every moment spent in the air, felt like an eternity to me. I listened to

REO Speedwagon's "Time for Me to Fly" on my Walkman and talked to Scott, trying to keep up my energy. I was nervous and excited, and the edge of adrenaline gave me confidence. But as the day dragged on, my energy waned. Scott and I sat in anxious silence, not wanting to talk anymore and give our feelings a name. By the time we pulled up to the school, at the very end of the day, I was ready for bed, not battle.

That changed the minute we got to the Academy and the bus stopped at the base of a big concrete slab with "Bring Me Men" printed above it. This, I was soon to learn, was the Bring Me Men ramp, named for the poem "The Coming American" by Sam Walter Foss. That poem was one of the first of hundreds of verses and slogans and sayings that we had to memorize during our six weeks of basic training. It read, in part: "Bring me men to match my mountains / Bring me men to match my plains / Men to chart a starry empire / Men to make celestial claims."

An upperclass male cadet was standing in the doorway of the bus, glaring down at us. (Only 10 percent of our class was female.) "*Shut up!*" he shouted. "Get up! Get off! And form up!" All but one of us candidates immediately scrambled to our feet and raced off the bus. I was sent in one direction and Scott in another. We didn't even look back, much less say good-bye. We were too scared of falling behind. I didn't know that that was just about the last I'd see of him for almost all of basic training. I was now completely on my own.

The yelling continued. "Fall in! Hurry up, you're late!" It never stopped. "*Cage your eyes!*" a cadet yelled at me. I stared straight back at him. "*Cage your eyes!*" he screamed. I looked at the ground. I had no idea what "Cage your eyes" meant. I was completely and utterly confused. "Hurry up!" he finally said, and pointed me toward a low nearby building. I went off blindly. I ran up to a desk, shouted out my name, and was given a huge tag that read "H." I was told to tie the tag to my duffel bag and throw it into the pile marked "H." The "H" stood for "Hellcats": my new squadron, my new home. I picked up my bag. It was packed according to the specifications in my "Instructions to Appointees" handbook: a razor, blades, and shaving cream, a hair dryer (for women only), and eight white bras, chosen, as the handbook required, for "support and comfort." And that was that. The rest of our clothes and toiletries were to be supplied by the Academy. I threw my bag into the pile, feeling as if I were casting off an old friend. Packing it at home in my room had been the last normal act of my old, familiar life. That seemed long ago now, and so far away.

I ran from the desk to a group of other candidates. "Fall in!" came the shout. "Wait." When enough candidates had gathered, an upperclassman paced in front of us and looked each of us up and down from head to toe. You could see that the candidates had made an effort to look as if they belonged in a military environment: many, like me, had cut their hair short; one brave soul had even shaved a "93" in the back of his head, for our class year; and we were all dressed neatly and conservatively. But there was no mistaking us for anything but civilians. By military standards, we were a sorry-looking group: some too fat, some too thin, some slouched, some tapping their feet or shifting nervously. All the haircuts were different, all the gestures, all the facial expressions. We were still individuals. We had a very long way to go.

The upperclassmen and -women began to teach us how to march in formation. First, we had to learn how to stand at attention: Heels together, toes out at a 45-degree angle, arms flat at our sides, fists closed as if curled around a roll of quarters, thumbs pointed down and lined up with the side seams of our pants. Chest out, stomach in, shoulder blades almost touching in the back. Chin pressed back against the neck, just as tightly as possible. Eyes facing straight ahead, focused on an object directly in front of us, never wandering up or down, left or right—"caged." The position of attention is completely unnatural and almost impossible to do correctly at first. An upperclassman had us strike it again, and again, and again. If your feet weren't lined up properly or were turned out too much or too little, he'd come up and kick them into place. As soon as he was satisfied, he led us in our first attempts at marching. Left foot down on the beat. Right foot following. Eyes straight ahead at all times. We marched up the Bring Me Men ramp and straight into the heart of campus.

The U.S. Air Force Academy is a grimly austere place in a sublimely beautiful setting. Its 18,000 acres are nestled at the base of the Rocky Mountains, on land donated by the state of Colorado. There's a cadet area with a big, flat marble-and-concrete surface, known as "the Terrazzo," surrounded by steel-and-glass academic and residential buildings. The buildings, designed by Skidmore, Owings & Merrill, are all very square and very flat. Very Cold War, very chilling. Even the chapel is eerie. Its seventeen spires look like the noses of F-15s—or like missiles. We always said they stood in for the twelve Apostles and the five chiefs of staff. Beyond all this spread the playing fields, the parade grounds, and the airfield off in the distance. When you looked out the window from the military-issue ugliness of your dorm room, all you saw was mountains. There was a sense of grandeur beyond the confinement. You dreamt of getting up in the air and soaring in the Rockies.

That first night, though, I didn't see any of this. Everything was a blur. I was completely disoriented, totally confused. I marched and was yelled at and then marched some more. I was told where to go, what to do, and where to look. There was

no time to think or ask questions. No time to try to make sense
of things or form a game plan. That, of course, was the idea.
The whole point of basic training, I would learn during the six
weeks of hell that ensued, was to break you down, rid you of
any individual characteristics you might cling to (like inde-
pendent thought), and build you back up again. To replace
your thoughts with Air Force slogans and ideas. To replace
your instincts with those of a fighter. To make you a part of a
team whose members always took care of one another.

We marched across the Terrazzo and into an administrative
building, where we were given green laundry bags full of gear.
Around our necks, the upperclassmen hung large cardboard
signs—"cowbells"—marked with our clothes sizes. Like cattle,
we moved passively and dumbly along, collecting boots and
uniforms, pens and papers and panties and briefs and sheets
and comforters. At one counter, a female cadet asked in a
bored monotone, "Pads or tampons?" I said yes—and got back
a stare cold enough to freeze nitrogen. You had to choose. I
quickly tossed the generic hygiene items into my laundry bag
and moved on to the next counter. Four laundry bags later, we
were finished. We were loaded up with gray baseball caps, gray
scarves, gray notebooks. And we had the little gray books that
would guarantee that, for the next year, we'd not only look alike
but think alike as well: *Basic Cadet Training Knowledge Book*
and *Contrails*. Both were full of quotes and songs and dates and
information about the Air Force and the Academy that we'd
have to memorize, word for word. For the first year of our life
at the Academy, the books would never leave our side.

Once we were outfitted, it was time to march over to the bar-
bershop for haircuts. The men were shaved to just about bald;
the women's hair was cut above the collar, tapering up to a row
of bangs. Since mine was even shorter than that, I was quickly
dismissed from the chair and told to grow it out.

It was too late for dinner or evening assembly. It was also too late for me to meet my new roommate, who'd been placed with some other girls for the evening. So I spent the first night in my new room alone. Before turning off the light, I memorized the Oath of Allegiance to the United States: "I, Kelly Flinn, having been appointed an Air Force Cadet in the United States Air Force, do solemnly swear (or affirm) that I will support and defend the Constitution of the United States against all enemies, foreign and domestic, that I will bear true faith and allegiance to the same; that I take this obligation freely, without any mental reservation or purpose of evasion, and that I will well and faithfully discharge the duties of the office on which I am about to enter. SO HELP ME GOD."

Heavy stuff for a college freshman.

I was exhausted, but couldn't fall asleep. I lay in bed, the events of the day running through my mind like a video. I played my good-bye to my parents over and over again. My mother had hugged me, kissed me on the cheek, and wished me good luck. Then my father had hugged me so hard, it seemed he never wanted to let me go. He had never held me so long or so tightly before. Finally, after one last squeeze, he'd patted my shoulder and said, "Bye-bye, baby. Good luck." I'd turned and walked down the long, carpeted jetway to the plane, choking back my tears. The display of emotion was so unlike my father. And yet I knew, as the plane taxied for take-off, that it was probably the truest moment my father had ever spent with me. The love had always been there. He just hadn't been able to express it.

I turned my head on the pillow. That morning now seemed to belong to another day. And yesterday seemed to belong to another life altogether. Just twenty-four hours earlier, Scott and I had gone for our last walk together as civilians. We had hiked up a small mountain and looked up at the stars. We were silent most of the time, both wondering about our future:

Would we become astronauts? Would we survive the Academy, much less basic training? Just before heading home we both saw two shooting stars dash across the clear night sky. I quickly made a wish that on June 2, 1993, Scott and I would both graduate and become second lieutenants of the United States Air Force. Now we were on our way. And, I saw, it was going to be a very long four years.

I finally fell asleep. And about a half-hour later, it seemed, was awakened by fists pounding on the door. *"Get up!"* voices were screaming, up and down the hallway. "Blue shorts! USAFA tees! Running shoes and gray baseball caps! You are late!" After the jump-start of my heart, I scrambled out of bed and into the required clothes, then ran down the hallway to my first morning of physical conditioning. Followed by shouts and yells all the way, all the basic cadets scrambled out the doors, down the stairs and onto the Terrazzo. An upperclass female cadet ran up and yelled *"Flinn!"* I abruptly stopped. She then proceeded to demonstrate the proper way of wearing a baseball cap: bill pulled straight down, bangs inside the cap, blue name tag smack in the middle. She pulled the cap down snugly across my brow. I never made that mistake again.

Morning physical conditioning, or PC as we called it, consisted of running laps, then doing sit-ups, push-ups, and jumping jacks. We started out with only one or two laps around the parade ground. Running at 7,200 feet above sea level was like nothing I had ever experienced in suburban Atlanta. I started to dry-heave the first morning because I wasn't getting enough oxygen. My back also ached from the strain of keeping my shoulders back and my chin tucked in when we stood at attention. But the hardest thing of all was learning to run in formation. That's a nightmare for everyone involved. If the tallest people lead the formation, their average stride is two or three times as long as the shortest people's. So what seems like a slow jog to them is a sprint for the little guys in back. Or, if the situation is reversed, the short people are comfortable while the tall ones shuffle as if their feet were in restraints.

I was never one of the top cadets in physical conditioning. I finished each run with my squadron, but I was always in the back. Unbeknownst to me, I had flat feet. This, combined with a hyperextended knee and running in boots or the generic government-issue running shoes, knocked me out with a shooting pain in my knee halfway through basic training. The doctor called it ilia-tibia band syndrome, gave me some arch supports, and kept me from running for a week. I was furious. The one thing you don't want to be known as in basic training is a sickie, particularly if you're a woman. So, once I was up and running again, I tried twice as hard to be twice as tough.

The first morning, though, we were all a mess. We muddled through the laps, the sit-ups, and the push-ups and ended with a motivational sprint up the Bring Me Men ramp, the finish line. Then we were shouted back to our dorms. We were told to change into our bathrobes and flip-flops. We had to place our folded white towel across our left arm and carry our soap and shampoo in the other hand. We had to form up in the hallway and stand at the position of attention for inspection. The upperclassmen and -women checked that our robes were fastened with the correct side folded over the other and the proper square knot holding the belt secure. I held my breath and prayed that I'd done everything right. I imagined that if the belt was tied wrong, the whole thing might be ripped open right there in the middle of the coed hallway. After the whole flight of basics—about thirty freshmen—had passed inspection, we were herded to the showers. The upperclasswomen stood in the shower room and watched our progress. "That's enough, ladies! Rinse off!" they began to shout after only a moment under the cleansing spray. "One more minute, rinse off! Hurry up, ladies! You're late!" In the coming days, they'd sometimes haze us by putting hot water in one stall and cold water in the next and making us go from one to the other.

Any modesty or inhibitions that you might have brought with you to the Academy disappeared within a few days. We were stared at all the time: marching, during inspection, in the showers. It would have been upsetting if you had time to think about it, but with all the rushing around you just didn't. So it became another fact of life, one low-level humiliation among many others. There was, for example, the problem for the female basic cadets only, of our Air Force–issue underpants. They were huge and white—always a "Large," no matter what had been written on someone's cowbell. They sagged at the waist and crept down our legs, and we had to wear them under tight, extremely short shorts. Figuring out how to hide them under the short shorts and the skintight USAFA T-shirts we had to wear was a challenge. Since we never had time to shave our legs, we were truly a sight. Maybe it was all an attempt to keep sex out of the ranks. With any group other than randy eighteen-year-olds, it might have worked.

After a few days, I learned the routine: Our alarm clock was a chorus of *"Wake up! You are late!"* "Wake us up earlier, then!" I always wanted to yell back. I never understood why we always were late, or what, exactly, we were late *for.* I never actually knew what time it was, since we weren't allowed to wear watches. That may have been a good thing, since the one time I did catch a glimpse of an upperclassman's watch it was 5:30 in the morning. It was better not to know, not to think about how early it was and how exhausted you were. You just had to think of how, in the five minutes allotted to you before inspection, you were going to get showered, dress, clean your room, and make your bed. And not just make your bed any old way, but make it the Air Force way: sheet folded six inches over the blanket, blanket folded eighteen inches from the head of the bed, and the crease ironed flat. Within a week, we all caught on to the one trick that made it possible: we safety-pinned our sheets and blanket in place and slept on top of them. It was hard to get used to, and a little bit chilly, but it was an essential survival skill for the Academy.

After we were cleaned up and presentable, we started training. During the day, we learned the basics of marching in formation, turning together, and staying in step. The Terrazzo was crisscrossed and bordered by marble strips against concrete. As basics, we had to walk along the marble strips that formed the outer boundary. We had to turn all the corners perfectly, marching in step. The upperclassmen analyzed, criticized, and corrected every move. "Attention to detail!" they shouted.

After marching and drills, we took placement tests for our classes. There were lectures on banking and money management—most of the basics had never been away from home before, and for some of them, managing even the little bit of spending money that we were allowed was a major challenge. In our downtime, we studied our little gray books. We had to memorize, word for word, long lists of inspirational quotations, the history of the Air Force, the names and specifications of all the planes, every code and pledge imaginable, the physical description and meaning of every badge, all four verses of "The Star-Spangled Banner," and the "Air Force Song." We memorized whole lists of staff personnel, from their ranks down to their middle initials. All this was called our "knowledge." You never knew when you'd be called upon to recite your knowledge. It might happen when you'd messed something up, or it might happen for no reason at all. Which meant that, during basic training, everyone was reciting knowledge practically all the time. This was called "being trained"—and if you saw a classmate being trained, you were supposed to gather around him or her in support. So it wasn't unusual to see twenty or thirty basics gathered around a classmate on the Terrazzo, joining him as he repeated the Code of Conduct for the Armed Forces of the United States as fast and as loudly as he could. That was teamwork. You helped out your buddies, and you expected that they'd do the same for you.

Mealtimes were marathon training sessions. We were constantly asked questions: about our upperclass cadets' names and ranks; about the number of days left to graduation; about the menu for breakfast, lunch, or dinner. Sometimes, we spent the entire meal reciting knowledge and never touched the food on our plates. And when we did get to eat, the training continued. We had to learn to eat just as we made our beds: to Air Force Academy specifications. We had to sit at a position of attention on the first three inches of our chair. Our chins remained in throughout the meal and our eyes were caged on the eagle at the twelve o'clock position on our plates. We had to place whichever utensils we used on our plates between each bite: knife on top, lying diagonally from the two to the twelve o'clock position, followed by the fork, then the spoon, spreading down toward three o'clock. If you did this incorrectly, you could spend hours with an upperclass cadet, studying the proper etiquette for utensils. And even if you mastered the silverware, you couldn't relax. The upperclassmen and -women would study your jaw, counting how many times you chewed. You were only allowed seven chews per bite. If you took eight, you were stopped and asked why you thought you were special. And if, during the meal, an upperclassman yelled "Fire in the hole!" you had to stop chewing whatever was in your mouth, swallow quickly, and then drain a glass of water in one breath. It was important that we not get dehydrated during basic training, so we drank four to six glasses of water at every meal.

Every meal then ended the same way: After dessert, the basics had to complete Form 0-96. This was a standard survey sheet—the kind of thing you might find to rate the service in a hotel. You always checked the same six responses. I'll call them "Excellent," "Clean," "Rapid," "Tasty," "Fine," and "Fine." I don't want to give away this Academy secret, because the responses are a kind of code. Academy graduates have been checking the top six boxes on Form 0-96 in the same way for such a long time that the six words, recited together, have become like a secret handshake. You can immediately recognize an Academy grad or an impostor by these six responses.

This came in handy during the Vietnam War. The North Vietnamese had some soldiers who spoke English very well and would sometimes use our radio frequencies to lure American rescue helicopters looking for downed pilots to a particular spot and then ambush them. Once the Americans were on to this, they waited to pick up pilots until they could check their ISOPREP cards. The ISOPREP card contained all of the pilot's personal information and gave the rescuers a way to positively identify him before attempting a rescue. (That's why, when Captain Scott O'Grady was shot down in Bosnia, they kept asking him in which squadron he'd served in Korea.) In Vietnam once, the story goes, a pilot went down and there wasn't time to find his ISOPREP card. He had to either be airlifted out immediately, or left to the mercy of the North Vietnamese. One rescuer, knowing that the stranded pilot was an Academy graduate, radioed to him: "Excellent, Clean, Rapid." The pilot replied: "Tasty, Fine, Fine," and was immediately rescued.

The last thing we had to do before leaving the table was "post"—tell a funny story or joke. This would have been simple enough, except that everyone at the table had to be in on the joke and say it together, so you had to get the joke around to everyone in advance. Often, you didn't know who was at your table until the meal started, or they'd switch a person on you at the last minute. And then, if the new person didn't know the joke, they'd start training you about classmates and team-work.

In the evenings, we usually went to Arnold Hall for a motiva-tional film or speech. This was the class bonding time and also a chance for the upperclass cadre to practice their leader-ship skills with motivational and inspirational speeches. One evening, we were told to take a good look at our neighbors be-cause one out of every three of us would not make it through the Academy. On another evening, a chant started in the back of the room. "Proud to be '93! PROUD TO BE '93!" It kept building in intensity. We repeated the words over and over again until we were inspired by them. Until we believed them. It became our unifying motto. We were, and will always be, Proud to Be.

All the training and reciting and chanting had an effect on your mental state. It mirrored the exhaustion of your body. Energy had to be preserved for the tasks at hand. Extraneous thoughts were chased away. The contents of the little gray books became the contents of our minds. Our intellectual in-dividuality went the way of our hair and civilian clothing. Our speech was shaved down to Air Force essentials. We were al-lowed only seven basic responses when addressed that year: "Yes sir!" ("Ma'am" for the females) "No sir!" "Sir, I do not know!" "Sir, may I ask a question?" "Sir, may I make a state-ment?" "Sir, I do not understand!" and "No excuse, sir!" "No excuse, sir" was what you said if asked why you had done something. The message was that it didn't matter why you'd done it. If you were guilty, you were guilty. There was no ex-cuse. That pretty much summed up the military's attitude to missteps. It was a valuable principle in time of battle. Less so in a time of peace.

ON THE SUNDAY halfway through basic training, we had a chance to actually leave the Academy for a few hours. The event was called Doolie Dining Out. It was our first opportunity to call home, eat candy and junk food, and nap in the afternoon at the homes of our sponsor families, people in Colorado Springs who had volunteered to be surrogate families to cadets during the school year. My sponsors immediately took another cadet and me to a store, where I bought envelopes and candy bars. I put two candy bars into each envelope, addressed them to myself at the Academy, put some stamps on them, and asked my sponsors to drop them in the mail every few days. As basics, we were not allowed to receive food or candy, and our mail was checked constantly. Sometimes, though, you could hide your food in your uniform before the upperclass cadets had a chance to check your mail. My sister Gail used to hide one small piece of gum in each letter she sent. Each time you could sneak some contraband back to your room, it was a small victory. And if I'd been found out, it wouldn't have been considered a violation of the rules. If I'd been discovered, I'm sure they would have tortured me in some way, perhaps by eating the candy in front of me while making me sound off for hours. But you could earn respect, too, for beating the system in little ways.

One morning shortly after Doolie Dining Out, I woke with the frightening sensation of having overslept. I wondered if our cadets had forgotten to wake us up, because I could hear the pounding fists on other doors down the hallway. We had a new group of upperclass cadre, mean-looking and clearly ready to drive us into the ground, and somehow I doubted they'd forgotten us. In fact, the second phase of basic training was beginning. This was the phase when we'd get down in the dirt and learn what it meant to be true warriors. If we hadn't known pain and exhaustion before, we would now. We needed the extra sleep.

That first morning, after we woke, showered, and ate, we ran over to the obstacle course. It was a total nightmare. We jumped, we crawled, we climbed. We ran and ran and ran. We ran to obstacles and ran between obstacles and while waiting in line for obstacles we double-timed, pulling our knees up to our chests. We ran through tires, jumped over water, swung over water, and swam in the water if we fell in it. If we so much as skimmed the water, we had to run in it, and the water in our clothes made us pounds heavier, as I discovered after I went swimming three times on the rope swing. The whole thing seemed to go on forever. After the course was over, I felt like I had died and gone to hell. But after I cleaned up, all I could think was: "I made it." And that made me want to push myself all over again.

A few days later, I got the chance. It was time for the big event of basic training: our ten-day stint in Jack's Valley, where we'd pitch tents and learn to fight for ourselves. Jack's Valley was a dusty, dirty place about two to three miles long on the Academy grounds. After our long march to the valley, we began to set up our tents. But first we had to clean up the dust. That wasn't easy in a dusty valley, and the upperclass cadre standing over us and shouting "MAKE THE PLACE PRETTY!" didn't help. We did our best. We moved the dust with our feet and swept it aside to some distance from the tents. Then, of course, it all blew back, and we started over. When our housekeeping was done, it was time to learn to kill. We grabbed our canteens and ran the half-mile or so to the Jack's Valley assault course.

This was the most terrifying run of basic training. Not only were we laden with gear, suited in heavy boots and long-sleeved shirts and pants, but also we were dreading what lay ahead. That dread was like a counterweight pulling us backward toward our tents. It was like carrying a hundred-pound backpack, only you couldn't take it off. We had heard that Jack's Valley was pure physical hell—that people got sick, got hurt, dropped out for good when they could not survive it. My stomach hurt with fear. If I couldn't make it through the next ten days in Jack's Valley, I knew my dreams of flying were all over.

We finally arrived at the assault course just as another group of basic cadets were finishing. I heard the upperclass cadets yelling at the basics, who were crawling through the mud. I could also hear the grunts from the basics as they parried with the bayonets. I knew instinctively that if I showed the fear in my eyes, I'd draw the upperclassmen's attention. And then they'd be sure to make it ten times harder for me. So I discovered a way to cover up: I moved through the course uttering the most vicious and guttural war cry I could muster. It made me feel better, and it made the cadet cadre move past me and onto the next suffering basic. And once I moved past the fear and into the spirit of the kill, I started to enjoy myself. It was like playing soldiers. We were learning to fight trench warfare. For the first hour, we crawled through the dirt and mud, under barbed-wire fences, and in and out of ditches. The air was full of smoke from simulated bombs. We learned to jump into ditches to avoid the smoke and how to throw a grenade properly from behind a sandbag barrier. We carried our rifles everywhere. They were M-1 rifles, loaded with lead, so they weighed about fifteen pounds. When we low-crawled, we held them in both hands and pulled ourselves along on our stomachs with our elbows. When we jumped into ditches, we learned how to touch down with our rifle butt, knee, and hand at the same time—a three-point landing that would prevent us from shooting ourselves with the guns or stabbing ourselves with the bayonets. We stabbed our bayonets into stuffed dummies and then learned how to kill with the butts of our rifles. "What's the spirit of the bayonet?" an upperclassman would shout. "*To kill!*" we would answer. Or, if we wanted extra attention: "To slice, dice, and make julienne fries"—though that

wasn't a recommended response. By the end of the day, everything was a blur. It was such an ordeal, with the smoke and the
noise and the yelling, that you didn't have time to think, to re-
flect upon, or to retain what was going on. And that was the
point of it all, really. When you're under that kind of physical
stress, you don't think about what you're doing, you just *become.*

After the assault course, we donned gloves, helmets, and
chest pads and held a pugo stick competition. This basically
meant using a heavily padded stick to knock each other down.
I won the competition for women of the Hellcat squadron.
This felt particularly satisfying because I was one of the smallest women and knew the upperclassmen still remembered
when I was a sickie. I felt a little glimmer of triumph when one
of my teammates told our flight commander that I had won.
He stared at me incredulously and said, *"Flinn?"* Then he
smiled, laughed, and wished me good luck in the overall competition. I lost the final competition, but walked away with a
white T-shirt that had "Big Bad Basic" printed on it.

A final victory awaited me back at the Academy. I wore my
white T-shirt proudly during dinner that evening and was
trained by an upperclassman who had harassed me a few
weeks earlier for not shouting loudly enough one day when
my throat was parched. He asked me how come I thought I
was so special that I could wear a white T-shirt when all my
classmates were dressed in green. I told him in a quiet voice
that I was the Big Bad Basic for the Hellcat squadron. He shut
up and never spoke to me again.

There were times during basic training when I had my
doubts about the military and its culture of learning through
abuse. Sometimes, while being berated by an upperclassman
(or woman) for some minor fault, I'd think, "This guy is just
one year older than me, and he's screaming his head off be-

cause I didn't square my corner properly." But I knew I couldn't take that kind of thing very seriously if I was going to get through basic training. I had to see it as funny, or as a game, or simply not think about it at all. And that's what I ended up doing most of the time. It was convenient not to think, and most expedient. There was too much of a sense of urgency in those six weeks, too much rushing around. You get so worn down that, by the middle of basic training, your emotional responses are pretty much limited to "My God, why are we running *again*?" Midway through the program, when I had my first, brief Air Force orientation flight, the experience washed over me like just another day on the obstacle course. I would have expected to be thrilled. But in fact, all I thought was that this was extremely peaceful and a whole heck of a lot better than running.

ON THE LAST day of basic training, we gathered on the parade grounds and formed up on the opposite side of the field from the upperclassmen. A drumroll started and slowly, one by one, our class units—called flights—started to march forward. The center flight went first, then the flights on either side of it, then the next flight and the next. In this inverted wedge formation, we looked, from a distance, like the wings of a giant airplane. When we finally reached the upperclass cadets we positioned ourselves in front of our new squadrons and stepped into the places set aside for freshmen. The formation was now re-formed, with all of us together. And afterward we marched off, complete squadrons of freshmen, sophomores, juniors, and seniors, to our new dorms, our new homes, and the new school year. You can't grin during a military parade. But I was glowing inside. I had done it. I had made it. I had survived what I thought was the toughest time of my life; I'd even thrived. It was time to move on. I was no longer a Hellcat. I was a proud

member of Cadet Squadron 31, Class of 1993. We called ourselves the Grim Reapers.

IF I THOUGHT life as a freshman was going to be any easier, I
was wrong. The end of basic training meant that we no longer
had to spend our days in a haze of running, yelling, and doing
sit-ups. Now we spent it attending classes, reciting knowledge,
marching to meals, playing sports, and studying. Not to mention ironing our shirts, shining our shoes, keeping our pants
perfectly creased and our rooms spotless, and watching our
backs around the upperclass. As freshmen, we were known as
SMACKs (Soldiers Minus Ability, Coordination, and Knowledge). The name pretty much summed up our status. We were
ignoramuses, the lowest of the low. We couldn't talk to,
couldn't date, couldn't socialize with anyone other than freshmen. For the upperclassmen, we were lackeys or whipping
boys. Mornings, we were their alarm clocks. We stood at attention in the hallway of our squadron dorms "calling minutes" until meal formation: "There are twenty minutes until
the morning meal formation. Uniform is: light blue short-
sleeve shirts, athletic jackets, gray leather gloves. The menu
for the morning meal includes French toast, cereal, fruit, and
orange juice. I say again, there are twenty minutes until the
morning meal formation!" This litany, or a similar one, was repeated at fifteen, ten, nine, eight, seven, six, and five minutes
before the formation. While you stood at attention, you held
your right arm at a 90-degree angle, with a copy of *Contrails* in
your hand and directly in front of your face. Like that, you
were fair game for any bored upperclassman who wanted to
test your knowledge.

Some squadrons "trained" like this for hours every day. My
upperclassmen limited themselves to a much more humane
two or three times a week. This was a blessing, because the

training sessions were brutal. To give knowledge, you had to stand at attention with your shoulder blades touching in back and your chin jammed into your neck. You had to cage your eyes and sound off, shouting at the top of your lungs. By the time you were done, beads of sweat would be running down your face, and your throat would be raw. Your fellow freshmen were supposed to come to your rescue as soon as possible. They'd form a tight crowd, standing shoulder to shoulder and back to back to keep other upperclass cadets from pressing in on you; sometimes, when a recitation was going on inhumanly long, another freshman would even create a diversion, sauntering down the middle of the hallway to attract the upperclassmen's attention. Then the first SMACK would be let off the hook. Covered in sweat, physically and mentally exhausted, he or she would scramble to the side of the freshman who was now the target of the attack.

Finding the time—and the strength—to study was a real challenge. I used to go to bed every night at eight P.M., sleep until two in the morning, then get up and study. My roommate worked the opposite hours, studying until two and then waking up at five or six in the morning. She could function on just three hours of sleep. A lot of other freshmen tried to. I would watch them dozing off in class, their heads drooping, then sinking lower and lower, until they jerked themselves awake.

Everyone had to find his or her own way to deal with the stress and fatigue. I kept myself awake by watching other people sleep; my stress outlet was soccer. The playing fields were the one place where freshmen and upperclassmen could mix and be friends. On the field we could laugh and blow off steam and release all our anger and frustration. My best friendships were formed on the soccer field. On trips to play other schools, some of the upperclass cadets would actually share rooms with the freshmen, because we were friends on the field. Once in the cadet area, we had to go back to being professionals. Still, the upperclasswomen on our team tried to take care of us as well as they could. Some of them would always stop by our rooms early on Saturday mornings to be sure that we weren't trained and could leave in time for the game. They looked after us and listened to us and made sure that we could survive.

Without soccer, I don't know if I could have made it through freshman year. For one thing, I was completely on my own. Scott had fallen in love with the girl he'd taken to our senior prom. She was also a cadet and he spent his free time with her, strengthening their new relationship. He disappeared almost entirely from my life. No notes in my mailbox, no attempts to sit next to me in church or the evening assembly. It hurt terribly. I wasn't jealous, exactly—there had never been anything romantic between Scott and me. But he'd been my other half, with whom I'd lived through all my hopes and dreams for the Academy. Now that we were there, I wanted to share that experience with him as well. I finally realized I would have to survive without him, and I learned, very quickly, to be alone and rely on myself for support.

I was under so much stress that I started losing weight. I lost at least six pounds in basic training, and continued at the same pace through the start of the school year. Midway through the first semester, my uniform pants were all but falling off. The upperclassmen noticed. Some of them cared, and others used my shrinking size as an added opportunity for hazing me.

"We're going to fatten you up," the senior at my lunch table declared one day. From now on, he decided, I wasn't leaving the table until I'd finished eating everyone's dessert. This, I quickly found, was cruel and unusual punishment. My classmates weren't allowed to help me, and I wasn't allowed to get up until I was visibly ill. After a few days I learned to make things bearable by eating nothing until dessert. Then I'd leave lunch on a sugar high, feeling sick, and fall asleep an hour later, between classes. This went on for almost two weeks, until finally someone noticed what was happening and intervened on my behalf. I think the senior was growing bored with the game, anyway. He wasn't getting any dessert, and I still wasn't gaining weight.

One good thing came out of this: I was protected from being the butt of the "fat cadet chick" jokes making the rounds of the dining hall. As everyone knew, freshman year is a bad time for female SMACKs' figures. If you weren't a very active athlete, it was easy to gain weight on mess hall food, which was loaded with extra calories, and by drowning your sorrows in ice cream and pizza on the weekends. And the minute you gained weight, everyone noticed. Our uniforms had been designed for men, without waistbands or pleats or extra fabric around the hips. If your hips widened even a fraction of an inch, the pockets would stick out. It was pitiful, really. Not that weight gain was a problem only for women. But when the men gained weight it was considered no laughing matter. I never thought it really was for the girls, either. The need to stay slim was just another pressure at a time when we were under enough to make any normal human crack. Too many women and even a few men caved in and developed eating disorders. Obsessed with Air Force weight standards, they lowered their own weights until they could meet and beat those standards. It was as though they'd internalized the terrible surveillance that we were always under. In a place where they were constantly being controlled, they'd found what they thought was a way to exert some control. And a way to remove any trace of femininity from their flesh.

I could relate to that. I'd quickly learned that being too much of a woman was a liability at the Academy. Anything you might do to remind people that you were different, not just one of the boys, could get you into big trouble. I found this out the hard way. I'd joined the track team after soccer season ended and befriended an upperclass male hurdler who taught me how to navigate the hurdles. He supported me and cheered me on, and at a party after a track meet during which I actually fell down, he spent an evening cheering me up and encouraging me to continue to race. When he left the party, he gave me a hug. The next day, rumors were floating around the team that we were dating—something that was strictly forbidden. Though the rumor was patently false, it created an enormous amount of tension on the team. My hurdling immediately grew worse, and I received no help or instruction from anyone; even the upperclass male who once helped me was afraid to talk to me. Accepting that hug was a fatal error. It was too intimate, too much a man-to-woman move. Instead, I should have gone for a slap on the shoulders—a gesture with the same meaning, but expressed in a purely man-to-man way.

The episode taught me that I'd get along better at the Academy if I could pass for one of the boys. So I did everything I could to fit in and cover up my femininity. I never wore makeup and kept my hair extremely short. I didn't date, either, not that that was much of a sacrifice. Dating at the Academy consisted of evenings spent at athletic events and in the campus pizza parlor. Off-campus passes were extremely hard to get until you were a senior. We weren't supposed to have TVs in our rooms, either. So while there was no ban on romance, there almost didn't have to be. No one really wanted to date in the fishbowl atmosphere of the squadron. As I've mentioned, freshmen could only date other freshmen, which meant pretty slim pickings. And if an upperclassman came on to you, you were put in the awkward spot of either accepting the pass and breaking the rule, or rejecting him and running the risk that he'd take out his hurt ego on you in a training session. One upperclassman came on to me when our squadron went away on a midwinter ski trip. We were sitting in a hot tub, filled with freshmen and upperclassmen, and I felt a foot running up and down my leg. I couldn't tell him to cut it out in front of every-one—that would have been bad form. And after the trip when he started leaving notes in my dorm room, I was caught be-tween being flattered and being scared. Finally, I told him to wait and ask me out after the end of the year. He never did.

Academy social life was caught in a time warp, somewhere between the 1950s and the 1990s. I'd heard that a couple of se-niors who were engaged to be married were caught having sex in one of their rooms just six weeks before graduation and their wedding, and ended up being expelled. People thought about sex all the time, but were not allowed to *have* sex—in the dorms, at least—so when they did have sex, it was dirty. And the girls who did it were considered dirty, too. Because it was taboo, sex was an illicit thrill, like underage drinking. And those people who had sex often did it destructively, or to ex-cess. Veronica, a cadet in my squadron, was absolutely ob-sessed with sex. She was tall, pretty, and athletic and would run down the halls squirting a water gun in the shape of a penis. She also had a condom tree. (Both items were gifts from her mother.)

Sometimes I woke up at night to find my roommate having sex. Both beds were top bunks, built over our desks, and the noise and movements were a bit too close for comfort. Twice, I managed to put myself into a deep sleep until it was over. Once, I just had to leave the room. I don't know if she noticed or cared that I was there. I never told her how uncomfortable her sex life (and its retelling) made me. I was still a virgin, and planned to stay that way, too. There was a legend concerning the eight-and-a-half-ton marble statue of Pegasus that stood in the cadet area: if a female virgin ever graduated from the Academy, Pegasus would fly away. My friend Elizabeth and I had vowed to each other that we would make Pegasus leave its plinth and take to the air. This was my way of being romantic: I held to the idea that I would have sex the first time with that one perfect person who would be my husband.

If Veronica and her friends had known about this, I would have been the laughingstock of the squadron. So I just distanced myself from those women—and from sexuality—as much as possible. I cut my hair even shorter: half an inch on top and shaved close to my scalp in the back, with short bangs in the front. But the truth was, you could only go so far in denying your femininity. If you were a woman, your sexuality was going to rise up and eventually strike you down. Because I didn't date and tried to fit in as one of the guys, people whispered that I was a lesbian. After my haircut, an upperclassman came up behind me as I was walking along the marble strip on the Terrazzo one day and hissed "Dyke!" in my ear. There really wasn't any way to play by the rules and win. Because the rules didn't take me and others like me into account.

I SUPPOSE that with time, had things peacefully taken their course, I would have become comfortable with myself as a woman at the Academy. I would have seen that there was a middle ground to femaleness between slut and tomboy. There were some nice guys at the Academy. I could have befriended them. Perhaps I could even have dated—if only I'd had a chance to find my way through the wilderness of becoming a woman in a man's world. But that was not to be. I was ambushed.

The trouble came, as troubles so often do, just as I was on the verge of triumph. It was the last week of freshman year. I'd gone through all the final rituals and the final hazing. My parents had come to Colorado Springs for the recognition weekend. I had never been so happy to see them. There was so much I wanted to show them. I wanted to share this life, let them see what I'd accomplished. We went out to dinner on

Friday night, right after my last exam was over. "You made it, Kelly," they said, toasting me over a glass of wine. "You survived. We all survived."

We made plans to meet the next day, and I went back to my dorm room, leaving the door unlocked for my roommate. She came in soon afterward, and also left the door unlocked. We often did that. No one worried about anything happening in the dorms. We were, after all, on Air Force grounds, surrounded by our nation's finest.

That night, I slept in my sheets. I allowed myself this rare treat because I knew that there were no more inspections for the remainder of the year. It was cozy, I thought as I fell asleep, to go to bed tightly wrapped in covers for once.

A few hours later I realized I was in a trap. There was someone pressing against me and holding me down. Something wet had been thrown up against my face. There was a terrible smell of sweat and alcohol, and hot breath against my neck. What was happening was so dreamlike that I could hardly believe it was real. I spent the next few moments in a kind of half-sleep, my mind refusing to wake up to what my body was going through. Water splashed against my face. I started up and tried to sit, but was forced back down by a large, muscular arm. I opened my eyes and saw a huge man standing over me, pushing me down. He was fully dressed and standing on the ladder that reached up to my bunk bed. He was covering my mouth with his hand. His other hand was wandering up and down my body. He pulled up my pajama top. He pulled down my pants. His fingers reached everywhere, touching every intimate part of my body. I twisted and turned and struggled, tried to rise and cry for help, but the man kept his hand clapped tightly over my mouth. I grabbed his wrists and tried to fight him off, but he was a solid, hugely muscular football player, and I couldn't win. My tightly pinned sheets held my legs immobile. I couldn't kick him off, couldn't push him off the ladder. While struggling with him, I caught a glimpse of my roommate's bed. She was being held down, too—but she was laughing.

My memory stops at this point. I don't know when or why my attacker left. He did not rape me. He didn't say anything to me. He may have expected me to laugh, like my roommate. And after a while, when I didn't, he may have grown bored or scared. I lay awake for the rest of the night. I didn't say anything to my roommate and I didn't move a muscle. I almost felt that if I didn't move or speak, then what had happened wouldn't become real. Now that it was over, it already seemed unreal.

"DID YOU KNOW those guys?" I asked my roommate the next morning.

"I think I knew one of them," she said, looking away. "He must have gotten the wrong idea."

He'd probably thought that since my roommate had a reputation as a willing partner, I would be one too, and had brought his friend along for some fun. I was furious.

"We should report it," I said.

"Report what?"

"They attacked us."

"No, they didn't."

"I'd call it an attack," I said.

"Oh, Kelly," she answered, turning away and preparing to leave the room. "It really wasn't so bad."

I WALKED THROUGH the squadron hallways wild-eyed. I couldn't sleep. I lay awake at night, afraid of letting myself go into the darkness of sleep. I remembered how, when I was a child, my brother Tim's rock band used to practice in our basement right at my bedtime. I would lie in bed, kept awake by the beat of the drums, and eventually fall asleep after using my imagination to create a wonderfully peaceful world. I tried to do that now— tried to go to a safe and calm place in my mind. But I couldn't. I just couldn't get away from the fear. A few days after recognition, the ceremony that marks the end of freshman year, an upperclassman called me into his room. Since freshman year was over and I was officially a cadet, we could now talk to each other like humans without shouting or reciting knowledge.

"Something's bothering you," he said. "You're not yourself these days."

"Well," I said, "something's happened."

I told him the whole story, right down to the fact that my roommate had laughed. I said that I wanted to report it.

"Did you scream?" he said. "Did you call for help?"

I was honest with him. "I don't remember," I said. "I don't know. I was in shock."

"Will your roommate come forward with you?"

I said no.

He said to let it drop. He'd been sitting at the Cadet-in-Charge-of-Quarters desk—posted as a kind of hall monitor for the squadron—that night, right near my door, and he hadn't seen or heard anything. That didn't mean he didn't believe me, but it did mean I had no witnesses. If I came forward, it would be my word against my roommate's—and against two other people's, if I identified our attackers. They were players on the Academy football team. No one would want to go after them. And with graduation coming up, he said, no one would want to investigate, anyway. No one would care.

No one cared. The best thing I could do was try not to care, either. So I buried the memory of the attack as far back as I could in my mind. What I didn't realize was just how deeply it had been burned into my flesh.

I WAS LUCKY that, unlike most college students, I couldn't spend the summer after my freshman year hanging out at home and napping. I don't think that I could have survived that. I needed not to think but to be busy, to be surrounded by rush and stress and sound so as not to listen to the rumblings of my mind or experience the misery of memory. Fortunately, the Air Force had plans for me. I was going to spend three weeks in the Rocky Mountains of Colorado, learning to stay alive by eating bugs and drinking mud.

The instruction started out on campus, at the Air Force Academy. For four days, we listened to lectures and watched slides showing all the grisly and disgusting things that can happen to humans shot down out of planes and trapped in the wild. There was a picture of feet rotted black and blistering with frostbite, the toes just on the verge of falling off. There was a leg with a compound fracture, the bones sticking out and the blood running down into a torn-up boot. There was a guy, still alive, with a twig sticking out of his eyeball. All around me in the auditorium, cadets from the Air Force Academy, Naval Academy, West Point, and ROTC groaned and writhed. The instructors, enlisted personnel from Fairchild Air Force Base in Washington State, simply loved it. As the country's best and brightest clutched their stomachs and tried not to lose their lunch, they grinned wider and wider and the slides got worse.

Then, when they'd struck the fear of God into us, they told us survival stories. Survival in the wild, we learned, was very largely a matter of will. Our instructors told us about a legendary man who was lost at sea. He spent weeks afloat on a tiny little raft, swimming every day to stay in shape even though there were sharks around. He had no drinking water. He had no food, except for the occasional raw fish he caught. But he lived for the weeks until he was rescued, because his will was so very strong. The counterexample was a pilot who crashed his airplane in Alaska. The plane landed with a minimum of damage. He had shelter, food, warm clothing—all he needed to stay alive. But he also had a gun. And after many hours of sitting on the ground wallowing in self-pity and wondering why he had not yet been rescued, he walked about a hundred feet away from the airplane and shot himself. A few hours later, the rescue plane arrived and gathered up his dead body. He had the means to survive, but not the will.

I was having some survival problems of my own in those days. Only two weeks had passed since my attack. The last thing I wanted was to be in close physical proximity to men—and now, of course, I was surrounded by them all the time. I had struck up an acquaintance with a Naval Academy midshipman, Kevin, who sat next to me in our training classes. We passed notes and joked, trying to keep each other awake while the instructors droned on about compasses and maps. But we rarely socialized together after class. And we never discussed personal things.

In the hallways, I averted my eyes from all men and veered away from them toward the walls when they passed. I had to keep a minimum safe distance between men and me at all times. Big, burly men who physically resembled my attacker made me actually jump away in fear. Kevin noticed this. But he didn't say anything. He just treated me kindly and kept a respectful distance, and soon enough the two of us became friends. When it came time to choose partners for our survival and evasion training in the woods, we decided to stick together. I knew it would mean bunking together in tents, eating and sleeping and going to the bathroom in the closest prox-

imity. But I thought I could deal with that. Kevin was solid
and muscular, with crew-cut dirty-blond hair and a quiet air
of self-assurance. After we'd spent hours together in the classroom, I instinctively trusted him. He eventually became a Ma-
rine. Back then, he was just like a point of quiet in a storm.

The day before we headed off to the woods, we made back-
packs out of used parachute packs and filled them with dry
uniforms and socks, a sleeping bag, and a jacket or sweater.
We had to travel light; we'd be carrying our packs for the next
ten days. I added some tissues and toothpaste anyway. Food
was strictly forbidden. So the last thing Kevin and I did was
stuff ourselves at the cafeteria. We had no idea how much food
we'd be getting out in the woods, but something told us that it
wouldn't be much. He looked at me thoughtfully as I ate. I was
antsy, tense, and touchy.

"Is anything wrong?" he said.

"I'm scared about this," I blurted. "I'm not sure how it'll be,
out in the woods."

And quietly, making sure that the entire survival training
program couldn't hear, I told him about what had happened to
me recognition week. Kevin was smart enough not to pat me
on the shoulder or hold my hand. He just shook his head. "I'm
really sorry that that happened to you," he said. "Not all of us
are like that. You'll see."

The next day, we loaded up into a small convoy of big blue
Air Force Academy buses and headed out into the woods. I
tried to sleep on the two-hour drive, as we'd been warned that
the first night would be extremely long. The bus wound along
a road lined with huge pine trees, which screened the mountain's perilously steep curves. When we reached our destination, we started hiking deep into the woods, and stopped when
we reached a small clearing. We were divided into groups of
twelve and would spend the next few days learning the art of
survival. We were told to sit, and immediately started looking

around for rocks or logs. We'd been told never to sit or even kneel on the ground. It wore out your clothing. And if you were going to survive you needed your clothing to remain intact. If we took care of our clothes, we could conceivably, like one World War II pilot shot down in the Far East, wander the woods for over a decade with hardly any wear and tear.

The secret to the art of survival, our instructors said, was improvisation. You had to learn how to get by with the materials you had on hand. If you ejected from a plane, the raw material you'd start with would be your parachute. The used parachute harness could easily be made into a backpack. The parachute cord could be divided into tiny strings that could then be woven into a fishing net. The wires contained in the parachute harness structure could be twisted into a snare to catch small animals. The chute itself could be made into different kinds of shelters: white side up if you'd landed in snow, green side up if you were hiding in the forest, orange patch showing if you wanted to signal for help. Pieces of the chute could also be used as a water filter. You could feel the ground for a damp spot and dig up some mud, then drain the water out of it through layers of parachute filters. The water would be black but drinkable. You could also get fresh water by wrapping the parachute around leaves, letting nature run its course through photosynthesis and condensation, squeezing out the water later in the afternoon.

That first night, after walking deeper into the woods, our group made two-person shelters with our rain ponchos. Kevin and I were partners and worked on our shelters together. Once the shelters were up and secured in place, the instructors had us fill them with "duff"—a mixture of dirt, tree bark, and pine boughs that, if piled high enough, could keep you warm. Alone in the tent with Kevin, warm and dry and safe, I felt almost as if I were on a camping trip, and I fell into a deep, peaceful sleep. That lasted about five hours.

The instructors woke us before sunrise. It was freezing in the mountains, and we dressed quickly: fatigue pants with running tights or long underwear underneath, a long-sleeved cotton T-shirt and camouflage sweater, a fatigue jacket, and two pairs of socks. We were given our food provisions for the next ten days: one MRE (Meal Ready to Eat) consisting of a foodlike patty, plus some crackers and dehydrated foods, and a couple of oatmeal-and-corn bars. Beyond that, we were on our own.

We learned to eat the protein most easily found in the forest: ants and crickets. Ants, I discovered, taste like lemon drops. If you squash enough of them in water, you can make lemonade. Otherwise, you have to pop their heads off. If you don't, they'll bite you on the way down. Crickets are stringy and crunchy like celery. They have to be eaten carefully, too; if you don't yank off their legs, they might grab on at the edge of your throat and fight not to go down. Of course, if you killed them first, you wouldn't have these problems—but if you're in the kind of situation where you're eating bugs, you're not likely to have the time to put much preparation into your meal. (You probably wouldn't want to get too close a look at it, either.) It is all personal preference. We learned to stay away from anything with more than six legs, and to identify all the edible plants and roots that grow in the forest. Some of them are pretty hard to choke down. Others, like the green onions that grow commonly in woods and fields, seem almost like normal food. The problem with those is that they make your breath and body stink. A few years later, when I was a survival training instructor, a couple of New York City boys in my group were disgusted by the MREs and ate the onions all day long. We always knew where they were by the smell. It wasn't a great evasion tactic. As a matter of fact, we had been warned that our body scents could give us away. During the Vietnam War, American soldiers hiding in the woods could be found by the Vietnamese because they smelled like soap, deodorant, and hamburger grease.

I didn't mind the wild salads. I liked them better than eating rabbit, which meant skinning rabbit, which was an experience that I definitely could have done without. So whenever I could, I bartered with the group, rabbit for vegetables or oat bars. There was usually someone who was happy to trade with me. And as long as we had enough to drink, I didn't find the lack of food all that terrible. But some of the bigger guys were really starving. Their little bit of a twelfth of a rabbit really mattered to them.

After five days of base camp, we camouflaged our entire bodies and set to work learning to evade. We learned how to navigate at night using our charts and compass. How to walk on the balls of our feet without breaking twigs, to move branches out of our way without rustling the leaves. There was an art to camouflage, too. You didn't only have to cover your face with green and brown camouflage paint; you had to mask the back of your neck, the insides of your ears, and your fingers. You had to cover up all the shapes formed by your body that were out of place in the woods. You needed, for example, to put some leaves and twigs in your hat and pockets to break up the shape of your head and body. Your legs make an inverted V when you stand still, so instead you had to crouch down and tuck yourself up into a huge ball to look like a rock. Or, if you were next to a tree, you'd cross your right leg over your left and try to squeeze into the tree trunk, thinking thin and small. You had to learn to move differently: if you heard a noise, you couldn't instantly drop to the ground, because the eye picks up movement. You had to very quietly slip away, fade into the darkness of the jungle. Or, if you were standing up, you had to melt to the ground and assume the shape of a rock.

On two of our evenings out in the woods we were stopped by "aggressors"—the cadets assigned to track us and act the role of enemy forces. We told them that we were out camping and had gotten lost. We had been taught to tell the enemy whatever it took to get away. Lying was perfectly acceptable if it brought you home safely with honor, which meant not defaming the United States or telling state secrets. One time, as planned by the training instructors, the enemy didn't believe us. We were taken prisoners of war, and held in confinement for several days. We were psychologically battered, spoken to in strange accents we could barely understand, and called criminals. Our every movement was restricted. With no rights whatsoever, we learned what it felt like to have every freedom and liberty taken away. It was all done so convincingly that, at the end, when we were released, the sight of an American flag made many of us cry. Just a taste of POW camp had been enough to make us realize the importance of all we were learning to fight for.

We understood, too, why so much of evasion and resistance is psychological. Surviving a prisoner-of-war situation is very largely a question of reining in your mind, because it's all you can control. And that's no small thing. It can be the difference between life and death. During seven years as a prisoner of war in the Hanoi Hilton, one pilot designed and built an entire house in his mind, right down to the last nail. When he finally returned to the United States, he bought all the materials and supplies, and he built the house. He found that he had imagined things so perfectly that he had only seven nails more than he needed. Another prisoner memorized the names of the hundreds of prisoners in the camp so that if he were ever set free, he could go back to the authorities and tell them who was there. And, of course, the POWs prayed.

I came out of the woods feeling renewed. It wasn't just that I'd survived an intense physical ordeal. I had spent ten days sleeping and dressing in a tent with a man, depending for my survival and safety on other men, and I'd come through unscathed. Back at the Academy, I headed straight to my dorm for a shower. Kevin and I had made a pizza date: we were going to eat just as much as our shrunken stomachs would allow. I looked in the mirror for a long time before I washed. Ten days' worth of dirt, sweat, and camouflage paint had created a pretty good disguise. In my rumpled camouflage suit, with my hair in a cap, there was virtually no way to tell that I was a girl.

But after I'd showered and changed, I was Kelly again. And as I walked down the hallways, I cringed.

CHAPTER 3

Learning to Keep Quiet

War is an ugly thing, but not the ugliest of things. The decayed and degraded state of moral and patriotic feeling which thinks that nothing is worth war is much worse. The person who has nothing for which he is willing to fight, nothing which is more important than his own personal safety, is a miserable creature and has no chance of being free unless made and kept so by the exertions of better men than himself.

—JOHN STUART MILL

I WAS HAVING A HORRIBLE TIME WITH MY SWIMMING CLASS— which was strange, since I had grown up on water skis and loved the water. All cadets have to take a swim class in order to graduate from the Air Force Academy, and naturally, we had to learn to kick, stroke, and turn exactly to specifications. I was a decent enough swimmer, but I had my own style. I had to spend an hour in the pool every day with the rest of the class learning how to swim just so. I perfected my breast stroke and my side stroke without problem. But I had real trouble with the dead man's float.

The dead man's float is a long-endurance water-survival position, which every young swimmer learns in summer camp: arms spread wide, feet dangling, face flat down into the water. The position is meant to allow you to expend the least energy possible while waiting to be rescued. To pass the Academy test, you had to spend twenty minutes in this position. Take advantage of it, the instructors said. Take it as an order to relax. But I simply could not relax and do the dead man's float properly. During one swim class we practiced it. But the first moment I put my face in the water and felt the wetness lapping up around my cheeks and insinuating itself into my ears, I jerked my head up and began flailing my arms and legs. I fought to remain calm. I tried again, and when I felt the water creeping up my arms and legs, I kicked and punched at it and gasped for breath. The third time, I made a conscious effort to take a deep breath, relax, float, and let the water carry me. Now it seemed as if thousands of hands were touching my body, invading my private parts. The memory of the attack came flooding back every time I let the water engulf me. It was the wetness—like the water that my attacker had splashed in my face to wake me up. I did not feel safe while being forced to float. I felt that at any moment the water would force me down and invade me.

For the next twenty minutes I struggled through the drill, trying to solve yet another problem on my own. At the end of class, I crawled from the pool and pulled my instructor aside.

"I'm having a hard time staying calm and relaxing during the dead man's float," I said.

"I can see," she said. "What's going on?"

"For some reason, it's bringing back horrible memories."

During the next swim class we worked through the fear together, and she helped me relax enough to hold the float. When I felt panicked, I calmed myself by reciting lists from biology class in my mind: bones, muscles, names of attachment points between bones and muscles, the nervous system, the digestive tract. Or I would raise my head and let the sight of her standing at the side of the pool reassure me that what I was feeling was not real, but just memories. Once I passed the test, the instructor said she was sure that my panic hadn't been caused by the water. Something else was bothering me—she thought so, anyway, since I could swim very well but hated to float. She recommended that I see a counselor to talk things through in private.

I made an appointment that very afternoon. The counselor was a plain woman, fortyish, and dressed in civilian clothes. She seemed nice enough. We made small talk as I told her the basic facts about myself and my family. Then we made another appointment to talk about the reason for my visit. That time, we got down to business right away. I told her all the details of the attack that I could remember. I could not remember, I said, how it ended, or even how it began.

"Well," she said, "let's trace the evening back." She was curious about the dinner with my parents. She questioned me on every moment, every detail. I was growing frustrated with these questions. When she heard of the toast and the glass of wine, she laid down her pen. She'd heard enough to offer up a diagnosis.

"You are a person who likes to control things," she said. "And in this situation, you were not in control."

That was a fact.

"You need," she said, "to learn that you can be with a man and have control and feel secure, even during a sexual encounter.

"Now," she went on, looking at me more closely, "what are we going to do about the underage drinking incident?"

I was speechless.

"I really should report you," she said. "Underage drinking is a serious offense."

"It was a glass of wine, with my parents."

"Are you sure that's all it was?" she asked. "Are you sure that you remember?"

I felt my face grow hot with anger. She didn't believe me. Not a word that I had said. To this "specialist," everything that had happened was about my getting drunk and blacking out while having sex. As if a single glass of wine six hours earlier could have made me fool around with a total stranger in the middle of the night! The counselor had one of the coldest expressions I'd ever seen in my life. It dawned on me that by coming in for help, I had walked into a trap and could end up expelled from the school.

"What are you going to do with this information?" I asked.

"Nothing, for now," she said. "But if there's another incident of this kind, I'm going to have to report this one, too."

NEEDLESS TO SAY, I did not make another appointment. I had learned an important lesson about asking for help in the Air Force: Don't. The doctor-patient privilege that civilians enjoy doesn't exist at all in the military. Of course, no one explains this to you until you've already poured out your heart to a doctor. Then you learn that if the doctor feels you are a risk to your country or to your squadron, he or she has the right to inform your commander. The doctor won't just reveal the diagnosis, either; he or she will divulge the details of whatever problem brought you in. So people in the armed forces learn very quickly to keep their problems to themselves. They may be depressed because they're away from their families sixteen hours a day or six months at a stretch, or because they don't sleep, are fighting with their spouses, are overworked and drowning in paperwork and worried about their career, but if they have any experience in seeing colleagues ask for help, they'll keep quiet. If a doctor diagnoses you as depressed in the Air Force, he'll recommend you be removed from flight status. Then, when you can't perform the job you love and were trained to do, you become more depressed. If this is noticed, someone will question whether you're fit for duty. You're likely to end up losing your job, all because you wanted to talk to someone about how to handle your stress. It's well known in the military: never ask for help unless you're ready to end your career. Despite an alarming increase in alcohol-related incidents and suicides, the military has done nothing to encourage its members to seek professional help. The consequences for having a mental health record are well known—if you seek help, your career is over.

I saw all of this with sickening clarity a few years later when one of my close friends, Tom, a senior captain and a distinguished graduate of Officer Training School, was suffering from mild depression because of marital problems. His performance on the job was never affected; he was never late or insubordinate, nor did he display any symptoms of despondency. But one of his colleagues, concerned about his friend, and aware of his problems at home, notified Tom's commander, who ordered him to see a psychotherapist at the mental health clinic on base. After two weeks of treatment, Major (Dr.) Brooks, his psychologist, recommended that Tom be returned to full duty. Tom was in the top 5 percent of his career field, had nothing but outstanding ratings on all his performance reports, and was well on his way to a successful career. But rather than reinstating him, the commander stated, "I had a sister once in your position, so I know how to deal with situations like these." He pulled Tom's security clearance, his job, his flight line badges (which allowed him access to his work area on the flight line), and transferred him to another assignment within the unit, where, for seven months, he endured over 600 hours of mental health evaluations and diagnostic testing costing the taxpayers over $7,000. The chief of the mental health clinic, in a memo placed in Tom's medical records, stated Tom has "a confusing and misleading mental health history, which prevents him from reaching his potential in the Air Force." After seventeen months, five doctors, and eleven separate diagnoses, Tom's history was described as "convoluted." The report went on: "The outcome of all his testing was within normal limits . . . he is fully competent to perform military duties as assigned by his commander with no restrictions . . . he is worldwide qualified. . . . His previous diagnosis was incorrect, [there is] no [need for] ongoing treatment or medications, no occupational, social, or financial impairment."

Despite these reports, Tom constantly battled to return to duty. For months, his psychologist, who had a Ph.D. and over ten years' clinical experience, met with Tom's command staff and encouraged them to return him to full duty, but to little avail. Tom's staff told Major Brooks he was "too close to the situation" and could "no longer be objective." Seeking more help, Tom went to the military judge advocate to inquire about his legal rights—which were none, since he wasn't being charged with a crime.

The protocol was not as clear as it should have been. The military base hospital did not have final say; despite five doctors' recommendations that he return to duty, he was at the mercy of his commander, who had no medical degree or psychological training. Despite the overwhelming evidence that Tom was fit for his job, he was still not allowed to return to work; rather, this time he was transferred to another base. In today's one-mistake Air Force, commanders are understandably afraid to make the "wrong decision." So they often simply make no decision at all, which can be the safest course. In effect, there is no accountability and they pass the buck on to someone else. Tom is still in the Air Force, slowly putting his life and career back together. He remembers the haunting words of one Air Force colonel: "We thought you, of all people, would understand sacrificing yourself for the betterment of the Air Force."

SOME PEOPLE recommend that, whatever your religion, a safe way to get help is to talk to a priest. Priests, one might assume, are bound to discretion by a higher law than the Military Code of Justice. And some priests and chaplains do adhere to a rule of secrecy. But others tell all, feeling it's their duty to keep commanders apprised of what's going on with their subordinates. And since the commanders write the chaplains' recommendations for promotion, there is more than a little incentive to keep the commanders happy.

This situation led to some sorry tale-telling recently at Whiteman Air Force Base. The chief of chaplains there learned that a young civilian who'd previously been a member of the enlisted corps was engaged to marry an officer, Lieutenant William Kite. The priest filed a complaint of fraternization against Kite, who wound up resigning from the Air Force with a general discharge to avoid court-martial for fraternization and a possible year-long jail sentence.

AFTER MY MEETING with the counselor, I went back to my dorm in a state of shock. I felt sick to my stomach. I was more scared than ever. Reliving the event had left me feeling dirty and disgusted. I wanted to take a long shower, but still hated the feeling of water on my face. I shied away from all the men in my hallway and tried to keep myself as hidden as possible. I so wished that I didn't have to be around men: since my world was 90 percent male, I was in a state of anxiety all the time.

Finally, my subconscious took over. After weeks of mental torture, something simply turned itself off in my head. I didn't repress the memory of the attack, but it went underground, buried itself so deep that it lost its emotional charge. That was something of a relief, except that, unfortunately, a lot of other emotions went dead with it. I was able to function now, but I went through the daily motions of my life in a daze. I was like a trained robot, living without thinking and feeling. I withdrew from my classmates and began calling home almost every day. I needed to hear those safe, familiar voices. My parents, hearing how unhappy I was, said that we'd talk about everything over Christmas break. I counted the days until I could leave Colorado Springs and go home.

This homecoming was so different from my first trip back to Atlanta, on Thanksgiving break of freshman year. Then, my brothers and sisters had laughed at me because I was so full of myself and the Academy. I'd talked the Academy talk, walked the Academy walk, spoken in acronyms and military jargon so naturally and incessantly that my brother Don had taken to making a buzzer sound every time I said something in indecipherable military-speak. I'd been so puffed full of pride and pleasure. Driving through the neighborhood, I'd stopped my car at the sight of a big American flag and thought: "I am fighting to defend this." I had been on my way to becoming a perfect little cadet.

Now I didn't think that such a thing existed. I'd seen too much in the past year. I'd always seen upperclassmen as something just short of gods. I'd been so proud, at the end of freshman year, to be able to call myself a cadet. But now I was seeing that upperclassmen weren't the perfect specimens of humanity that they seemed, in their crisp uniforms, with their sharp gestures, their perfectly creased pants and shined shoes. They were simply college students living in a very strict environment and sometimes sneaking downtown at night without a pass, climbing the walls to get some extra space. They launched fruit against the walls of their dorms. They broke all the rules, and then some. To blow off steam some nights, they held "gross-out contests," during which the men did things like drink, get sick, and eat one another's vomit. Or they'd pour honey down each other's backs, stick an apple in the crack of their butts, and then lick what dripped out the bottom. They drank like fish. They had casual sex. Some male cadets even hid in closets and watched their buddies having sex. They even had hidden families—wives and children whom they'd "rediscover" the day after graduation.

And even when cadets played perfectly by the rules, their way of being left a lot to be desired. Living by the honor code, for example, was often far from what I considered honorable. The honor code created a completely outer-directed sense of morality. Most cadets didn't make moral choices based on deep-seated feelings of right or wrong, but on the basis of blind adhesion to a set of values that were spoon-fed to them. We swore: "We will not lie, steal, or cheat, nor tolerate among us anyone who does. Furthermore, I swear to do my full duty. So help me God." But, often enough, the vows were applied selectively and in ways that I didn't consider honorable at all. I saw friends turn in other friends for honor code violations. I saw squadrons torn in half because of honor inquisitions. I saw excellent cadets who would have made superior officers brought up on honor code charges because of unsupported claims and forced out of the Academy. Very often, these accusations were made just to curry favor with superior officers. Prosecution was just as random and extremely selective.

One cadet I knew accused another of having glanced at her paper and copied an answer. The accused cadet went before an honor review board. The teacher testified that he'd seen no cheating and, judging by the test results, believed that none had occurred. The tests were compared and there were hardly any similar answers. Yet, despite the overwhelming lack of evidence, the accused cadet was found guilty and dismissed from the Academy. At the same time, I saw cadets who'd been investigated for rape and sexual harassment graduate from the Academy and go on with unblemished records to pursue their military careers.

We lived in fear of unexpected fiascoes. If I drew a blank during a test, I was very careful not to give the wrong impression while I stared off into space. I had to make it crystal clear that I was not staring over someone's shoulder. So I would raise my head briskly, in one swift, solid movement, and stare directly at the ceiling. If I wanted to glance at the time, I would raise my head to look at the ceiling, turn my head in the direction of the clock, lower my head only slightly to see the time, then repeat the same movement in the opposite direction. This was a waste of time and a real concentration breaker. It had nothing whatsoever to do with honesty. But it was typical of what happens to your behavior when the letter of the law is more important than its spirit. You live by the rule of fear, not of honor or even common sense.

All this made me completely question the institution that I'd fought so hard to join. Was learning blind obedience to rules and a callous disregard for the gray areas of real life and real feelings the best way to prepare for leadership? Would an education in brownnosing and groupthink give us the right stuff to defend the United States? I didn't think so. In fact, it seemed un-American to me. After all, our country had fought hard for the right to freedom of opinion.

Down the line I would learn that my nineteen-year-old instinct was correct. The Air Force succeeds beautifully in teaching its members how to operate complex machinery, but is utterly incapable of imbuing them with a sense of how to be human beings in the modern world. Meanwhile, I was coming more and more to think that the whole Academy experience was not for me. For one thing, being a perfect cadet seemed to me to mean being a not-so-great human being. And, on a more basic level, I didn't *like* being a cadet. I was an upperclassman now, but as a sophomore was still the lowest on the upperclass totem pole. That meant that whatever paperwork there was to do, the juniors and seniors passed it on to us. Also, sophomores were responsible for checking that the freshmen knew their knowledge. But in their frightened shouts of "Ma'am!" I rarely heard genuine respect. Some of the freshmen even called me "sir" just to get my goat. Nobody disciplined them for it. It was as though saying "Ma'am!" was such an unusual effort that they had the right to refuse to acknowledge me as a woman. I got so sick of it that finally, when one too many freshmen called me "sir," I had him write an essay on the differences between men and women. The next offender had to make a list of the ten major differences between men and women. Other freshmen I just had scuttle around the Terrazzo carrying big, fat basic biology textbooks.

I talked about very little of this with my family. We just discussed the academic problems I'd been having: notably, in passing my one required course on economics. My teacher had said that my reasoning made sense, but not economic sense. I barely passed the class. That amused my family.

But I could not tell them about the attack. We'd never talked about sex at all; I would not start things off by discussing the attack. Besides, I had buried the attack deep in my memory and did not want to relive it. I also just couldn't bring myself to tell them how seriously I was now thinking about leaving the Academy. They were all so proud of me. My parents had already reserved five rooms at the Embassy Suites hotel in Colorado Springs for my graduation in June 1993. They bragged of my experience to their friends. It would have been awful to let them down. And it would have been a terrible letdown for me, too. There was a real stigma attached to quitting: it meant that you hadn't been strong enough to endure the agony of the institution and take the pain like a man. I knew that if I quit, people would believe it was because I was too weak for the Academy—not because I simply didn't like it.

In the end, I didn't have the courage to quit. I told myself that I had to stick with it, because at the time I thought it was the only way I could fly. And I so loved flying. The summer after freshman year, I had spent a few days at McDill Air Force

Base, Florida, and had had my first ride in a military aircraft—
an F-16. The F-16 is a sexy plane—sleek, lithe, maneuverable—
and it's extremely versatile, too. It can drop bombs on enemy
targets, then turn around and shoot down an enemy fighter
with its missiles. Plus, it gives an intense ride: fast, purposeful,
packed with firepower. As the pilot, an Air Force major, pushed
his throttle all the way up for takeoff, a thrill rushed through
my body. The afterburner kicked in, and I felt a jolt that threw
me back in my seat. We rushed forward then as the engine lit
and exhaled its powerful force. I could not stop smiling as we
streamed down the runway. Then, suddenly, we were in the air,
the pilot easing the plane's nose higher and higher as we
climbed with easy grace. He shouted back to ask how I was
doing. I could barely make out what he was saying. The radio
traffic was all babble to me, too. So I just looked out the window and enjoyed the ride. The sky was clear and you could see
for miles.

As the pilot rolled into a turn and adjusted the throttle once
again, I could feel myself getting a bit light-headed. Gravity
was working against my body, causing the blood to pool in my
lower legs and feet. This is a major danger for fighter pilots; if
it isn't corrected, they may "gray out"—which makes their vision cloudy and gray—or black out entirely. Like the pilot, I
was wearing a G suit. Its holsterlike pants wrapped around the
leg and contained air bladders. When the force of gravity became too severe, these filled, forcing the blood up from the feet
and back into circulation. As I felt the air bladders inflate, I
also took quick breaths and released them forcefully, straining
until the forces diminished. Then the pilot did a series of loops
and barrel rolls. We flipped ourselves around wing over wing,
doing aileron rolls. After a few demonstrations, the pilot let
me have a chance. I put my left hand on the matching throttle
and my right hand on the stick in my seat behind the pilot. I

felt as if I were in a moving La-Z-Boy chair. I flicked my right wrist very slightly. We abruptly veered off to the right and into a nosedive. I tried to correct subtly to the left, and we rolled over. Once we were level again, I pulled back and we started to do a loop. It was amazing how responsive the instruments were, almost as though you could think your direction and the plane would follow. Power flowed from your fingers. For the first time in my life, I had a truly macho experience.

"Did you puke?" the crew chief wanted to know when I climbed down from the plane. Nope. I'd been careful to eat an extremely light breakfast, just to be sure I wouldn't see it again during the flight. I shook my pilot's hand. The crew chief gave me a thumbs-up. And I walked away from the F-16 with a swagger in my step. I hoped that in a few years the plane would be mine.

Did I *have* to stay at the Academy to fly? Not really. I could have gone to college anywhere and then possibly become a pilot through the National Guard or Air Force Reserve. Had I done that, I might have been able to fly a fighter for one of the units. But I just didn't have the strength to start again or the courage to leave. Nor could I see myself doing anything differently—applying to other schools and becoming a civilian.

I was on the bus coming back to the Academy from the Denver airport after a soccer trip away from the school, when a familiar pit opened up at the base of my stomach. All the cadets around me had suddenly fallen silent. "There's that feeling again," I overheard a senior say. Her seatmate nodded in agreement. That's when I knew I wasn't alone in my feelings about the Academy. I'd always thought that my discomfort had to do specifically with *me*, with my fears of training, of the assault course, or of men. But it wasn't true. The Academy was more than a school, or an experience. It was a feeling—a feeling of agony, of pain, dread, and hatred. Many cadets experienced it. Many continued to live it long after graduation.

I COULD NOT, I knew, hope to have a career in the Air Force if I continued to live in fear of men. The counselor had said I needed to learn that I could be in control around men. I particularly needed to know that I could be in control sexually. I took that to mean that she thought I should go and have sex so I would realize that it didn't always have to be forced and frightening. And that's what I set out to do. I'd been wondering about sex, anyway. My two best friends, who had made the Pegasus vow with me just a year earlier, were no longer virgins, so once again I was the odd one out. I had lunch with a male friend whom I trusted. He knew about the attack and had noticed my unease in the hallways; he'd said I should let him know if there was anything he could ever do to help. He'd probably never expected me to take him up on it. Or at least, not in the way I had in mind. I told him that I'd gone to see a counselor.

"She says I need to gain control," I said, "and to feel comfortable in an intimate situation."

There was a long silence in the conversation.

He instinctively knew what I wanted and asked, "Would you like to go out?"

On a Friday evening, I dressed in civilian clothes and met him at his car. We drove off base for a nice, relaxing dinner and then went to a motel. The room was a generic motel room. The bed was firm and there was a minibar. We watched television for a while. I drank a wine cooler, and he had a beer. We were both so nervous and awkward that for a moment I thought we'd let the whole thing drop. But then he leaned over and kissed me. We were U.S. Air Force Academy cadets, after all. We knew how to perform under stress. I just kept telling myself that this was therapy. Even though it contradicted the moral code by which I'd been raised. Even though it brought me no pleasure. It was something that I had to do.

After a few moments of awkward silence, I knew Pegasus wasn't going to fly because of me. It was all purely clinical, with no seduction, no romance. My friend was kind, though. "Is this okay?" he'd ask. "And this?" It was as if we were following the Antioch College code of sexual conduct.

When it was all over, we dressed in silence. I was expecting to feel somewhat different, as if I'd changed. Become a *woman*, as the romance novelists put it. But I felt exactly the same. In an odd sense, I felt as if I'd ended up, once again, in the camp of the men. Women, I'd always heard, got an emotional charge out of sex, while for men it was purely physical. I wondered if that was just a stereotype. Or if by having meaningless, casual sex without a relationship, I'd just, once and for all, become one of the boys.

"SHOULD I STAY or should I go now?"

The music came blasting across the Terrazzo. A couple of seniors were leaning out their windows and grinning. The joke was on us. Classes were starting the next day: the first classes of our junior year. The rule was that if you attended that class, you were officially committed to the Air Force. If you left before it, you wouldn't owe a penny toward your education. If you left afterward, you'd either have to repay the cost of your education to date, or serve as an enlisted member to pay back your tuition. I'd decided to stay. I just loved the flying too much to quit. I'd learned to fly a glider my sophomore year. I'd soloed before my parents, mastering the bizarre sensation of aero-tow—taking off while attached by rope to another aircraft. It was my first experience of feeling that click of recognition when something all of a sudden feels just right and makes you able to do what before seemed impossible, like when you're learning to play tennis and for the first time feel the ball hit the sweet spot in the center of the racket. At that moment, you can hit the ball with control and direction—and if you keep practicing, you'll never hit it with the side of the racket again. It had taken me about seven flights to learn to use the stick and rudder properly to keep my wings level and my glider centered behind the propeller plane towing me. Then, all at once, it was as if someone had turned on a light-bulb. I had the feel and could hold the glider behind the plane with no problem at all. "It just hit you, right?" my instructor had said.

"Yes."

He explained that it happens that way with everyone. From there, it was just a tiny step to my first solo. I flew around, did some stalls and some turns. I listened to the air slip across the wings and heard the perfect silence—the lack of all human noise. I was in heaven. I felt I'd been admitted to a celestial so-ciety whose lucky members, through the mastery of air and space, win the right to cruise high above everyone else. The light that had turned on so naturally in my head was an indi-cation that I was in fact good enough, coordinated enough, natural enough in the sky to make it as a pilot.

I'd also, at the end of sophomore year, had an experience that left me with the happy thought that there was more to life in the Air Force than the Air Force Academy. There was, for one thing, camaraderie. I'd been sent to Kunsan Air Base in Kunsan, South Korea. The F-16 pilots stationed there were on remote tours: one-year hardship assignments abroad, without their wives and children. Every day, they dealt with the stress of flying missions in the airspace right next to a hostile nation. Every night, they relieved some of the pressure by partying, and while I was there, they brought me along.

I should, I suppose, have found their life of working hard and playing hard alienating. Every night we went to bars where women danced naked and swung from poles, or stripped on a stage in the center of the room. As the men sidled up to the bar to order drinks, they were immediately set upon by a wave of "juicy girls"—prostitutes wearing short silk dresses. "Juicy? Juicy?" they'd ask, rubbing and bouncing themselves against the officers' laps. The nights were like marathons. In bar after bar, we drank *soju*—an Everclear-like grain alcohol—and OB Beer, a Korean beer that, judging by its smell, probably contained a fair amount of formaldehyde. My group of four cadets, honorary members of the Panton Squadron, earned our call signs, nicknames, one evening after a certain late-night drinking binge. Basically, the men vomited and blew chunks off the second-floor balcony of a restaurant. Since I enjoyed going out and drinking hard with the boys, I was quickly integrated into the group and given a nickname of my own, although I did not get sick. Joining comrades named Chunk Nose, Chunk Lips, and Chunk Face, I was called Chunk Tits.

I didn't make an issue of it. In truth, I didn't mind. I wasn't offended because, for once, there truly was no offense intended. I put my call sign on my name tag. I answered to the call of Chunk T. Some feminists might say this was the equivalent of sleeping with the enemy. But I would answer: You have to pick your battles. And you have to be able to distinguish between enemy attack and friendly fire. Because, in Korea, for the first time in my short Air Force career, I encountered real support, sympathy, and kindness. In our long nights of hanging out and drinking, the pilots listened to me when I talked of my fear and loathing of the Academy. Rather than calling me weak, they said my observations were astute. And they told me not to lose hope. The Academy, they said, pits every cadet against every other. In the *real* Air Force, the enemy was external. The need to fight—or to prepare to fight, as the case now was—brought members of the military together. It was true: I could see it all around me. There was none of the splitting up into groups of African Americans, Irish Americans, Jews, Catholics, and WASPs that I knew in America. Faced with an outside enemy, *all* the Americans came together and rallied as Americans. All the people stationed at Kunsan, enlisted and officers, went out together at night. They paid for rounds at the bar and in the jukebox, playing "American Pie" night after night and shouting "Bullshit!" and "Fuck you!" whenever Don McLean crooned, "This'll be the day that I die-aiy-aiy." They were scared of dying—they had reason to be—and that fear united them into the greatness of being Americans. They even brought me into the fold. No one cared that I was a cadet—and the only woman—out drinking with them in the middle of the night. No one pulled rank on me or harassed me. They mentored me.

"Don't sweat the little stuff," my favorite F-16 pilot told me. Captain Brian Green was a graduate of the Academy, class of 1980, which was the first class to include women. He had two little girls and one little boy. He was a real believer in women. "The Academy is all about rules and regulations and minutiae," he said. "The real Air Force is about defending freedom and liberty. Try to keep your mind on what matters. Otherwise, you'll go nuts."

In Korea, I saw that real discipline—real, morale-boosting discipline—had more to do with reason and judgment than with brandishing a punitive but largely empty honor code. On the infamous evening of blowing chunks, a cadet in my group came back to our hotel extremely drunk and disoriented. He walked into the hallway leading to his room from the direction opposite to his normal route, walked past the usual number of rooms, and inserted his key into what he thought was his door.

The lock turned, and he entered the room. As soon as the door closed behind him, he vomited on the bed. He walked out, left his key on the floor, and went into the bathroom, where he passed out. In the morning, he discovered not only that he was sleeping on a tile floor, but that he had thrown up in a visiting major's bed.

The major filed a complaint. The next morning, during a briefing, the cadet was handcuffed by the security police and dragged down to their building for questioning. It turned out that he'd accidentally been given a master key to the rooms. He was released to his squadron commander, who told the security police and the major that he'd handle the situation and take disciplinary action. After questioning the cadet, who apologized, the commander took the security police report and put it away in his desk drawer. He told the cadet not to drink during the rest of his stay in Korea and to apologize to the major. If he made it through the next few weeks without incident, the commander would tear up the report instead of sending it on to the Academy.

The cadet took his second chance and went on to graduate at the top of his class. He's a pilot in the Air Force today. If the Academy had had its way with him, his career would have ended right there. Fortunately, someone with a more developed sense of the human side of morality intervened.

Before leaving Korea, I had another ride in an F-16. We flew in formation, three feet apart. I looked out my window and saw the other pilot staring back in my direction. The sun shone off his gold cockpit, illuminating his dark visor. He moved the plane gracefully with the smallest, most delicate gestures. Then the clouds moved in and enveloped us in whiteness. I was struck once again by the peace. It was like having your faith renewed. I knew what I wanted to do with my life. It wasn't enough anymore just to want to be a pilot. I wanted to be an *F-16* pilot. And I was willing to grin and bear what I had to, to become one.

LITTLE DID I KNOW that forces beyond my control were about to change the rules of the game altogether. A few months after we made our commitments to the Air Force, Chief of Staff General Merrill McPeak came to the Academy to give a special briefing to all cadets. We filed into Arnold Hall in our blue cadet uniforms. General McPeak demonstrated the new service-dress style that he'd just decreed was the future look of the Air Force. He'd done away with name tags and changed the shoulder rank insignia to stripes on the sleeves. He looked like an airline pilot, I thought, staring up at his jacket sleeves from my seat in the front. All around me, cadets were shifting and whispering uncomfortably. McPeak wasn't known for making bold command decisions; we thought he'd come to talk uniforms.

Once we were all seated, though, he turned on a slide projector and started showing us graphs of planes and pilot spots. He pointed to charts showing a huge surplus of pilots for 1993 and 1994. He pointed to charts showing a deficit of planes. What was the point of having pilots without planes? Not much, he indicated. There were going to have to be cuts. Starting right here and now, with us. The current seniors, the class of 1992, he said, would be spared the ax. All who were physically qualified would enter pilot training. Slightly over half of them would enter pilot training immediately after graduation, while the rest would wait for one to three years. For my class, the news was much more grim: Only a third would be allowed to enter pilot training. Period. A pilot board would make the selection on the basis of our grades, military performance, physical fitness scores, letters of recommendation, and flying scores.

We sat with our mouths agape. None of us had ever dreamed that the Air Force, that great institution, would put one over on its future officers like this. We'd come in to be pilots. We'd suffered the indignities of basic training and freshman year because we had the faith that we'd all come out of it pilots. We had planned our activities, marshaled our energies, managed our time and academics according to the old rules. There had always been a saying: "2.0 and go"—which meant that, with no more than a 2.0 grade-point average, you would be sure to go to pilot training. Now, all of a sudden, some fine potential pilots simply wouldn't have the grades to go on and learn to fly. The Air Force had clearly made allowances for this. They had an easy out ready and waiting: quit now, and repay only one semester's tuition, without having to serve out the rest as an enlisted member.

Before we'd had a chance to catch our breaths, McPeak wound up and dealt the final blow: the Air Force wasn't just cutting back on training pilots, it was cutting back on training *fighter* pilots. In the past, all Academy graduates who entered the year-long pilot-training program (which, once again, was virtually everyone) first spent six months learning to fly the T-37, a side-by-side-seat aircraft with low, fat wings and a distinctive engine whine that all pilots can identify immediately. Then they'd spend six months flying the T-38, a low-winged two-engine jet with tandem cockpits that resembled a jet fighter. Afterward, they began training on the aircraft that they'd actually fly in the Air Force.

Now, all that was changing. Since the Air Force had an abundance of fighter pilots, it saw no need to send everyone to T-38 training—the one part of pilot training, of course, for which we were all holding our breath. Instead, they'd purchased a new trainer: the T-1, a two-engine plane that resembled a Learjet. From here on in, all the pilot-training classes would be ranked, and only the highest-ranked trainees—four or five out of each class of twenty-five—would be allowed to go on to fly T-38s. *Those* pilots would then compete to fly fighter planes and bombers. The others could expect a career flying tankers or transport planes. As for those cadets not selected by the pilot board, they faced an even worse fate: an Air Force career on the ground or even underground, working twenty-four-hour shifts in a missile silo, watching videos or playing cards and waiting for the highly unlikely call to punch a few buttons and launch a missile. This job was the stuff nervous breakdowns are made of.

McPeak finished speaking and asked if anyone had any questions. A slowly dawning realization had left a sick feeling in my stomach. It was 1991; women still weren't allowed to fly combat airplanes, but it was a topic of hot debate in Congress and in the nation, and the situation seemed highly likely to change in the next couple of years. Faced with growing numbers of women in all areas of professional life, Americans were slowly coming to grips with the idea of seeing their daughters held as prisoners of war and young mothers coming home in body bags. They weren't quite there yet, but they were close. It was clear to me that if some cadets were going to be shunted out of T-38 training, the first to go would be those on whom, for now at least, the training was wasted: women. I raised my hand. McPeak called on me. "Does the new training program mean that women, regardless of their performance, will automatically be sent to T-1 training and the tanker-transport program?" I asked.

"You got it," he said.

The room went completely silent. McPeak stared at me, expressionless. "What if a woman is number one in her class and earns the T-38?" I said.

"Let me be clear," he responded. "All women will fly the T-1. None will get T-38 training."

I sat back down. Looks of shock were trained on me. "I can't believe you asked him that," one of my neighbors said.

"I can't believe he responded," I answered. It was the first time that I'd heard a straight answer from a general. Clearly, blocking women from combat planes was so nonsensitive an issue that he could afford to be candid. But it was a highly sensitive issue for me. It meant, essentially, that even if Congress changed the laws and enabled women to fly in combat planes, I wouldn't have the training to take advantage of the change. This was the first time in my life that my gender had ever held me back from something that I wanted to do. It was a shock to my sense of myself and my place in the world.

As it turned out, just two months before I graduated from the Academy, Congress enacted legislation allowing women to fly all combat aircraft except those used in special-forces operations. (Ironically, women still can't be involved in the first, highly risky and secret special-operations forays in a war. They can, however, fly the helicopters that pick up special-forces wounded just hours later.) Once more, as had been true my entire life, I didn't have to fight for my basic right to equal treatment. I inherited it from the pioneers who went before and had enough of an edge of anger left in them to fight for women my age. Perhaps if I'd had more of that kind of anger, I would have become alert much sooner to the subtler forms of discrimination that I was subject to every day. But I didn't. I believed that so long as I didn't make an issue of my gender, no one else would, either. I was starting to learn that I was wrong.

BY SENIOR YEAR at the Air Force Academy, I had learned how to fly a plane. I had learned how to survive in the forest and resist interrogation in a POW camp. But I had learned less than nothing about life as it's lived beyond the confines of the military command structure. I barely knew what to do on a date. I had no clue about how to have a serious relationship. The simple fact of putting on a dress made me strange to myself. How to be a woman beyond the narrow confines of military-issue acceptability remained an utter mystery.

The bounds of what was acceptable for a woman at the Air Force Academy basically came down to this: you couldn't have sex. If you had sex you became, in the eyes of your male classmates, not just a fallen woman but a fallen cadet. I had sex once, with a friend, and the word spread afterward that I was loose. It became harder to command respect in the classroom and in training. The problem, I'd soon learn, didn't go away when you graduated. Members of the "real" Air Force, too, tended to view women either as worthy virgins or incompetent whores. A friend of mine named Allison learned this the hard way a few years later. She was a pilot—such a good pilot that she qualified to fly special operations, or would have, if she had been a man. But she was a single woman, and a woman who also enjoyed sex. She was always unhappy with the treatment she received from the men on her Air Force base who rated her flying performance. Until she discovered a remedy: she stopped going out, stopped dating, stopped wearing makeup, and stopped sleeping with anyone. "It was a choice," she told me. "I could either be Allison the pilot, or Allison the woman pilot. And Allison the woman pilot wasn't a great thing to be." It seemed to both of us that to be successful in the Air Force, men were given condoms, and women wore chastity belts.

To this day, I don't know how you were supposed to get through life in the Air Force as a woman. If you slept with men, you were called a slut. If you slept with no one, you were called a lesbian. Things became utterly confused in my mind. As far as men went, I'd barely moved forward since the attack at the end of freshman year. It would take a trip across the Atlantic to start to straighten things out. And once I glimpsed a different world and a different way of being with men, it was harder than ever to come back.

I'd decided to participate in a semester-long exchange program with the French Air Force Academy in southern France. I had to get away. By the end of junior year, the stress had become absolutely untenable. We'd been rushed into early flight training so we could complete the screening program in time for the new pilot boards. That meant stress on top of stress on top of stress—an irony, because the Academy's flying program was designed to make us learn how to handle stress.

We did learn the basics of how to fly. Training on a single-engine propeller plane, a T-41, we learned to take off and land, maneuver in steep turns, and recover from stalls. But what we spent most of our time drilling on was emergency procedures: memorizing airplane manuals and checklists for all flying procedures and emergency formulas right down to the last letter and hyphen. It was all about attention to detail. One detail, after all, could be the difference between life and death in the air. I prepared myself as well as I could for the pilot boards. I passed the T-41 flying program, scoring well above the cutoff. I dropped one of my organic chemistry classes because it was lowering my grade-point average. I worked harder at everything I did, and enjoyed myself even less. When I'd done all that I could and the opportunity came, I jumped at the chance to go to France.

The exchange program was an indirect gift from French president Charles de Gaulle. In 1969, after de Gaulle removed France from the military side of NATO, some French and American colonels, not sharing the general's pique, met over coffee and decided they had to do something to maintain congenial military ties between their countries. They formed the exchange program.

Eight cadets were selected to attend classes at the Ecole de l'Air in Salon-de-Provence. We were to study survival training and engineering and, above all, to learn something about the way the military operates in a foreign culture and make lasting friendships and ties. The differences I saw at first were amusing but largely superficial: The French ate much better than we did. They drank wine with their meals, and they drank well. The purpose was pleasure, not to get falling-down drunk. Their academic level in engineering was much higher than ours in all areas but electrical engineering, where we had them beat. This last made no difference for me, though. It was such a struggle for all the Americans to learn advanced aeronautical engineering in French. Lucky for us, all the exams were open book, and we were able to understand some of the questions and find the answers in our books. We all passed. Some of us, every once in a while, would even score higher than the French who were taking the same open-book exam.

My French improved during survival training. It had to. We were out in the woods, hiking all over the Pyrénées, until we were captured, taken prisoner, and put inside a dark, dungeonlike tunnel. You can learn a foreign language pretty quickly under these conditions. I figured out enough to be able to work with the others at finding a window, rappelling down from its frame, and escaping. Fortunately, the survival and evasion skills we used in France were largely the same as those we'd learned in the States. With a couple of memorable exceptions: While the Americans had learned to eat bugs, the French were taught how to bake bread. And while we tried to walk as invisibly as possible, cutting through trees and streams and underbrush, the French marched comfortably right alongside their roads. It was a whole lot easier. But not, I thought, the best way to avoid attack.

There were other, more fundamental differences, too. For one thing, the French cadets had no tolerance for brownnosers. They saw many of the Americans trying to curry favor with our commanders, yes-ing them on everything and offering up no opinions of their own. "Don't you learn to think for yourselves?" one of the French cadets whispered to me. I didn't know what to tell him. The French Armée de l'Air treated its cadets completely differently than did the United States Air Force. They were actually considered to be adults. There weren't regulations monitoring their every movement and utterance. There was a sense of trust. There was a respect for each cadet as an individual. There was even respect for me as a woman.

That was the greatest shock of all. The male French cadets took me and the other female Academy student, Susan, under their wings right away. They tried to befriend the American men, too—but the Americans would have none of it. Out of their element, many of them simply fell apart. They retreated into their own little pack, drinking beer and counting the days until they could return to the States. The French at first found them comical, then simply rude. But they enjoyed spending time with Susan and me. They'd come around to our room on base after dinner and drag us out to the local cafés. They'd gently tease us about the way we dressed—if we weren't in our uniform pants, we wore shorts or jeans—and demand that we put on skirts and do our hair. We spent many hilarious evenings in front of our mirrors, trying on outfit after outfit, until the French guys approved. "Why don't you want to look like women?" they'd ask, each time they saw us fall back on our big T-shirts and jeans. "We want to be taken seriously," we'd answer.

"And so?"

The notion that you couldn't dress like a woman and be taken seriously at the same time dumbfounded them. "Typical American puritanism," they muttered. As far as they were concerned, we *were* women: it was a fact. And we were also excellent cadets: that was another fact. There was no contradiction between the two. There was only the question of how much fun or how grim we wanted it all to be.

So we decided to have fun. On rainy nights, we drank red wine and ate Roquefort cheese in our rooms. When it was clear, we sat in sidewalk cafés and drank pastis. The French cadets didn't hit on us. They *flirted*, which was something else altogether. It was sweet, complimentary. It had none of the undercurrent of disdain or danger that attention from American military men often contained. It didn't mean anything, either. You could flirt for the fun of flirting, without anything further being expected or required. You could even gossip, tell tales, without it turning outright vicious.

I used to walk into the classroom every morning, sit down next to one of my good French friends, and say, "Let's have it. What did I do last night?" And out would come an absolutely unbelievable story about me and several men and wild, marathon sex. I wondered how I'd have been able to actually get up and walk in the morning after a night like that. "Does anyone really believe this stuff?" I once asked him.

"Of course not," he said. "What a silly question."

The American men, of course, believed everything. It didn't matter that they knew me and saw what I was really like. It didn't matter that Susan had repeatedly told them that it was all silly locker-room talk. A group of them actually called the Academy and told the officer in charge of the exchange program that they wanted me removed because of conduct unbecoming. When I found out about this, I cried in my room for hours, trying to understand their motive. It had, I decided, to be petty jealousy. While they were festering in their rooms with their American flags and American music and American beer, Susan and I were out having fun. We'd both found boyfriends. We didn't need the Academy guys. And fortunately, as it turned out, the officer in charge of the exchange program had heard it all before. Every year was the same thing: the women adapted to France; the men dug in their heels; and before long, the orgy stories were finding their way back to Colorado Springs.

My boyfriend—what a thrill it was to use that word!—told me not to worry about the Americans. They were fools, Vincent said. They didn't know how to appreciate women. He certainly did. In the evenings, we would walk for hours along the streets of Avignon, discussing life, philosophies, and my difficulties getting along with the American men. He said all the talk was just innuendo, and none of the French ever took it seriously. He would smile confidently at me and pull me closer toward him. *He* definitely knew the rumors weren't true, since we spent all our free time together. We would then walk hand in hand quietly up and down the streets, staring off at the distant ruins. He would caress my cheek and smile lovingly at me. We would share a bottle of wine, stare at the night sky and then deep into each other's eyes. He treated me wonderfully and genuinely cared for me. I felt truly appreciated and loved. With him, the difficulties of the day were washed away. This was part of the French experience, I told myself. The best part of France. Looking back, I must have been falling in love.

Granted, there were limits to our relationship. Vincent and I could speak, but it was painfully difficult. I almost always had to ask him to repeat things two or three times before I understood. He didn't really seem to mind. And I was in heaven. I felt pretty, I felt sexy, I felt appreciated—both as a cadet and as a woman. It wasn't just Vincent. The French took me flying in the backseat of a Mirage 2000, a Jaguar, and an Alpha Jet. I proved to them that a woman does not necessarily get sick flying fast jets (at this time, French women were not allowed to be pilots in their air force). They loved showing off for me, and I loved showing off for them. When an American guy in my group got sick doing acrobatics, we all felt a sense of triumph.

Something began to eat away at me in the evenings, as I walked in the hills of Provence with Vincent. I was surrounded by vineyards and cherry trees, enjoying life in one of the most beautiful regions in the world, just a few miles away from where Van Gogh had lived and worked. My French sponsor parents spent hours and hours smiling and laughing with each other. They were so happy and so incredibly in love. What was life really about, anyway? Was it about living like a fighter pilot: being ranked, checking off lines on a checklist, performing to perfection, being stressed to the gills, and soaring high above all earthbound relationships? Or was it about living well and falling in love? I'd been programmed for the first life for as long as I could remember. It was the way of my family, my culture, my own personality. But taken to extremes, it was also the way to madness. There had, I thought, to be a way to live more happily. And when I flew back to America and returned to the Academy, I felt driven to find it. I didn't realize that I was up against forces much stronger than I. I could will myself to make it through the Academy and into the Air Force. But I couldn't will myself to be happy.

FOR THE PILOT selection board, I put together an application package containing my grades, a list of military and athletic activities, a T-41 performance sheet, and letters of recommendation. I also had to include a "dream sheet," a list of other jobs I wanted if I didn't get a pilot slot. I filled in some biology-related jobs and prayed to get none of them. Then I waited. It was an agonizing, miserable wait. We all knew that only five or six people out of the twenty-five in each squadron would be selected for pilot training. We went through the weeks before the decision like robots. No one talked about it. No one admitted to the stress. But it surrounded all of us like a ring of fire. We could think of nothing else.

The board announced its decisions on a Friday. We all gathered within our squadrons for the announcement. In some squadrons, the names were read out loud in front of everyone. In mine, things were handled more privately. We gathered in the squadron room, poker-faced and whispering furtively, like guests at a funeral. Some cadets paced. Others leaned against the walls. Our AOC—air officer commanding, the officer in charge of the squadron—walked slowly into the room. He was carrying twenty-five small strips of paper, about a quarter of an inch wide, wadded up in a ball. He uncoiled the first strip, just far enough to read the name. That cadet walked up to the front of the room and collected his strip of paper. He walked slowly back to his seat with all eyes on him and unrolled the paper. His face remained impassive. Fortunately, we had been trained in public stoicism. The AOC continued calling names until everyone knew his or her fate. When I heard my name called, I took a deep breath and dizzily walked up to the front of the room. I didn't unroll the paper till I was back in my seat. My name was typed across the left side of the paper. I continued to unroll. I saw one zero, then another and another, and then the number six: "0006"—that was the Air Force code for pilot training. I wanted to dance up and down around the room and sing. But I kept my face immobile. It was agony to be so happy when I knew that others were suffering. No one said a word until the last strip had been handed out and the AOC had left the room. Then we decided to go around the room one by one and announce what we'd received. I was shocked to hear one particular woman announce something other than pilot training. Her GPA was close to mine and she had a high-status job on campus. I saw the sadness and shock in her eyes. When I announced that I had been chosen, she leaned over graciously and said, "Congratulations." I did not know how to answer. Thirteen of the 225 cadets chosen for pilot training were women. We were 10 percent of our class, but only 6 percent of those chosen to go on to fly.

Instead of celebrating, I walked back to my room. The mood in the squadron was somber. I could see the despair in the eyes of my classmates all up and down the hallway. I dreaded having to ask some of my closest friends whether they'd been selected or not. It was a horrible feeling, wanting to celebrate, but watching classmates see the end of their dreams.

I dreaded talking to my friend Elizabeth. She desperately wanted pilot training too, and I knew that her GPA was even lower than the other female in my squadron who was not selected. I did not know what I was going to say to her. I sat in my room, staring out the window. Fortunately, Elizabeth called and told me that she had in fact been chosen. A surge of joy and relief passed through my body.

When it came time to choose our new bases, I elected Columbus Air Force base in Columbus, Mississippi. It wasn't too far from home, and it hadn't yet changed over to the T-1 training program. There, I knew, I'd be guaranteed a chance to learn how to fly T-38s. One month later, all the female cadets chosen for pilot training were called into a room and told that Congress had at last decided to pass the bill allowing women to fly in combat roles. We were thrilled. Some of the top-ranking women were especially excited because if the selection process was redone in view of the new law, they'd be able to select EURONATO, a joint U.S.-European pilot-training program that virtually guaranteed its graduates they'd fly a fighter. When we'd made our base selections, only men had been allowed to select EURONATO. Now, in a new selection process, the women who had scored higher than some of the men selected for EURONATO could get in. Also, one of the men who'd selected EURONATO had decided to go to graduate school at Harvard, so his slot had opened up.

But the commanders decided not to hold a new selection. Instead, they simply took the one open spot and gave it to the highest-ranking woman. Because my T-41 training score was too low, I wouldn't have been in the running anyway. So I voiced my opinion to the colonel in charge of selection for the program.

"Why not give a chance to everyone who deserves it?" I asked.

He dismissed me with a wave of the hand.

"Too much paperwork," he said.

I sat in stunned silence. The Air Force clearly handled the principle of equal opportunity the way it applied its honor code: it made a good show but believed in nothing. If the EURONATO slot had not become available, I am certain the colonels would not have redone the selection process, despite the new laws. They'd do it next year. I had never suspected that people's lives could be made or broken over issues like convenience and paperwork. I had quite a lot to learn.

I'D COME TOO FAR to quit the Air Force Academy now. The thought of leaving after junior year, with so much learned and so little time left, seemed just ridiculous. Many of my classmates felt the same way. We stayed on out of inertia, nursing old dreams that were quickly becoming more phantoms of the past than hopes for the future. As the seniors of the class of 1993 approached graduation, we were not the same proud, confident basics who had once roused Arnold Hall with the chant "Proud to be '93." We were bitter, exhausted, soured on the Air Force. It had brought us in on the promise that every physically able person among us would become a pilot, and it had broken that promise. It was hard to keep faith with an institution that would do this, hard to serve an organization that didn't want you. Everything we did now, every tradition that we tried to uphold with our chins held high and minds uplifted, was tainted with that grimness. Our pessimism about the future had carried over into the inscription that we'd chosen for our class ring: "Nonus Supurates," "None shall surpass." We liked it because it sounded so much like "None shall pass." That became our unofficial motto, a nod to the new pilot boards and to our class's record-high attrition rate. I took the class slogan one better. I had a few additional letters engraved on my ring: "IHTFP." You saw this abbreviation in discreet places all over the Academy, and it was often muttered by cadets. It stood for many things. The nicest: "I'm here to fly planes," or "I have truly found paradise." The nastiest: "I hate this fucking place." All of them applied to me.

The class of 1993's attrition rate was particularly high for women: of the nearly 200 who had started out in 1989, only 92 were left to graduate with 870 men (out of approximately 1,200) in 1993. This was so dramatic a loss that it actually caught the attention of the Air Force brass. They'd been rattled by a recent gang rape near the athletic fields that separated our gym from the dorms. The victim didn't know the cadets who attacked her, but had done her best to identify them to the security police, who were circulating composite drawings. During the investigation, they heard more and more stories about forced sex on campus. Times had changed since my freshman year. The Anita Hill story had shaken the nation. The term "sexual harassment" had become commonplace. Even my freshman roommate had had her eyes opened. When we'd studied sexual discrimination and harassment in a constitutional law class junior year, she'd leaned over toward me one day and whispered, "Maybe we should have reported it, after all."

The Office of Special Investigations—the Air Force equivalent of the FBI—was called in. They brought all the Academy's women into a lecture hall for a briefing, no men allowed. They handed out some forms, to fill them out anonymously, describing any sexual harassment or abuse we had experienced.

I certainly had a story to tell. So did my friend Elizabeth, the only woman left on the Academy parachuting team. The harassment on the team—the lewd jokes and crude comments and even indecent exposure—had been so bad that the two other women had quit. After that, the officer in charge of the team had launched an investigation. One of Elizabeth's teammates had threatened to kill her if she told investigators anything.

And in the end, both the men *and* the women on the team were punished equally, the men for indecent exposure and sexual harassment, and the women for underage drinking. Both men and women were restricted to base for a few months and forced to spend hours marching around the Terrazzo with their rifles in their hands. It was as if the commanders couldn't bear to let the hammer fall too heavily on the men. After all, they couldn't come down too hard on their boys for just being boys.

After we finished filling out our forms we were told to pass them around the room until they were randomly mixed. "Now," the officer in charge of the meeting said, "if you're holding a piece of paper that tells a story of harassment or abuse, raise your hand." At least 75 percent of the women in the room raised their hands. The Special Investigations people looked aghast. This was much higher than they'd ever expected. And it proved to them that little of what actually went on around campus was being reported.

How, I wondered, could they have been surprised? I'd seen firsthand what happened to women who came forward: victims were blamed again and again. Commanders and investigators found it hard to believe. I found it hard to learn my lesson.

And at the end of senior year I got myself punished for speaking up once again. There were one hundred days left until graduation. It was a special Air Force Academy holiday weekend. There was a class dinner planned, and the freshmen were going to wreak havoc in our rooms. That was a tradition. On the Thursday night before the weekend revelry began, I returned to my dorm room from classes, stopped short at my door, and blinked. I could not believe my eyes: someone had written "Cunt" on the message board. I tore the board off the wall and marched down to my squadron commander's room. Also a senior, he'd been selected for the job because of his superior qualities as a leader. I tossed the board on his desk. "I want this investigated," I said.

He looked at the board, read it, and said, "I'm sorry this happened, Kelly. I'll look into it." I thanked him and left the room.

The next morning, we had an inclement-weather formation—that is, it was crummy outside, so we had to form up indoors. During the formation, the squadron commander announced that as of the moment, the entire squadron of one hundred people was restricted because of what had been written on my door. When the culprit was found, he said, we could all go off campus again. If looks could kill, I would have died that morning of ninety-nine fatal stab wounds. After the formation, I asked the squadron commander and the AOC why they were doing this. Had I realized that I would be punished for asking for an investigation, I told them, I would never have done it. I was part of the squadron, they said, and had to take my punishment like everyone else. This was ridiculous: the perpetrator wasn't necessarily someone from the squadron. Even if he were, I couldn't imagine why he would have come forward. What they were counting on was that someone would rat out a friend under the honor code. It was the easy way out. They never had to launch a formal investigation. And despite the Special Investigations team's interest in the issue, they never called.

I finished senior year completely ostracized by nearly everyone in my squadron. One woman came up to me and whispered, "You did the right thing," but everyone else pretty much froze me out for the entire weekend—and for many of the hundred days until graduation. One person's opinion of me was now universally shared. The Air Force certainly had a talent for creating esprit de corps. The problem was, there always had to be an enemy.

CHAPTER 4

Too Close to the Sun

No bird soars too high, if he soars with his own wings.
—WILLIAM BLAKE

I LEFT THE MOUNTAINS OF COLORADO WITH A SAD MIX OF RE-gret and relief. I saw the mountains fading in my rearview mirror every time I looked up to check out my new haircut: it was short and sleek, cut above my collar and worn without headband or clips, all to pilot training school regulations. Cutting my long hair—it had grown out since basic training—into a bob had been like basic all over again. Only now I had chosen the style. I needed whatever sense of control over my life I could get. The rigors of pilot training, I knew, would make my Academy education look like a joke. Veterans always likened the experience to a fire hose: information was blasted at you so fast and furiously that it was all you could do to withstand it. You absorbed some of it, swallowed some of it, and had to relax and let a lot of it just wash over you. Otherwise, you'd be knocked out by the flood.

Columbus, Mississippi, was swampy and flat. We spent our first four weeks there in a classroom, studying aerodynamics:

thrust, drag, lift, and gravity. Basically, the way an airplane works is this: The sheer power of the engines creates thrust and moves the plane forward. Air rushing over and under the wings creates lift. Working against the thrust and the lift are gravity and drag—the pull against all the surfaces that hinders the plane's movements forward and up. Flying the T-37 would mean learning to master all these forces. So we studied its engines and learned how they produce thrust. We studied the hydraulics system, the electrical system, the power sources, and the backup systems. We learned every system and subsystem imaginable. Then we moved on to cockpit instruments. Ground speed, indicated airspeed, true airspeed, calibrated airspeed. Indicated altitude and calibrated altitude. We learned how to use our navigational aids to find our position in three-dimensional space. We learned what kind of weather we could fly in and out of, and the damaging effects of natural phenomena like lightning and hail. We climbed into an altitude chamber and learned to recognize the effects of hypoxia, or lack of oxygen: tingling in the fingertips and toes, giddiness and uncontrollable laughter, sluggish motor skills. If you don't recognize and treat hypoxia instantly, we learned, you'll die. And if you're flying a fighter, you'll take a multimillion-dollar taxpayer investment down with you. The antidote is to put on your oxygen mask and force as much oxygen as possible into your lungs and blood. We also studied the physiological effects of motion on the body. If you're in a spin, the body can think it's straight and level when it's actually in a right turn. The body's instincts can't be trusted in a plane, particularly with respect to direction and movement. After a spin, you can think that you've righted the plane when in fact you're spiraling toward a violent death on the ground. Message: Trust your instruments. And know how to read them.

We did all this studying on the ground, before we had even entered a plane or a flight simulator. We were tested at the end of every week. As in baseball, we were allowed just three failures—"hooks," we called them. Three strikes of the same kind and you were out of the program, for flying tests and for on-ground training. If you failed three tests, you were out. If you failed three training flights in a row, you were out. If you failed three check rides, you were out. If your instructor held his thumb and forefinger up in a "U," with the other three fingers bent in toward the palm, you had hooked. This was my introduction to pilots' sign language. In jets, we often communicated by tapping our fingers on our helmets, cutting down on radio traffic and foiling any enemy fighters who might be listening in.

If you had two hooks, you knew your days were numbered. You'd often fail a third time out of nervousness. It was a sink-or-swim approach to learning. Many people quickly sank. We were forced into the most intense possible kind of competition. We were competing constantly for rank. The higher your rank, the better your chance of flying the plane of your choice. Almost everyone wanted to fly fast, sexy fighters like the F-16. Only a few students really wanted to fly cargo or transport planes, which were the military version of commercial jet liners. We were graded every single day on absolutely everything that we did. We were graded on academics, on physical fitness. We were even graded on our social skills. If we didn't get along well with our classmates, we lost overall points.

That factor particularly frightened me, because it wasn't entirely clear to me how, as one of two women in my class, I was supposed to get on well with the guys. The name of the game on base was male bonding. Our very presence was a monkey wrench in the machinery. Take the first bonding experience my class had: designing the class patch. The patches had great symbolic value. We wore them on our right shoulders after we completed our first solo rides. They were supposed to sum up the unique spirit of the group. They also caught the spirit of the times. The old class patches hung up on the Columbus Air

Force Base walls were like minitestimonials to American pop cultural history. There were cartoon characters ranging from Donald Duck to Beavis and Butt-head. Psychedelic colors from the sixties. Vietnam themes. And, of course, lots of women. Big-breasted women sitting on top of airplanes or holding T-37s and T-38s in their hands.

The best drawing produced by our class was done by a Portuguese student stationed in Columbus for the year. It showed a woman wearing a short red miniskirt, fishnet stockings, and spiked high heels. She was bending over and glancing over her left shoulder, showing off her flowing black hair and solid backside. Her feet were shoulder-width apart, and from between her two legs flew a T-37 and a T-38. The men in the class just loved it. Tracy, the other woman in my class, and I looked at the floor.

"Come on," the guys said. "It's funny,"

"What would be funny," I said, "would be a knife and a cucumber." Lorena Bobbitt was all over the news at that time, and my comment brought an angry silence. The other trainees knew that one way or the other, they wouldn't get their girlie picture. On superficial matters like this, the Air Force was doing its best to be politically correct, so a demeaning picture of a woman wouldn't fly. Eventually we all just settled on an Elvis patch: Flying Elvises, Mississippi Chapter. But the resentment of Tracy and me didn't go away.

It was so easy for the students to do something wrong, so hard to know how to play by the rules. They were so variable, so open to interpretation; part of the bonding experience was knowing how and when to bend them. When it came to passing our classes, bending the rules was almost required behavior. The point was to counteract all the competition with cooperation. "Cooperate and graduate," the instructors chanted. We were fighting each other for rank, but we wanted everyone in our class to pull through. So we studied together and helped each other over rough spots. During tests, an instructor would walk by and check our answers. Stopping at my desk, he'd shake his head and point to the correct answer, then walk around the room doing the same for everyone else. Students used hand signals to pass answers around the room. Instructors would say, "I am leaving the room. Tomorrow's test is sitting wide open on my desk. Take a hint." This was known as mutual support; it built a sense of complicity. In the classroom, Tracy and I were included.

But bending the rules socially was another game altogether. The men made an art of it. For example, students weren't supposed to socialize with instructors. It was too sensitive a relationship; it was too easy to give the impression that you were trying to curry favor or gain an advantage. But in fact, students and instructors drank together all the time. They bought each other Pig's Eye beer and traded stories about women; on Mondays in the flight room, they reported back on their weekend conquests. They even went out in search of women together, trawling the bars for students from the local women's college, which every year offered new pickings for the men on base. I'd sit back and watch them find women, hit on them, and leave with them. "Drink a Pig now, do a pig later," I once overheard an instructor telling a student in a bar. Of course, if I had ever had a conversation with an instructor that included any sexual innuendo, the rules would have been completely broken. If I'd even bought a drink for an instructor, it would have been seen as going too far. Once I drove an instructor home because he'd had too much to drink, and even that was suspect. The rules of the game were completely different for me.

In a world built around male bonding, I was necessarily an outsider. But because we were all together all the time—training, or studying, or drinking, or recovering on Saturday mornings at a Columbus lunch place called Profit's Porch—I was in on all the conversations. So I heard the talk about a girl in a class just a few months behind mine who had dated a number of the guys in my group. They talked all the time about "scoring" with her. And not just about sleeping with her, but about her feminine hygiene techniques, where she shaved, what shape she shaved. What was I supposed to say to that? Talking about a woman instructor whom they considered "hot," the men would discuss her underwear and guess at its color. One guy even told me he could distinguish certain colors of underwear through my flight suit. I asked him to tell me which colors so I could avoid wearing them again. He said no, it was a guy thing. I couldn't be let in on the secret.

How was I supposed to find a place for myself among men like that? I didn't want to date. On the one hand, I was too busy trying to tame the fire hose. I had one relationship, with a handsome graduate of the Citadel. We fought about Shannon Faulkner and massaged each other's necks as we studied our general flying knowledge together night after night. We had fun being together and drinking at the officers' club Friday nights, and we truly cared about each other. But our classmates ruined things for us. People saw us dancing together and commented on it, saw us studying together and had something to say. We tried to deny that our relationship was romantic, but of course people saw through us. I was teased constantly, even by instructors. And of course, since I couldn't afford a bad flight grade, I kept my mouth shut about it. The pressure from our peers—and our work—finally drove us apart. We tried to put things on hold for a while, and ended up never getting back together again.

That pretty much soured me on dating. Besides, I'd seen what could happen to female students who dated. You could have been the best pilot in the program; it wouldn't have mattered. If you slept with a few of the guys, you were *fallen*, never to be respected again. So I did my best to pass unnoticed as a woman. I picked up a male pilot's jaunty way of walking, talking, holding myself. In my heat-resistant Nomex flight suit, my leather boots and gloves, my sunglasses, I looked as cool as any guy. And as the weeks went by and I learned the lingo, I sounded cool. I talked fast and low. I kept my intonation flat and my tone all-knowing. I learned that the key to impressing people straight off was to talk as though you knew everything and had seen it all before, even if you had no idea of what you were saying. I learned to hold my alcohol like a man. I could go to the fifty-keg party that some of the instructors threw at Profit's Porch every year and stay up all night with the guys, finishing off the kegs. I just didn't go home with any of them. That would have blown my cool.

And I worked as hard as I could at learning to be a pilot.

Every weekday began with a morning briefing in the flight room, a small classroom with a podium and screen at the front, a large, gray oval table in the center, and instructors' desks all around the back. In front of each instructor's desk were two chairs for students; as the moment of the briefing approached, we stood in front of our assigned seats, facing the center of the room. The class leader would knock twice, assertively, on the instructors' private office. As soon as they filed into the room, the class leader would call the room to attention. Then the instructors would take their places at their desks, behind our backs. The class leader would say, "Morning, sir, Warhawk flight all present and accounted for." The rest of us would chime in with a motivational expression of the day—"We feel the need, the need for speed," for instance. Then we'd turn around and salute our instructors. It was like being a freshman at the Academy again.

Once the protocol was done with, the flight commander would read all the flying notes (closed flying areas and a safety tip) of the day. Then it was time to practice emergency procedures. The students took a moment to catch their breath. Then we'd snap to attention in our seats. I'd put on my Air Force–issue eyeglasses and get my pen and paper ready. The instructors purposely made this part of our training as stressful as possible, so that we'd be prepared for the real stresses of emergencies that we might encounter in the air. Anything, after all, could happen: flaps might not come down; the engine might catch fire; the landing gear might not extend. We had to know the safest way to bring a plane back down under these conditions. We had to have them not just memorized, but *embedded* in our minds, like muscle memory.

On the ground, though, we weren't afraid of dying, but of showing weakness or ignorance and embarrassing ourselves. Also of being grounded: if you made a mistake during the emergency-procedure scenario, you couldn't fly that day. Three hooks in a row, of course, and you flunked out of the program.

A typical morning's exercise might go like this:

"You are on the runway and have started your takeoff roll," an instructor says. "Suddenly you hear a loud bang and notice the airplane yaw"—pitch—"to one side. Lieutenant Flinn, you have the aircraft."

I rise, grab my checklist detailing all the specifications and normal procedures for my airplane, and stand at attention at the end of the oval table, facing the podium. I can almost hear the other students sighing in relief.

"Roger, sir, I have the aircraft. What are the weather conditions and runway conditions today?"

"It is clear and a million and the runway is dry," which meant there wasn't a cloud in the sky and you could see forever.

"First thing I would do is maintain aircraft control. To do this, I would use the rudder pedals to ensure I maintained runway centerline."

Next, I analyze the situation. "Sir, what do my engine instruments read?"

The instructor turns on the overhead projector and displays a mock-up of the engine instruments and their present readings. I write down all the numbers.

"Sir, do I see any lights in the cockpit?" I ask.

"No."

"Do I notice any vibrations or other noises?"

"No."

"What does my airspeed indicator read?"

"Forty knots."

I ask questions until I have a complete picture of the emergency. I need to know whether the plane is keeling left or right, whether I smell smoke or see any flames. I have to know how far down the runway I am. My exhaust gas temperature, my oil temperature. My Go/No Go speeds: If I am under a certain speed, I can still abort takeoff. If not, I have to take off, solve the problem in the air, and then land. I see that there's an arrow on the right-engine RPM gauge indicating that the engine is winding down. And that the engine exhaust temperature gauge shows a reading within normal range, with no fire lights illuminated. And so I give my diagnosis (hoping I am correct):

"Roger, sir, from the engine instruments and indicator lights, I have determined that my right engine has failed and is winding down. There is no evidence of an engine fire at this moment." Now that I have analyzed the situation I must take the proper action. "Since I am on a dry runway, below the single-engine safe airspeed, and below the maximum speed for abort, I will abort the takeoff."

Emergency procedures always had a set formula, called a boldface. You had to have the boldface memorized, down to the exact position of the dash.

"Sir, the abort boldface is 'Throttles—Idle'; Wheel Brakes— As Required.'" I talk my way through performing the boldface, even carrying out the motions of my hands and feet:

"I am pulling the throttles back to idle using my left hand. I am using my feet to apply the wheel brakes as necessary to slow the aircraft down to a taxiing speed. I am using my rudder pedals to keep the aircraft aligned on the centerline of the runway."

Once I have the aircraft slowed down to taxiing speed, I make a radio call and inform the runway supervisory unit officer that I am aborting the takeoff because of an engine loss, and taxiing clear of the runway. Once clear of the runway, I stop the aircraft, shut off all engines, and evacuate the aircraft in a controlled, safe manner. I have to run through the order of aircraft shutdown in detail, even specifying how I unstrap my safety belt and climb out. If the instructor is in a picky mood, and I forget to say that I opened the canopy before climbing out, he might say: "You hit your head on the canopy." The key was attention to detail.

"All right," I finally hear. "Take your seat."

If the scenario had put me in the air, I would have discussed looking out the window, clearing for other aircraft, and making all the required radio calls. If I made a critical error, I would be told to sit down, and another student would take over. If everything went well, the instructor would give the class a critique of my analysis and handling of the situation. If I forgot to ask a question or missed something, he would point it out. If there was another way to handle the emergency, he would tell us. If there was another possible analysis of the situation, he would tell us that, too.

In addition to the daily emergency procedures, we had a weekly exam covering emergencies and basic aircraft knowledge. If you hooked one of these tests, you would not fly until you retook it and passed. Before you could fly solo, you also had to pass three emergency-procedures scenarios in the flight simulator—an enclosed capsule, moved by hydraulic lifts, that almost exactly resembled the cockpit of a T-37, only with video screens in place of windows. We commonly referred to these scenarios as Dial-a-Death. You sat in the podlike simulator with an instructor next to you, and you watched him out of the corner of your eye. You scanned your instruments cautiously, searching for an emergency. Just when you thought things were calm, all hell would break loose. Lights would come on; the plane would shake and roll to one side. The instructor had input a scenario into the simulator's computer program. You had to fly and deal with the emergency at the same time. Rather than talking through the maneuvers, you had to *do* them. And your actions had to be in real time, since you were actually flying a simulator. The stress was intense, but it eventually paid off. Flying in the simulator was actually harder than flying a real airplane. When I started flying, I was never scared: the emergency procedures had become reflex.

Our last form of training was known as chair flying. This meant sitting in a chair, or on the couch, or on the floor, and visualizing being in an airplane. We would talk ourselves through the flight and practice everything from adjusting our imaginary throttles to making radio calls. Sometimes, we would practice the landing pattern together in the classroom. We'd stick tape on the floor in the shape of the runways and flight patterns, then walk around the tape, talking through all our actions. One of the instructors would clear us for takeoff and landing. We'd hold our arms in the air if we were at the higher altitudes and at our hips if we were coming in to land. Practicing like this helped us visualize how the landing pattern worked in the air and how aircraft are kept from hitting each other.

Once we had mastered the basics of flight in the classroom and simulator, we were ready to go on our first real flight—called a dollar ride, because the tradition was that you gave your instructor a decorated dollar bill afterward. In those days, the back of the bill was often decorated with naked women. I spent the evening before my first flight cutting out all the new terms we were learning—VOR, TACAN, ILS, spin, closure—pasting the pieces of paper onto the bill, and then cutting it into puzzle pieces.

On the morning of my first flight, the weather was cloudy, as was typical of Columbus, Mississippi. I was nervous and excited. I did not want to get sick. If you got sick in the air, you had to enter a special program that would try to eliminate the problem by teaching you how to fight the motion sickness. I could barely sit through the morning brief: flight objectives, events of the day, more expert knowledge, and details, details. After a while, important though it was, it all just sounded like so much blah blah blah. Sometimes, when a person's mind is saturated with information, it simply shuts down. Today, all my brainpower was reserved for flying.

We picked up our life support equipment—helmet, mask and hose, and parachute—and headed out to the plane. We placed our parachutes and flying gear gently on the ground. The instructor followed me around as I began the exterior inspection checklist. I looked at every nook and cranny and moved each flight control. I tried not to take too long. "You are not buying the plane," we were always told. After the walk-around, I placed my helmet bag on the wing, just within reach of the cockpit, and climbed into the plane. I tried to be as graceful as possible and look cool while I swung my leg over the side of the plane and tumbled into my seat. Okay, I could have used an extra inch or two in height. I pulled the rudder pedals all the way toward me and raised my seat as high as possible. I put on my helmet and plugged the oxygen hose into the airplane's supply. I rechecked my mask and verified that the ship's oxygen was working, too. I took a deep breath and tried to calm my anxious nerves. I then began the interior pre-flight inspection. I checked all the knobs and switches and made sure they were in the proper position for engine start. I was nervous and hoped I was running my checks properly. The instructor watched carefully over my shoulder, taking notes on the pad affixed to his knee. Once I finished the check, I pulled on my gloves, strapped my checklists and knee pad to my thighs, readjusted my glasses, and gave my instructor a thumbs-up. It was time to start the engines.

I signaled the crew chief; he stepped into position, cleared behind the airplane, verifying that no one was behind the engine, and gave me the go-ahead signal. I held up my forefinger and drew a a horizontal circle in the air. The crew chief echoed it. I looked left, then positioned my fingers on the controls and my left hand on the left throttle. I held one switch up with my right forefinger, waited for the engine to wind up a bit, then pushed up the second switch with my right middle finger and held them both in position. Once the engine reached a certain speed, I moved the left throttle out and over the stop into the idle position and waited for the engine to ignite. I released the switch under my right middle finger and waited a few moments, monitoring my engine instruments, then released my right forefinger and checked the instruments. The instruments and engine gauges were functioning properly. All was well. I held up two fingers and drew a circle: I was starting the second engine. I followed the same procedures. The T-37's engines make an incredibly high, piercing whistle; most pilots wore earplugs to block it. I held the brakes with the balls of my feet and finished the checklist. "Cujo One One, taxi with Information Bravo," I radioed to ground control. The instructor took over the controls to steer us out of the confined area where all the planes were parked. Once clear of the other planes, I began to taxi. I felt so tiny passing the larger T-38s. And anyone watching could tell I was a new student, because I could not taxi straight. I kept swerving from one side to the other of the yellow line, as if drunk. I was overcorrecting my movements—braking too hard, too. The first time I applied the brakes, our bodies lurched forward as the plane stopped. It reminded me of the first time I tried to drive a car. Once I was in the air, though, I wouldn't have the luxury of stopping to adjust the radio or temperature controls. I'd have to learn how to maintain my course and altitude while simultaneously changing the radio controls or reading my checklist.

"Cujo One One, Number one, ready for takeoff," I said, keeping my voice as low and cool as possible. Once we were cleared, I rolled onto the runway, set the plane on the center line, and stepped on the brakes. "Four green, no red, no amber, line on line point on point on point, two good engines, the time is now eleven-thirty-three," I said out loud: a mnemonic for checking all the instruments and indicator lights. I released the brakes and pushed the throttles up. The plane lurched forward—picking up speed, but not nearly as quickly as in my F-16 rides. And there was no extra kick when the afterburner lit: T-37s don't have an afterburner. At takeoff speed, I eased back on the stick and climbed into the air, awkwardly reaching for the handle to raise the landing gear while keeping the plane at the "climb-out" angle. Then I raised the flaps and had a look at where I was going—for this, I'd plotted out landmarks on the ground.

My mind was racing. I didn't have time to enjoy the freedom of flight. I had to just concentrate on flying. I had done this many times in my chair, but the chair was not racing through the air, and it was a whole lot quieter. My instructor was talking to me and there was endless babble over the radio. I just nodded and tried to follow directions. I was trying to keep my head from spinning. Now, in a jet aircraft traveling much faster than the T-41, I wasn't having quite the calm experience I had anticipated. I looked at the instruments and calculated my position, heading, altitude, and airspeed.

I turned left and climbed to the cruising altitude; there, the instructor took the controls and helped me level the plane. For the rest of the flight, he would demonstrate, then turn over the controls, and I'd imitate his actions. I was all smiles, but I had no time to really enjoy the flight. I was busy fighting the controls, trying to sound cool during my radio calls, and fumbling to switch instrument settings. I was also trying to figure out where I was—it's a lot harder to navigate in three-dimensional space. In sensory overload, I tried to take in as much as possible; the rest I tucked away in the back of my mind.

Finally we practiced landing, with me imitating the instructor. I managed to land a few times during our touch and goes, and was pleased with myself.

Back at our parking spot, I cut the engines and ran through the postflight checklists. I took off my helmet, shook out my matted-down hair, grabbed all my gear, filled out the postflight paperwork, and headed back to the flight room for debriefing. I could barely contain my excitement. I had now officially started the flying program. The instructor critiqued my performance, telling me what I did wrong and did right. Afterward, I handed him my dollar and asked him if he could help solve the puzzle of flying. He looked at it and grinned. Then I took a few deep breaths and, for the first time in hours, relaxed.

Your first ride is an ungraded "freebie." But from here on in, everything you do in the airplane is evaluated. Our days were filled with endless briefs and debriefs. We listened hard, trying to clear away the cloud of confusion that covered us. Slowly, we were catching up with the fire hose, retaining more and more of what we were told. After each briefing, we practiced our maneuvers. We learned the basics of acrobatic flight and how to fly and land the plane in all types of situations, including single-engine landings. We learned how to do loops, barrel rolls, aileron rolls, stalls, and spins. My favorite exercise was spinning the T-37. Flying becomes an adventure once you've adjusted to seeing the world spin 360 degrees. First, you stall the airplane and kick in some rudder. The nose of the aircraft falls over and points to the ground; then the airplane starts to spin around an axis pointed straight at earth. "Idle, neutral, aft, spinning left, needle left, full right rudder, one full turn, slam, slam pull to the horizon," I'd say to myself. Translation: Once I realized I was in a spin, I had to check that my throttles were in the idle position. I'd move the stick to neutral so that there were no other forces working on the plane, then pull it to the aft position to raise the nose and slow down the oscillations. If I was spinning left, the needle of the turn-and-slip indicator would be pointed left. In that case, I'd step on the right rudder and take a quick mental snapshot of the earth to find a reference point. I could hold the rudder in place for just one full turn. Once I spotted my reference point coming around again, I'd release the rudder and use all my strength to slam the stick forward for the briefest moment, then jerk it back to neutral. This would break the stall, and then I'd gently pull the nose back to the horizon to avoid another. If I had held the stick forward too long, I could enter an inverted spin—that is, spin toward the ground upside down. This would be very bad news because sometimes you can't recover from an inverted spin; you have to eject. So any time you were spinning, you had to remain calm, think through your procedures, and execute them properly. Do one thing at the wrong time, and you could spin out of control.

After demonstrating my proficiency with all the emergency procedures and different types of landings, I was ready for my first jet solo. I geared up and sat in the cockpit, humming the theme from *Top Gun* and feeling on top of the world as I taxied down the runway. Takeoff! Next thing I knew, I was piloting a jet plane, solo. But I didn't take a lot of time to enjoy myself; I was too scared of messing up and hooking my solo ride. I came in for some landings, concentrating my hardest. I wanted to read "EXTD"—"Excellent touchdown"—on my landing comment sheet the next morning. Seeing that next to your call sign makes you sit a little taller in your chair. I also wanted to hear the faint double-click of my radio, which would mean that the controller had rated my landing excellent.

I finished my postflight checklists and paperwork, headed toward the flight room, and took off my patches and emptied my pockets of money and keys as fast as I could. I knew what was coming next. As the Flying Elvises approached, I tried to run. I didn't get very far. There was no escaping my squadron's *après*-solo tradition: I was lifted and carried off to the dunk tank. This was a huge converted feed trough painted with our class colors and filled with extremely dirty water. I was squirming and trying to get away, making things tough on my classmates, so they stopped by the local mud pit and dragged me through that a few times first. After I'd learned my lesson, they bore me off to the dunk tank, held me just over the water, then let me fall and jumped away to avoid my huge splash. I stood up in triumph, with my wet flight suit hanging off me. I had done it. I had soloed a jet. I could now proudly wear Elvis, the class patch, on my arm. Also, I owed my instructor a bottle of his favorite drink. That was a more enjoyable tradition.

I loved flying solo. I flew much better with no instructor and no one watching me on the ground. I could do whatever acrobatics I pleased, in a broader swath of airspace. I could also simply play. Sometimes, instead of practicing my acrobatics, I would just fly circles around clouds. I spent some of the happiest moments of my life like this in the sky, just being alone and enjoying the peace.

Formation flying was a fantastic thrill, too. It was a war exercise—the way planes would fly into battle for mutual protection and support. The perfect formation position was three feet away from the lead plane—and at first, this was flatly terrifying. One false move and two huge white monsters would collide in the air. My first formation instructor was all too aware of the possibility, because he'd been in a serious midair accident. Though no one was killed—all four pilots ejected safely as the planes smashed to earth in a fireball—he'd been seriously shaken up by the experience. The first time I flew in formation with him, I felt as if I were fifteen years old and being taught to drive by my mother. Just as my mother had sat with her hands around an imaginary steering wheel, air braking every time she thought I was going to crash, my instructor sat cringing beside me, doing all he could not to air brake and snatch the controls away. Once you get past the fear, though, formation flying is incredibly satisfying. The planes fly in harmony, in perfect synchronicity. It's like an air ballet.

Halfway through this contact flying and learning the acrobatics phase of T-37 training, there was a "check ride" with an evaluator pilot. Check rides were the most dreaded and stressful activities of pilot training because how you performed on them largely determined your overall rank at the end of the year. The check ride system is extremely stressful. Grading was idiosyncratic; some evaluators were known to be tough, others to be cool, and all were subject to moods—and didn't hesitate to let their moods affect their judgment. One instructor, I recall, had just been assigned to fly an A-10, a slow, low-flying attack fighter. He was so happy, you could have flown into a tunnel and he would have passed you. The grading was incredibly complicated, too. You received scores on all your maneuvers, plus an overall grade for the ride, and one grade might have nothing to do with the other. For instance, if you performed every maneuver perfectly but messed up a landing, you could fail the ride. One more wrinkle: the baseline grade for maneuvers was "excellent." The equivalent of "good" was called a "one downgrade." Not very encouraging.

On the day of my check flight, the weather was clear. I was nervous. My check pilot was not known as a Santa Claus—far from it. He never smiled, he gazed at students with an air of superiority, and he didn't pass many students.

I tensely performed the prebrief and ran through the flight profile—a description of the coming flight—with my evaluator, then took a deep breath and walked out of the flight room and into life support to get my gear. The evaluator took note of the check I made on my parachute and helmet. *Everything* was graded, including the way I walked to the jet, including my attitude. I performed all my checks, then double-checked.

Once we were taxiing, though, I started to calm down. I was now in my element. I flew cautiously, setting up the maneuvers so I would not fly out of the designated box of space I was supposed to fly within. Sometimes, if you flew one foot above the ceiling altitude, you'd hook the flight, while another evaluator might let you fly 300 feet out the top and not even notice. Carefully, carefully I went through my maneuvers—so far, so good—and started back to the base, feeling pretty confident. I set up for the single-engine landing, and was beginning the final turn to line up with the runway. I checked my configuration, the flaps, and the landing gear, and checked my alignment with the runway. The next thing I heard, halfway through the descending turn, was "I have the aircraft." I gave up the controls to the evaluator and quietly, inside my helmet, I began to curse. I wanted to hit myself. I had just made a mistake, but what was it? And I had hooked the check ride.

Trying to shake it off, I just kept flying my jet. My other landings went perfectly. Maybe there was hope: sometimes, when you make a mistake, an evaluator will let you try the maneuver again. No such luck. I landed, finished my postflight checks, and turned in my equipment. Then I walked into my flight room to take a breath and get a drink while I waited for the evaluator. It was a bad sign, we had been told, if the evaluator went immediately into your flight commander's office and shut the door. My evaluator did just that.

"How'd it go?" the other students asked.

"No idea," I said, fearing the worst.

When the evaluator finally called me, he spent half an hour quizzing me and discussing emergency situations, then pulled out the grade sheet. I received mostly excellents for the maneuvers, but on the single-engine landing I hadn't cross-checked my airspeed, and it had dropped too low. I felt sick to my stomach. I was devastated. My first check ride: hook.

I walked out of the evaluator's room and into my flight room. All the other students looked up at me in anticipation. I held up my thumb and forefinger in a U. They all nodded solemnly. Tracy came over and put her arm around me. "It'll be okay," she said. I thought, "Yeah, whatever."

My flight commander called me into his office. "You'll fly with me tomorrow, Flinn," he said. This was called an 88 ride, a second evaluation. If I failed it, or ever again failed any other check ride, I would have to fly with the squadron commander. If I failed *that* ride, I'd have to go before a review board, which would determine whether I was fit to go on with the flying program. From now on, every check ride I took in a T-37 would be an 88.

"Do you understand the procedure?" the flight commander said. Yes, I did—and the ramifications as well.

"Calm down, Flinn. Get some rest," he said.

I just shook my head.

I couldn't go home because we hadn't yet been released as a class. I stepped outside for some air, and began to cry. I was devastated. I'd been totally unprepared for the possibility of failure. I'd never failed at anything before in my life. I'd never doubted myself before. Now the ground had opened up under my feet. I was sure that my life was over. I'd never fly an F-16— or anything else, for that matter.

After a few minutes, one of the instructor pilots came outside to sit next to me. "Look," he said, "I've seen this happen dozens of times before. Calm down. You'll get back in the game." I thanked him for his encouraging words, but still felt I had just blown all hopes of ever being a fighter.

I waited until I could convincingly wear my cool-pilot poker face. Then I returned to the flight room, trying to walk with my usual swagger. But I was fooling no one.

I passed my 88 ride the next day with no problem. My shoulders were low, my confidence was blown, but I flew well. The flight commander shook my hand. "Get back into it and keep doing well."

As it turned out, I wasn't the only person who had hooked this first check ride: more than half my classmates had, too. And I'd learned an important lesson: I wasn't infallible. No pilot is. There was an expression at flight school: "There are those who have, and those who will." That is, sooner or later, everyone hooks a check ride. That was only human. I acknowledged it. But I didn't feel I could afford too much humanness.

In the second phase of contact training, we worked on the acrobatic maneuvers and added a few more complicated ones, like tracing a four-leaf clover in the sky. We also began to train at an auxiliary field called Gunshy, a small landing strip in the middle of Mississippi used by both the Air Force and the Navy for landing practice. Our final contact check ride was called the potluck, because some of us would have to fly to Gunshy and others wouldn't. Having to fly to Gunshy put you at a real disadvantage, because the landmarks were difficult to recognize. As luck would have it, I, of course, was scheduled for Gunshy.

I woke up on the morning of my check ride to dismal weather—too dismal to fly. It held for several days. Finally, just before the delay got long enough to force me to take a refresher flight, I was scheduled to go. The weather was still hazy and I was worrying about passing the ride. The closer we came to Gunshy, the lower the clouds. Our forward visibility worsened. I was concentrating hard, looking for a clump of trees that stuck out of a larger grove a little. At this stage of flying, we used ground references to navigate. Later, we would learn how to use the navigation instruments. Finally, thinking I'd spotted them, I made my radio call to the Gunshy tower. Wrong clump, by a mile or two. The instructor said over the radio, "Disregard," took control of the plane, and pointed out the right group of trees. I began to curse inside my helmet again.

But I had an entire ride to finish, and a small hope in the back of my mind that if I executed all the maneuvers well, the instructor would give me a break on account of the weather. I flew some of the best landings I had ever done. I performed my maneuvers very well, too. It made no difference. Hook.

What was going on? I knew what I was doing. I knew how to get to Gunshy, and I knew how to fly. My next flight would be with the squadron commander, an 89 ride, to determine if I had the potential to continue the program. I woke up the next morning and groaned: the weather was once again cloudy and dismal, to fit my mood. The squadron commander did his best to relax me with some words of encouragement. We climbed in the plane, but were delayed for a few minutes on the ground because the weather fell below our landing minimums; the clouds were too low and the visibility too poor. I was hoping and praying that the commander would cancel the flight. No such luck. The weather cleared up a bit, but not much. I could see nothing but clouds in every direction. I started toward Gunshy, flying right at the base of the clouds. Through the light haze of clouds, I could make out some landmarks. Once I thought I had the proper entry point, I called on the radio for clearance to land.

"I have the aircraft," the squadron commander said.

This time, I knew my days of pilot training were numbered. We continued to Gunshy. I did some great landings once I got to the airfield. Then, as I started my acrobatic maneuvers and stalls, there were clouds everywhere. We were completely surrounded by them—tall white cumulus clouds, rapidly growing into huge towers. No acrobatics: they require a clear sky above and below. All we could do was fly around in circles. Over the radio, we heard that planes were being diverted from Columbus because of the weather.

The squadron commander looked over at me. He was a happy fellow, with a smile always on his face. "Someone must be watching over you," he said. Because as of that moment, the evaluation was over and incomplete. We would fly together again the next day. I breathed a sigh of relief.

The commander was basically prohibited from teaching me anything on this flight, since it was an evaluation ride as opposed to an instructional ride, but he could critique and give pointers. He suggested some other landmarks for Gunshy. Then he took the controls and started dancing in and out of the clouds—flying directly toward a cloud, as if to go through it, then banking to one side and sliding past, in the clear. We were chasing the clouds and I was thoroughly enjoying myself. I was feeling a little lighter about flying, and a little more confident.

That afternoon, one of my instructors spent hours with me, pointing out every single possible landmark for Gunshy. He even taught me a trick on the instruments for determining the clump of trees. I thanked him and headed home for a good night's sleep. The next morning, the weather was clear. The storm had blown through. I found Gunshy with no trouble. My acrobatic maneuvers were fine, and so were all my landings. Afterward, the commander shook my hand. "You've done very well," he said. I felt relieved and happy. I knew I could fly, and

I had finally shown others. I had been given another chance. The Air Force, I thought, believed in second chances.

I learned to fly relying solely on my cockpit instruments, learning to trust mechanical buttons and dials while my field of vision was restricted by a cloth visor. I mastered flying in formation, and passed my last T-37 check ride without difficulty. Then it was time to move on to T-38s.

The T-38 was more sophisticated than the T-37. It looked like a small, sleek fighter aircraft. It had afterburner engines and a pressurized cockpit. The seats were tandem, one behind the other, not side by side as in the T-37. You had to climb up a ladder to reach the cockpit, rather than just stepping over a railing. That was much more cool.

T-38 training began in July in as rigorous a manner as T-37 training had, with the fire hose of systems, mechanics, and emergency procedures, simulator flying and checklists. But the atmosphere in flight training had changed. Our new instructors strutted when they walked and took a tone of superiority when talking to the students. They were the guys with the big jets, and they let everyone know it. The cockiness was catching. Everyone stood taller, looked tougher, in a G suit. I felt powerful, too. But with the extra machismo came added competition. The famous esprit de corps melted down into every man for himself.

You started T-38s with a clean slate, no strikes recorded against you yet. I was still having my old problem with check rides. I'd do extremely well on all my maneuvers and then fail the overall ride. Each time it was something different. Once again, I came within a hairsbreadth of being kicked out of pilot training. I had 88 and 89 rides with my commanders. I passed—but my classmates were no longer standing by me. Not a single one waited in the flight room on the afternoon of my make-or-break flight with the squadron commander to see how I'd done. No one seemed to care anymore whether I made it or not. It was as though, if I wasn't a winner, I wasn't worth bothering with at all. Sometimes I had the distinct impression that they were rooting for me *not* to make it. Conversations would come to a dead halt when I came into the room. Or I'd walk out and the room would burst into laughter. My few friends in the program told me people were laughing at my incompetence and hubris. "She's crazy if she thinks she's going to get a fighter," they would say. "She should just focus on getting her wings. She'll be lucky if she gets to fly a helicopter."

Slowly, the disrespect crept into my instructors' attitudes as well. One instructor, a former B-52 pilot who had come slightly unhinged, told me that I'd better know my checklists extremely well because he did not want to be "sweating his balls off" waiting for me to finish my preflight checks. One morning, while Tracy and I were discussing the day's emergency procedure, my new flight commander snapped at us: "Why don't you two girls quit your yapping?" I put my hands on my hips. "We are trying to complete an emergency procedure, *sir!*" I didn't want to make waves and file a complaint, but I did change my attitude. I stopped trying to please. I stopped hanging out with the guys and refused to kiss up to instructors. I didn't seek out conflicts, but I stood my ground when they arose.

Sometimes I felt that no matter what I did there was someone waiting in the wings to put me in my place, as if I were being punished for daring to think I could compete like one of the guys. I got that message in no uncertain terms one evening when I wandered into the officers' club with friends after attending a formal graduation dinner. I was, for once, wearing a dress—a long black dress. The club was packed. I was standing, talking to friends, when suddenly, I felt a hand on my rear end. The hand tightened and squeezed, then quickly slid away.

I looked around and noticed a flight commander ducking away with a sly grin on his face. He glanced back at me with a knowing look.

"What's the matter?" asked one of my friends. I was so angry, I was shaking. "Nothing," I snapped, and walked away. I knew from experience that if I complained, I would be the one to suffer. Everyone would question my motives and what I had done to lead the commander on. And given my spotty check-flight record, he would make or break my class ranking: 25 percent of it was based on his opinion. So angering him was the last thing I wanted to do. I went home and changed from my dress to jeans. I didn't want to hear any comments about how nice it was to see me in a dress. I didn't want to attract any more attention.

Soon a strange thing started to happen: at least once a week, I'd hook a flight. The failures were so regular that I started calling them my "Once a week plus iron" flights, spoofing the old vitamin commercial. Sometimes I hooked for good reason; but at other times I wondered if there wasn't some ulterior motive at work. I would hook for a performance that would have earned another student a good grade. I felt cursed, and everyone else expected me to fail. When it came time to partner up for our formation-flying check ride, no one wanted to fly with me. I was assigned a partner who was visibly afraid to be stuck in the air alongside me.

Maybe it was just to spite them all, but on the check ride I flew sensationally. I made no mistakes landing and passed with flying colors. My partner and I ended up with the second highest grade in our group. But when we returned to the flight room and announced the grades, no one congratulated me. My flight commander stared at me in disbelief and said, *"Flinn?"*

But, interestingly, after that I never hooked a daily ride again. Certainly, my confidence had been restored; but I think there's a darker explanation. The instructors had formed the impression that I was a student who hooked rides. I'd seen this with other students as well: once you hooked, you kept hooking. Now I was a winner. And I remained a winner all through the rest of pilot training.

IN DECEMBER, the Air Force sent over the list of aircraft and air bases that currently needed pilots. Forty students—twenty from Columbus and twenty from Vance Air Force Base—would choose from forty available planes. There were nine fighters on the list, several Learjet-like C-21s, which were used for shuttling around VIPs; some KC-135 and HC-130 air-refueling planes; C-130 and C-27 cargo planes; helicopters; and the B-52 bomber. We were told our rank the night before the formal selection. I was number 10 selecting from Columbus, which made me number 20 overall: right in the middle. I knew I had no hope of a fighter, but I still wanted to fly a combat plane. I hesitated among the HC-130, one of the few planes women could fly in special operations; the C-27, which would have meant being stationed in Panama; and the B-52. Now, that B-52: Historically, it had proven itself as the ultimate symbol of America's post–World War II fighting power. It was one of the most hated and feared planes ever built. The Vietnamese and Iraqis still talk of its massive destructive power. Every one of the bombers has served in war—most recently, launching conventional missiles on Iraq. The B-52 is time-tested and true, and not likely to be phased out anytime soon by Congress. It has proven itself. And it's a great deterrent to war. All we have to say is that the B-52s are up and running, and people get scared.

I liked the fact that flying the B-52 would put me in the center of the action in wartime. I also liked the fact that I'd be flying a plane that could carry all types of weapons. It was a powerful feeling. I had always wanted to be a combat pilot. I wanted to be at the heart of a war, pulling my own weight. Flying the B-52 would let me realize that dream. But the B-52 base was in Minot, North Dakota, and I'd seen pictures: flat and bleak. It wasn't, I thought, the kind of place people lived in by choice.

When I talked to some former B-52 pilots who were now instructors on base, though, they urged me to take the plane. Minot wasn't so bad, one of them told me. There was a lake and hunting and fishing. Great place to raise a family. That wasn't at the top of my agenda, but if Minot was a nice place for it, I figured that was a good sign.

On assignment night, the Flying Elvises formed up in the hallway outside our flight rooms, in rank order. We were going to announce our choices in a telephone conference with the students at Vance and with the military personnel center, which would record our choices. At the front of the conference room was a large screen displaying the list of available assignments. Each line was numbered, with the name of the plane and its base location. Around the perimeter of the room sat the students' chairs, and in the middle of the room was a large conference table for the colonels. We filed in and remained at attention until all the commanders and colonels entered the room.

The wing commander, a Colonel Trexler, sat at the head of the conference table with the phone in his hand. The number one student from Columbus started things off. He was a guy who wore a black leather jacket and drove a Harley-Davidson, with his girlfriend attached in a sidecar: clearly *Top Gun* material. He stood at attention, said loudly, "Columbus picks line nineteen, F-15E to Seymour Johnson," and sat back down. Colonel Trexler repeated the choice into the phone, and line 19 was crossed off the selection choices. Next came the number one student from Vance, and so on as the ranks wound down. I held my breath each time a student ahead of me made a selection. Soon, all the fighters were gone. When my turn finally arrived, I stood proudly at attention, said, "Columbus picks line two, B-52 to Minot," and sat back down. Colonel Trexler looked at me questioningly, and I nodded. He repeated my choice into the phone. Across the table, another colonel glanced my way, his mouth agape. Clearly, they'd never expected me to pick their big, manly B-52. "I figured you for a C-21 pilot myself," my squadron commander said as we filed out of the room after the selections. After all this, that's what they thought I was good for: A cushy job. A girlie job. "Live and learn," I thought.

At the Officers' Club we drank eight kegs of beer. I let loose, too—I could finally celebrate. All the former B-52 pilots on base congratulated me and bought me beers. For once, the restraints were off. I could drink and party with the guys. I had proven myself as one of them.

The following Monday morning, I was called to a meeting with my squadron commander. "Do you realize what you did on Friday, Flinn?" he asked. I searched my mind, trying to remember. Had I done something stupid while I was drinking? Had I drunk so much that I couldn't remember? What was it? I drew a blank.

"No, sir," I finally said.

"You became the first woman ever to select a bomber," he said. "You are the first female bomber pilot."

I nodded. The word "female" didn't really catch my attention. For me, being female wasn't much of an achievement, but earning a bomber was. And there was one check ride left before pilot training was officially over. Given my track record there, I couldn't relax until it was done.

"There'll be some publicity down the line," he said. "Be sure to pass that check ride and graduate."

What a recipe for disaster: a final check ride, a B-52 in the balance, the entire Air Force apparently watching.

The weather that day was predictably miserable. This was a navigational ride—a flight out to another base and back—and all the nearby Air Force bases were weathered in except for Dobbins, in Georgia. The weather there was terrible, too. I had to check and double-check every aspect of my flight plan. My evaluator had a reputation as a stickler for the rules. So, once in the air, I followed every rule and procedure to the letter. No individual technique. No personal judgment. As I started my landing at Dobbins, I worked on keeping my descent perfectly within the altitude restrictions. I glanced at my altimeter and saw the needle pass through 14,000 feet. At 11,000 feet I'd have to react and slow my descent or I'd pass through one of the altitude restrictions and possibly put the aircraft in a dangerous situation. The altitude restriction is a safety precaution to prevent a pilot from flying into a ground obstacle, such as a tower or mountain peak. Once safely past the obstacle, you can continue your descent. I knew that would take a few moments. I stared down at my leg, reading my checklist and thinking about what to do next. I became fixated on my approach plate, the chart that mapped out all the information I needed to land, and must have lost my sense of time. The next thing I knew, a voice from the deep recesses of my consciousness screamed, *"Wings!"* It was like I'd been knocked over the head. I looked up. The altimeter was just about to touch 11,000 feet, and we were descending quickly. I yanked back the stick to stop the descent. A split second later, I felt the instructor's pull on the controls.

"I have the aircraft," he said.

I knew I had beaten him to the controls by a quarter of a second. Would he acknowledge this? If not, it was all over.

Without a word, he gave back the controls and I finished the approach and landing. We refueled and headed back to Columbus. All went well.

Back at the squadron, I found, to my surprise, that many of my classmates were waiting for me in the flight room. I wondered why they were there, since they had never done this before. The evaluator had to attend a meeting for an hour before the debrief, and meanwhile he wouldn't tell me whether I'd passed the flight. That hour turned into four. My classmates took off for other duties. Finally, I was called back to the evaluator's office.

"That altitude restriction is a problem," he said. "I did take the controls." He went on: For the past few hours, he had been debating whether or not to pass me. But I *had* reacted a split second before him. I *had* acted to correct the situation. So . . . he passed me—not, mind you, with a great score.

It didn't matter. I'd made it through. I would soon wear the silver wings of an Air Force aviator.

In recent months, I've learned that people are saying I passed that last check ride only because I'd picked the B-52 and the Air Force wanted its first female bomber pilot to succeed. The story has circulated as far afield as Germany, and has made the rounds of bases in the United States as well. Supposedly, even my evaluator has said that I shouldn't have passed. Would an evaluator have let an unqualified pilot go on to fly a plane that carried nuclear weapons? Or is this just a smear campaign, like the later stories that said I cheated my way through B-52 training?

I'd like to believe the latter. I know that, my fear of check rides aside, I was an excellent pilot. My performance reports from pilot training and from B-52 training prove it. Here's my training squadron commander's report for pilot training: "Lt. Flinn met or exceeded standards for all phases of training. Her efforts were especially noteworthy in the instrument category. . . . Lt. Flinn is an excellent junior officer. Exceeding all standards, her strong desire to excel was contagious." My evaluators and squadron commander from B-52 training wrote: "Her airmanship and leadership were dynamic and a very positive influence on the student class. . . . Kelly displayed outstanding situational awareness during the flight line phase of training. Lt. Flinn achieved the maximum possible score on all stan/eval [standardizations and evaluations] tests and the highest rating on her in-flight evaluation. This along with her outstanding performance throughout the academic and flight training allowed her to be recognized as the Distinguished Graduate."

I have trouble believing that all these evaluations could have been part of a PR campaign meant to show how much the Air Force loves to have high-flying women in its ranks. But I'll always feel that tiny doubt. And that's why I never wanted to be "the first female bomber pilot." Or a "female pilot" at all. I just wanted to fly.

CHAPTER 5

Poster Girl

*When once you have tasted flight you will always walk the
earth with your eyes turned skyward: for there you have been
and there you will always be.*

—LEONARDO DA VINCI

I HAD HOPED THAT WITH THE END OF FLIGHT TRAINING, MY
anxiety would decrease and my flying would improve. I never
had a chance to find out. No sooner had I pinned on my pilot's
wings than the media barrage began. The public affairs personnel at Columbus Air Force Base called me in for a meeting:
"We have to talk about this 'first female bomber pilot' issue."

"There is no issue," I answered. "I'm just a pilot."

I knew where this could lead. I had seen what happened to
Jeannie Flynn, who'd had the bad luck to be the first female
fighter pilot. She'd been brilliant, second in her class in pilot
training. She'd picked her plane just before Congress changed
the law and permitted women to fly in combat, so she'd bounced
around flying cargo aircraft and then instructing T-38s until finally the Air Force discovered her and assigned her the F-15E
she'd earned. And then the press started following her *everywhere*. Anything and everything she did became news—particu-

larly her mistakes. People said she was mean. She didn't fly that well. She had hooked lots of rides. I don't believe any of this is true. When a formation of F-15Es crashed over the ocean, her presence made news, even though she had nothing to do with the story.

I did not want this happening to me.

"What if I don't meet the press?" I asked.

"Well"—and the once-admiring faces shut down; the eyes narrowed—you can either tell your own story, or you can let us tell it for you. Let's just say that it would be wise for you to co-operate with us.

I was given to understand that, no matter what I said or did, the Air Force was going to the media about me. "You're making history," I was told. "This is big news for the Air Force." But if I cooperated, I could at least have a hand in shaping the story people told about me.

That story as told by the Air Force, I saw, was quickly shaping up to be one about a woman who fought for her rights and won them, a kind of "women can do anything" fairy tale. It was nice, but it wasn't me. It didn't resemble me, it didn't sound like me, and it wasn't how I had lived my life. I had never considered myself a feminist. I'd always thought that all the shouting and screaming about women's rights actually got in the way of women's advancement. For one thing, it created a lot of resentment. For another, it made women different—separated them into "women pilots," not just pilots—and different very rarely meant the same thing as equal. I'd always believed that I was equal and had achieved all that I had achieved because I'd done my best as a person, not a woman. I'd been a person all my life. I wasn't going to start being a *woman* now.

The public affairs people weren't very happy about this. "This is your opportunity to send a message to the world," they said. "You are a woman, you're in a man's world, and you're the first in your job. There's a message there, whether or not you want to see it."

In the end, I had to do what they wanted. They were only acting on orders from the Air Force brass. And, in the end, it didn't really matter what message I wanted to get across. The press seized upon the "first female bomber pilot" issue and ran with it. In early press conferences I tried to set the agenda, delivering a statement I had prepared for the children of America. In America, I said, anyone—regardless of race, creed, or sex—can do anything if he or she takes advantage of the educational opportunities offered to them. "I feel that this country has given me so many opportunities that I want to give something back," I would conclude.

There were never any follow-up questions. My statement virtually never made it into print. Instead, every press conference turned out the same:

"What's it like to be the first female bomber pilot?"

"What's it like to fly with an all-male crew?"

"How do you feel about women in combat?"

And even, incredibly enough, "What's it like to be a female?"

Nothing in my education had prepared me to answer *that.* "The airplane," I would say, "doesn't know the gender of the crew. The bombs don't know, and I'm sure those on the ground don't care, either." I tried, as much as possible, to deflect attention from my gender. Asked to answer a question "as a female pilot," I'd be sure to answer "as a pilot." The Air Force didn't appreciate my playing down the "first female" aspect of things. They wanted to milk the poster girl possibilities as much as possible. But I insisted: If they wanted to make a poster girl of me, fine. Only, I said, let it be because of my achievements. Not because of my sex.

After a few weeks of jumping through hoops for the media, I needed to blow off some steam. My friend Elizabeth, another pilot, and I met for the weekend at nearby Randolph Air Force Base, in Texas, and decided to have some fun. Randolph was known for its officers' club, the Auger, which had great music, outstanding Long Island iced teas, and a rotating population of swaggering fighter pilots. Like me, Elizabeth had recently completed pilot training and had earned the plane of her choice: a cargo plane used occasionally in combat missions. She was feeling pretty giddy. Both of us have blond hair and blue eyes, and we'd always joked about passing for dumb blondes. That weekend, we decided to see if we could take some fighter pilots for a ride.

We entered the Auger and checked out the scene. The room was dark, with a few tables and chairs, and a pool table tucked away in a corner. A thin layer of cigar and cigarette smoke was forming just under the ceiling. Pilots were swaggering around the room in their green flight suits. They'd stop and stand in a cluster with their friends, gripping their beers, crossing their arms, nodding and pretending to talk, while checking out all the women in the room. Larger groups of women clustered around them, looking up fawningly and waiting for the pilots to take notice. In the towns around Air Force bases, I knew, it was considered a coup to snag a pilot. And what catches they were, I thought, in their unzipped flight suits, caressing their bottles of beer. Were they prized because they could defend our nation against its enemies, or because they could fly low and fast? Were they cool because they had sharp reflexes, or because they knew how to wear their Air Force–issue Ray-Bans? Elizabeth and I caught each other's eye. This was going to be fun.

We bought ourselves a couple of Long Island iced teas and stood at the bar. After a few minutes, some men in green flight suits approached us. "Hey," they said, "what're you guys doing here?"

We smiled at them with our big blue eyes.

"Are you a pilot?" I said to the guy who'd placed himself squarely in front of me.

"Yes, ma'am," he said gravely, keeping his voice in the low, flat tones we'd learned for talking over our radios. "I'm an aviator."

"What kind of flying have you been doing recently?" I looked up and did my best to bat my eyes. "If it's not *classified* . . ."

"We did something called navigational proficiency," he deadpanned. (This meant he had taken off in Utah and landed in Texas.) "Real complicated. Extremely tough."

"Oh, wow." I had to bite my bottom lip to keep from laughing.

I talked to half a dozen "aviators" this way. Then I went up to the bar for a refill on my Long Island iced tea. I saw a guy standing against the bar with a Minot patch on his flight jacket. "Great," I thought. "This will be fun."

"What is this patch?" I said, sipping my drink.

"Minot, ma'am. Fly a B-52."

I fingered the patch. "And this one?" I opened my eyes a bit wider. "And this one?"

The pilot eventually walked away and joined his friends. He watched me from across the room, nodding and elbowing his buddy. "I can't let this go on anymore," I thought. I bought a beer and walked back over to him, replacing his empty beer bottle with my fresh one.

I stuck out my hand. "Nice to meet you, I'm Kelly Flinn."

He shook my hand. My name didn't mean anything to him— yet. "I'm going to be stationed at Minot." He stepped back, looked at me oddly.

"Oh, yes?"

"I'm a pilot."

"Really?" he said, still trying to get his bearings. "What plane?"

Dummy, I thought. (There's only one plane at Minot.)

"The B-52."

"Ohhh!" he said, recognition dawning. The Columbus press people had done a good job getting my name and story into the *Air Force Times*. He started pointing at me drunkenly, over and over again, laughing and shaking his head.

"That was awesome," he said. "That was very well done." And he handed me his squadron patch.

I grew tired of the game after that. I decided to stand quietly and watch Elizabeth flirt for a while.

"Let me buy you a drink." The pilot who walked up to me had been talking to Elizabeth before. He was about my height and muscular, with a great smile, a slightly receding hairline, and a funny gleam in his eye. He flew an F-16.

"What do you do?" he asked.

"I go to the community college," I said.

He grinned wider. "What do you study?"

"Biology."

"Tough stuff." He kept grinning, as if keeping a secret, while he went to the bar to buy me another drink.

"Did you tell him anything?" I asked Elizabeth, who was holding court while a circle of pilots explained the sexiness of cargo planes.

"Yeah," she said, looking surprised. "He knows who you are. Didn't he tell you?"

He had beaten me at my own game.

"Let's cut the bullshit," I said when he returned. He handed me my drink. "You can buy me all the drinks in the world," I went on. "But I'm not going to sleep with you."

He laughed out loud. "Talk about dropping a bomb. No wonder you're flying the B-52."

I liked him. We thought alike. We shared a sense of humor. He flew the plane I'd once dreamed about, and he described it interestingly.

"Let's get out of here," he said as the evening wound down. "Let's go to my room."

I declined, but I did agree to exchange phone numbers. I figured I'd never hear from him again, not after he'd bought me four rounds of drinks and gone home to an empty bed. But I underestimated him. He left a message on my answering machine. He sent me a card wishing me luck with the B-52. When he returned to his base in Utah and I moved to B-52 training in Louisiana, we wrote letters back and forth.

I never really looked for anything more. I didn't want a long-distance relationship. I thought if it was meant to be, then it would be. We did get together one weekend when we crossed paths by chance. It was wonderful, and we decided we wanted to see each other again. But our Air Force lives made a serious relationship impossible. There was no point investing in a relationship, only to have to separate days later. I'd observed the ugly side of too many Air Force romances: distance bred infidelity bred broken hearts. Finally, we decided to be just friends, making peace both with our feelings and with our lives.

But the sense of what might have been ate at me. It reminded me painfully of the end of my love story at pilot training school. I'd broken up with my boyfriend because I had too much work to do, not enough time for him, and not enough patience to explain over and over why I had to keep studying. I was midway through T-38 training, while he was still a few months behind, in T-37s. I had twice his workload. "I'm sorry," I had said. "In a few months, you'll understand." After I graduated and long after we'd stopped seeing each other, I did run into him on a trip back to the base, just as he was struggling with T-38s. "I understand now," he'd said. "I'm sorry." It was too late. We moved on with the careers that had driven us apart in the first place. There was just no way to be the pilots we wanted to be and also stay together. I had the sense now that this story and stories like it were likely to be repeated all through my Air Force career. I understood why so many pilots married young. But how many husbands would have been willing to drop everything and travel to Minot, North Dakota, with me?

IN APRIL 1995, I moved to Barksdale Air Force Base in Shreveport, Louisiana, to start B-52 training. My reputation preceded me. On the first day of classes I was treated to the sight of people staring at me as I passed them and whispering "Is that her?" behind me in the hallways. I kept my head down and tried to be inconspicuous. In the classroom, we'd been given assigned seats, as if we were in grade school or flight school. Of course, mine was in the most visible and inaccessible spot: first row, far left corner, next to the window. I had to physically squeeze past two people to get to it. So much for passing incognito.

Our instructor came in, looking kind of nervous. "Gentlemen and, uh, ladies—I mean, lady—or whatever," he began. "Welcome to the B-52."

It was the same in every class. The instructors were tense and uncomfortable. "Guys—and uh, girls, ladies? Gals?" they'd begin. Each time they fumbled, I felt more and more uncomfortable. These adults couldn't even handle a simple introduction. " 'Guys' is fine," I would say. I said it so much that, by the end of the first week, I was considering having " 'Guys' is fine" printed up as a name tag. But the question of how to address the class was just the tip of the iceberg. Everyone was deeply uncomfortable around me, afraid of saying or doing the wrong thing. It was so easy, after all, to slip up. Half the B-52 flight lingo seemed to contain terms like "balls" or "tits." Everyone was cleaning it up now, for fear I'd lodge a complaint, despite the fact there were a few female crew chiefs who had been doing maintenance on the B-52 for years. And that self-policing pretty much killed all casual conversation.

It didn't help that the Air Force simply refused to let me just settle in and be one of the guys. I was constantly singled out for special treatment. During the academic part of our training, instead of being paired with another lieutenant, I was assigned the one lieutenant colonel in the class. He was a very interesting man: a Strategic Air Command warrior who had flown B-52s in Vietnam and afterward during the SAC days when the planes were on call twenty-four hours a day. He'd flown the D-model B-52, an older plane that had a tail gunner. He was requalifying on the B-52-H, a newer model plane, because the Air Force now needed pilots. He constantly interrupted lectures with questions and stories about how things were done (better, it seemed) on the D-model. Usually, once he started, we threw down our pens and sat back, because we knew he was going to go on a long time. But once when he mentioned that he'd been flying with a tail gunner who had actually shot down a MiG during the Vietnam War, the Academy graduates immediately snapped to attention.

"Airman First Class Albert C. Moore," we all chanted, then started to laugh. Freshman knowledge never left you. The lieutenant colonel couldn't remember his gunner's name, but we'd never forget. Albert C. Moore was the tail gunner on *Diamond Lil,* the B-52 now on static display at the Air Force Academy.

My classmates could probably have overlooked my pairing up with the lieutenant colonel—we were, after all, the oddballs of the class—if I had just been allowed to get on with my training afterward. And I *was* left in peace for a couple of weeks, while we studied the B-52's complex and antiquated systems. The plane was a remarkable feat of engineering. Its design had held up since 1961, the last time it was manufactured. It had a 185-foot wing span and could carry up to 70,000 pounds of bombs. There were twelve fuel tanks; the copilot manually controlled the movement of fuel through the engines. If you did not follow all the proper procedures to the letter, the plane's center of gravity and balance would be upset, and the plane could stall and fall from the sky. The electrical system was also mind-numbing in its complexity. Part of flying the B-52, my instructor said, was accepting that sometimes the more than forty-year-old system would do strange things and no one would be able to figure out why. He called these strange electrical occurrences queertrons. That pretty much summed things up.

My time as a normal student ended one day when we were preparing for a test on the hydraulics system. My squadron commander pulled me out of class and took me down to public affairs, where I was told that I'd be giving a press conference the next day.

"Can't do it," I said. "I have a test."

"Forget the test," they said. "This is important. You can have all of next weekend to prepare for the test."

That night, while the other students crammed, I shined my boots, polished up my media platform and reread my prepared answers to reporters' questions. In the morning, while everyone else zipped hurriedly into their flight suits and gulped down their coffee, I took extra time with my hair and put on makeup. I never wore makeup in uniform; it made me look like too much of a woman. But I wanted my skin to be clear for photos. The other students stared hard at me when I walked into a class right before the test period and sat down.

We were reviewing for another test the following week. I couldn't follow along. I had homework to do that I'd neglected the night before. I was getting further away from what I was supposed to be there to do. It dawned on me that if my performance started to suffer, I'd have the Air Force to thank.

With an apology to the instructor, I left class early and headed out to meet my squadron commander and the public affairs officer while my classmates finished cramming for the test. We climbed into a van and headed out to the flight line, where the B-52s stood waiting to fly. The rules of engagement were explained to me. I would stand in front of the plane while the reporters snapped photos and asked questions. It was utterly absurd. Some of the seasoned military reporters in the group probably knew more about the B-52 than I did. I had never even seen one up close before. It was *huge*. I had to tell myself not to gape. Instead, I tried to look cool and confident. I struck my best pilot's pose and pretended I knew what I was doing. Some cameramen asked if they could film me walking around the plane, as if performing a preflight check. I looked at my commander, and he whispered in my ear where to begin. I kept my eyes on him as I toured the plane, trying to interpret his signals and improvise some semiplausible procedures. I didn't even know which side I was supposed to begin with. I ran into the bomb bay, where the cameras weren't allowed to follow me. Some weapons loaders were there working. I startled them. "Hey," I said, "can I just come in here for a minute and hide?"

I sat there for a moment, nervously giggling, then stepped back out into the blinding lights of the cameras. After an eternity, I finished my walk-around, and the questions began. The reporters wanted to know what the hardest thing was about flying a B-52. "I don't know," I said. "I've never flown one."

How was I going to go to the bathroom?

"Same way I always have, I suppose," I said.

I really didn't want to share my peeing techniques with the national media. And I really didn't know. How to adapt a B-52's rudimentary toilet facilities for me was a problem that the Air Force thought they had to devote considerable man-hours to solving. All the B-52 had ever been equipped with was a urinal and a bucket, and it was considered very poor form to use the bucket because many of our flights were about twelve hours long and there was nowhere to dispose of the bucket's contents. In fact, there was really nowhere on the plane to even *use* the bucket. The B-52 had been designed to carry and drop bombs—as many bombs as possible—and virtually every inch of space inside the plane was used to store its cargo. The bucket was kept in the cockpit in a tiny space under one of the extra seats. Far from private.

What happened, by the way, was this: Without consulting the one person who would have to use the result, the Air Force developed its own solution. The idea was to provide a plastic liner for the bucket (a garbage bag) and a curtain to go around it. I would throw the bag away after each flight.

"I hope it's pink," I joked, trying to cut through the pea-soup-thick tension the subject aroused.

The bucket-and-curtain contraption seemed plausible, until I tried it. This was a couple of months later, when I was actually flying.

"Copilot clearing for relief," I announced to my panicked crewmates, and settled myself in behind the curtain. It was pitch-dark and I held a flashlight in my teeth. In the space available, it was virtually impossible to unzip my flight suit, pee, and zip up again without total disaster. Then I looked in the bucket: no plastic bag. I had to scrounge through my gear for a Baggie. I would have to develop some other solution.

After the flight-line tour, we returned to the classroom building so that the reporters could take pictures of me practicing in the B-52 cockpit mock-ups that we used before we were ready to fly. While I climbed the stairs, followed by the gaggle of reporters and colonels, my classmates were cleaning the room and scrambling to hide the tests they were taking. They'd just been told by the base commanders to make it seem that I was only missing a lecture. The Air Force didn't want the general public to think I received special treatment.

Some of my classmates were asked by the press what it was like to be around me. "She's just like the rest of us," they said. I looked at them across the sea of reporters. I so wished that it could be true.

Strike two against me came on the day of my first official flight as a B-52 copilot. Three copilot students and our instructors were to spend two to three hours practicing landing procedures and techniques. The week before the flight, I learned that I was scheduled to fly not with my regular instructor pilot, Captain Mark Ewart, but with the squadron commander. The explanation was that the squadron commander always flew on the first flight and my crew was scheduled to take off first. But there were two other copilots on the flight. Not only did they not get to fly with the colonel, they had to wait until I was done to get a turn at the controls. "Flyin' with the colonel, huh, Kelly?" one of them barked to me, raising his eyebrows, as I checked out the flight schedule. "Flyin' first, I suppose?"

What was I supposed to do? In an effort to ease the tension, I showed up for the flight with a bright pink publications bag. A publications bag is a huge briefcase, like the kind attorneys carry, filled with every single technical document and checklist needed for the B-52 and all its systems. The T-37 and T-38 technical orders were about an inch thick. The B-52's filled a three-ring binder about eight or ten inches thick. I had spent the whole weekend painting my publications bag pink. If they wanted me to be a female pilot, I thought, I'd give them "female pilot."

I stopped by life support to collect my helmet, and the technicians noticed my bag and started to laugh. For the first time, I sensed them finally starting to relax around me. One of them helped me secure my bag, adding some red duct tape to its worn edges.

I walked out and joined the crew waiting for the big blue Air Force bus that would bring us out to our airplane. The other copilots started to laugh; the instructors tried to stop themselves and failed. This was the least tense that anyone here had ever been around me. I was feeling more comfortable than I ever had before, either. Then the squadron commander showed up. "How are you going to evade with that thing?" he asked. I stared back at him, dumbfounded. Was he serious? First of all, if I had to bail out of a plane in enemy territory I sure wouldn't take the briefcase. Second, I doubted I'd be evading the enemy in Louisiana unless something was happening that we hadn't been briefed on. I sarcastically muttered something to myself about changing into the heels and dress that I also had in the bag and going out to dinner.

Finally, we arrived at the airplane and unloaded our gear, and I hoisted myself into the cockpit.

One of the first things I noticed was the smell: thirty years of sweat, fuel, oil, and hydraulics fluids—the mechanical equivalent of how an athlete smells after a strenuous workout. It wasn't foul, though, just peculiar. I was amazed at how small the cockpit was. On one side of the stairs that led to the front of the plane were the pilot and copilot's seats. On the other side were the gunner and electronic warfare officers' stations. Their area was almost completely dark, and their ejection seats faced toward the back of the plane. The ceiling was so low that I could not stand completely upright.

I climbed up the ladder and pushed my gear forward toward the front of the plane. The walls were covered with endless rows of circuit breakers. I checked the settings. Just under the circuit breakers, on the left-hand side of the cockpit, was a bunk about two feet wide, with about a foot of space above it to lie down in. The worn mattress that covered the bunk was topped with the ten spare parachutes required by safety regulations—which, unfortunately, hadn't specified where to store them.

I took a swig from my water bottle and tossed it in a side bin next to the copilot's seat. Already I was starting to swelter. It was early June, and the Louisiana summer was upon us. The sun was shining directly into the cockpit, and only a slight

breeze entered the tiny windows. I grabbed a hot-pink bandanna and tied it around my head to keep the sweat from
building up under my helmet and running into my eyes. The
colonel shook his head. I checked the oxygen system. Moving
around the cockpit from right to left, I verified that all the engine ignition toggle switches were off. These eight switches
would generate a spark that ignited the fuel, starting up the engines. Once I was set, the pilot and I nodded to each other. He
was a stately-looking man, with perfect posture and slightly
graying hair. He turned on the battery and interphone switch.
We would now use the interphone to communicate with each
other. To talk to him, I would push a toggle switch on the back
of the yoke, or steering wheel, with my right forefinger. If I
pressed the switch down, I would send a radio broadcast to
the world, so I was always careful to toggle up. Together, the
pilot and I talked through the endless series of checks, while
outside, the crew chiefs helped check external systems that we
could not see from inside the cockpit. I had to crane my neck
and twist my body around to even see the edge of the wings. I
was thirty feet off the ground and was longing for my tiny little T-38. How in the world was I going to land this thing? It
was like being inside a department store. The wings, weighed
down with fuel, sagged to the ground, resting on the tiny
wheels at the end of each wingtip.

Once the colonel and I had finished our checks, the rest of
the crew came on board. I checked the radios and informed
the ground controllers that we were starting engines. I wanted
to sound cool, since all ears would instantly recognize my
voice and attribute any and all radio faux pas to me.

The engines came to life and a huge roaring filled the cockpit. The eight TF-33 turbo-fan engines made the huge plane vi-
brate. Without earplugs and a helmet, the noise would have
been unbearable. I had to crank up the volume on my helmet
to hear the colonel and instructor. I could faintly smell the

JP-8 fuel fumes wafting through the cockpit. I love the smell of jet fuel. It smells like speed.

Once the engines were started and a few more checks completed, we were ready to taxi. In the cockpit I readjusted my huge flight gloves, moved the rudder pedals all the way up to me, and moved my seat as far forward as possible. I could not see beyond the nose of the aircraft to the ground directly below.

The colonel wanted to demonstrate the taxi procedure from the parking space. I had no objections; the last thing I wanted to do was have a fender-bender in the parking lot. He pushed all eight throttles forward to increase our momentum, then pulled them back to idle. We started forward—a slow, lumbering movement, like trying to roll a safe, but even with the engines at idle, you could feel the plane wanting to pick up speed and momentum.

The colonel gently tapped the brakes. They squeaked and the plane jerked to the side while the wheels slowed down. I heard a few comments from the crew in the back, but we would soon learn that this jerky motion was just part of the B-52.

Once we were clear of the other planes, I took the controls. I placed my left hand on the throttles and spread my fingertips across all eight throttles. It was like trying to reach a full octave on the piano. My palm pressed against the edge of each throttle, while my fingertips rested along the top and edges. I gently bumped the throttles forward and the plane responded with more speed. I tapped the brakes and once again we jerked and squeaked. I tried to imagine the centerline running through my right leg—an adjustment, because I was used to sitting along the center of a plane instead of off to one side. Turns were even more difficult. Instead of starting when the plane's nose reached the place where you wanted to turn, you had to wait until you thought the tail of the airplane had gotten there. To an observer it looks as if you've missed the turn, but a B-52 almost pivots in place, making close to a 90-degree angle. The first time I experienced this, I was shocked.

I took one last swig of my water, attached my mask to the helmet, and pulled down my visor. I tightened my seat straps and reviewed the takeoff data for the entire crew. Ready. The pilot had the controls and I called for clearance. "Tuff zero one, number one, ready for takeoff." We were cleared onto the runway. I checked that no other aircraft was approaching the runway, then made sure the wingtip wouldn't hit anything on the way. The colonel pushed the throttles forward and slowly guided the BUFF ("Big Ugly Fat Fucker"—or "Fellow," for the tasteful) onto the runway. He swung the nose around and lined up on centerline, then slowly began to push the throttles forward. You could feel the momentum building. My left hand followed his right on the throttles, and my right hand was poised on the interphone switch, careful not to grab the yoke and interfere with the pilot's control inputs by possibly holding the yoke in place. Inside the plane, the only sound was the roaring engines. As we gathered steam, the plane seemed to wobble back and forth on its landing gear. You feel as if you're on a skateboard, trying to keep it from tipping and using your arms for balance. We were just using wings instead of arms.

Once the pilot called "committed" (meaning that we were past our Go/No-Go speed and had committed to the takeoff), he removed his right hand from the throttles and put it on the yoke to help with the control inputs. At this point, you needed both hands to get the airplane off the ground. I now had control of the throttles and watched the engine instruments carefully. Ten knots below the takeoff speed, the pilot gently began to pull the yoke toward him, and you could feel the tail end of the aircraft settle back on the ground. A B-52's back end initially starts to rise in the air well before the front end, so you have to counteract this tendency, otherwise the tail end may flip over the nose. At takeoff, the pilot pushes the yoke forward and the airplane starts to climb. This is one of the weirdest sensations I've ever experienced. I had learned in pilot training that when a plane takes off, you pull back on the stick or yoke, the nose points high into the air, and the aircraft climbs into the sky. "Pull back, houses get smaller. Push forward, houses get bigger" is the mantra. But when you're taking off in a B-52, the nose is pointed directly at the ground, so you're staring at concrete instead of blue sky, but you're climbing.

I shook my head and focused on the instruments. This was another big difference between flying the B-52 and flying T-38s. In pilot training, we had spent 75 percent of our time scanning the horizon outside, occasionally cross-checking our instruments for altitude, heading, and airspeed. In the BUFF, even on the clearest day, you spend 75 percent of the time scanning the instruments. Because of the physical design of the cockpit, you can't use the sky and ground references to guide your flight, and the altitude indicator is the only guide for turns and banks, climbs and descents. I felt a bit insecure, not being able to look outside and orient myself to the real horizon.

I continued the checklist, raising the landing gear when the pilot asked me to. We reached the designated pattern altitude (the altitude you fly in the landing pattern), and the pilot gave me the controls. I took a moment to congratulate myself, then had to concentrate on flying. The ride inside a B-52 is never smooth. You always feel some vibration, either from the rumbling engines or the weather. I always chuckle during a commercial airline flight when the pilot turns on the "Fasten Your Seat Belt" sign because of turbulence. Usually, the natural rattle and hum of the B-52 is a lot rougher.

I started a left-hand turn. The first thing I noticed was how long it took the airplane to react to my input. We'd been warned about the reaction time and seen it in the simulator. Now I was really experiencing it. In a normal airplane, if you want to make a right turn, you lower the yoke or push the stick to the right, which lowers a mechanical piece on the left wing to create more camber—wing curve. The slipstream hits the lowered part of the wing—the aileron—and produces more lift on the left side. This makes the left wing rise higher into the air than the right, which makes the airplane turn to the right. A B-52, unlike almost every other plane in the world, does not have ailerons. Instead it uses spoilers. These are airfoils that stick up from the top of the wing into the airstream; they "spoil the lift" on the wing. If you want to turn right, you raise the right spoiler, which makes the wing drop down and puts the B-52 into a right-hand turn.

But back to my left turn. After I initiated it, aerodynamic forces pushed the plane to climb, so I pushed forward a little on the yoke to maintain altitude. Farther into the turn, the plane wanted to descend—the normal reaction of all planes in turns. I pulled back on the yoke and added some trim to hold the elevator in the position I had set, alleviating some of the air pressures over the air surfaces. I tried to look left to check that the sky was clear in front of me, but my view was blocked by the metal frame of the B-52 cockpit and my pilot's head and body. I could not see to the left at all. So I reverted to the instruments for the rest of the turn and asked the pilot if we were clear. He nodded, and I rolled out to the wings-level position, ending the turn. The colonel began the landing checklist. He lowered the gear, checked the fuel, and determined the landing weight, which would determine our landing airspeed. I kept scanning the instruments, getting used to their positions in the cockpit.

We were almost fifteen miles from the runway. At the air traffic controller's direction, I started another left turn and slowly began descending to the specified altitude. I tried to line up with the runway, but the lumbering dinosaur I was flying wouldn't let me. First I overshot to the left. Then I over-corrected to the right and we sailed past the runway. Then, zing again, out to the left. I was on what felt like an endless zigzag, swaying back and forth, like a skateboarder on a ramp, and despite all my attempts I could not get the plane to stop in the center of the bowl. This was hard physical work, too. I was sitting stiffly upright, like a mannequin posing for display, with my right arm raised and almost parallel with my shoulder. This awkward position is necessary to fly the plane and control your movements. Your right arm moves all as one, rising and lowering as you turn the yoke. Your left arm moves from the elbow joint forward, gently applying pressure to the throttles. I began to notice how many muscles I was using to fly this plane, all of them in the shoulders, back, and upper arm. I was glad I had been building up my back muscles.

After a few of my zigzags, the colonel took the controls. I guess I was making him seasick. Keeping our airspeed constant as we approached the runway, he focused on the landing aimpoint. Aimpoint and airspeed are the key to landing an airplane, any airplane. As he neared the runway threshold, he kept the plane's nose pointed at the aimpoint and gently pulled the throttles back to the idle position. That makes a plane's nose want to drop. Gently, he pulled back the yoke and added two clicks of trim, counting to himself: "One potato, two potato." The trim button, just under your thumb on the yoke, electrically moves a mechanism in the back of the plane which holds the attitude the pilot designates, almost like an autopilot. He continues to drive the aircraft down to the ground, down toward his aimpoint. When we were only a few feet above the ground, he shifted his gaze to the horizon, gently pulled back on the yoke, and began the "curved roundout" phase of landing, leading into the flattened-out flare. This is the art again. If you start the roundout too late, the front gear (the nose) of the aircraft will touch first and you'll bounce. If you start it too early, you'll approach the ground, then start to rise again before you've touched down. If you've risen too much when the plane stalls, as it's supposed to do during landing, you'll fall too far and hit the runway too hard. Pretty obvious why *that's* dangerous. To land properly, you want to stall just a few inches to a foot or so above the ground, so the fall is short. Of course, even a short fall in a B-52, 290,000 pounds of metal and fuel, is a crash.

Once the front wheels touched down, the pilot still had to "fly the wings" to keep our balance. We were on that skateboard again, cruising down the runway. Then he pushed the throttles forward and we headed back into the air. My turn.

I flew around the landing traffic pattern. This time, I was able to keep the plane much steadier. I repeated to myself, "Aimpoint, airspeed; aimpoint, airspeed." I cross-checked my instruments, chewed my bottom lip, held my arms in the awkward position that would one day become natural. My movements were small—barely detectable, I knew from watching the pilot. Approaching the threshold, I noticed my aimpoint wandering and tried to correct it. Out of the corner of my eye, I could see the pilot following me on the controls, ready to grab them if I did anything remotely dangerous. I started my roundout a tad too soon. We hung in the air momentarily as the airspeed bled off and the plane finally stalled, a little higher than it ought to have. *Thud.* "We're here," I thought, as if there were any doubt. I tried to keep the wings level, we bounced from tip gear to tip gear. I pushed on the rudder pedal to correct back to the centerline and the aircraft jerked left, taking us with it. Trying to correct, I jerked us right. I had no finesse whatsoever on the controls. It didn't matter, though. I had landed a B-52.

My bandanna was soaked with sweat. My gloves were crinkled around my fingers and the palm of my hand. I could already feel the calluses developing on my palms. I removed my

"The Clan": Flinn family Christmas photo, 1970s.

Before I encountered the Academy's strict eating rules.

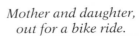

Mother and daughter, out for a bike ride.

"What am I supposed to do with these?"

Tommy and me, planning our next adventure.

Playing with the boys: my first soccer team.

The ReBelle traveling soccer team.

"Always a comedian": at St. Monica's grade school— I'm the one in the middle, with my hand over that girl's head (and someone's hand making horns over mine).

"Wonder if I'll ever wear a real one of these": at space camp.

My hopes and dreams hanging on the wall: my bedroom, during high school.

At the senior prom, with my pen pal.

"Miss LHS": my high school graduation.

Proud to be . . .'93.

"There are twenty minutes till the morning meal formation!": calling minutes, freshman year at the Academy.

Demonstrating the three-point landing on the assault course.

"Do we have to shower before dinner?" Logan and I return from survival training.

"Is this how you apply makeup?": me, after ten days in the woods.

"Besides eating the meat of the rabbit, you can make puppets too!" Here I am, as a survival instructor, demonstrating to one of my students other uses for the rabbit.

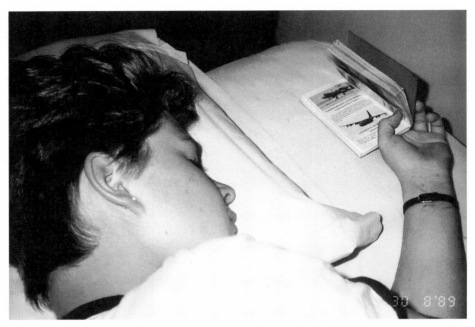

Learning Contrails *by osmosis.*

"I did it!": after my first time flying solo in the glider— I'm running toward my parents, who were watching.

Partying hard: a sweep of the bars in South Korea.

Pegasus is still safely grounded: that's me in the middle, with two of my friends.

"The Kun": at Kunsan Air Base, Korea.

"She shoots!": on the Academy soccer team.

*True friends: Jessica, Krissy, and me
after beating the Naval Academy in a soccer game.*

Proud parents and the baby, in France, posing in front of a Cap-10.

Big bingo winnings: my friend Mo and me.

"C'est la vie!": enjoying the day with the French cadets.

Celebrating our wings: Kristin and me after pilot training graduation.

"Let's get going!" Kristin and me awaiting graduation.

My wish did come true:
Neal and me after graduation from
the Air Force Academy.

"Am I wearing this correctly?"

*"Uh-huh": the Flying Elvises,
Mississippi chapter—
this is a T-38.*

The Bomber Baron.

B-52-H at Minot.

Air refueling.

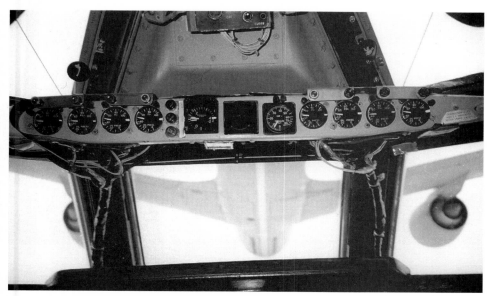

View from the cockpit of a B-52-H, getting ready to refuel.

Signing the "honorable" discharge resignation paper.

Enjoying my new civilian life: Jessica and me.

helmet inside the cockpit and tried to brush my matted hair into something presentable. No hope. It was plastered to my head, with a definite part down the middle and several unco-operative wisps sticking straight up. "Guess I'll get used to this look," I thought as I climbed out of the cockpit. I grabbed my gear and got on the blue bus. The instructor pilots made fun of my hair and I teased them back. It was such a relief to be able to laugh. Captain Ewart slapped me on the back as I packed up my gear and headed home. I thanked my lucky stars that he hadn't given me a hug.

I LOVED FLYING the B-52. I learned to anticipate, thinking well ahead of the jet so it had time to respond to my input. This was my airplane—we clicked. I would fly about twice a week, each mission nearly twelve hours long. During the flight, we would spend an hour in the air refueling, then spend two hours skim-ming the ground at just 600 feet.

Flying low-level and practicing bomb runs give you power-ful feelings. The plane's rumbling and shaking increase as you accelerate to bombing speed and the bomb doors open. The noise from the roaring engines intensifies while the pilot holds the plane steady. I search the horizon for the target and for advancing simulated enemy fighters. The radar navigator calls "Hack" and begins to release the bombs, which shake the plane from side to side as they are forcefully ejected from the bomb bay. As soon as the bomb doors close, the flight becomes smoother and I would smile to myself with a feeling of exhila-ration, because we had successfully completed our mission.

I was very happy with my instructor, Captain Ewart. He was the first person at Barksdale to treat me like a regular pilot. He was never nervous around me, never tried to give me any spe-cial treatment. Whenever he was asked about me, he replied,

"She's just a copilot." I don't think he ever knew how much that meant to me.

THE WEEKS OF TRAINING passed quickly. It was time for another check ride. As always, Murphy's law was in effect. We were delayed on the ground for about two hours by maintenance problems. We kept the engines running for a long time and I watched the fuel run down. There were storm clouds building in the distance. All our fuel curve estimates and schedules had to be reworked. Matters didn't improve when we were airborne. Our refueling tanker arrived late, and we had to reschedule again in the air. Then the tanker wasn't where it was supposed to be. The radar navigator and the electronic warfare officer scrambled to find it and I said a silent prayer for them. We were all being evaluated together as well as separately; if one of us failed, the whole crew might fail. Even my instructor pilot was being evaluated that day. So we really had to work together as a team.

The navigator had a superior attitude toward enlisted men, and in the past, I'd been annoyed with our radar navigator as well; he had a tendency to shout out "Centerline!" as I was trying to land. But now we put all that aside. Teamwork: it was my job to call for a check of all systems every half hour. If I was a minute or two late, one of my crewmates—the navigator, the radar navigator, or the electronic warfare officer—would speak up with a code word to remind me to call the check. My instructor pilot noticed that whenever I was at the controls, the evaluator set aside his magazine and started taking notes. So he did most of the flying, and the evaluator read.

I felt relaxed through most of the flight. But when the time for my landing approached, I snapped to attention. The evaluator was poised between the pilot and copilot seats, pencil in hand. I did not want a repeat of my earlier check-ride fiascoes—especially not now, when I knew I could fly this plane and fly it well. As we approached the runway I could see the landing in my mind. It was a *physical* sensation. Everything clicked. Up till now, I had flown mechanically, relying on outside indicators to tell me when to flare. Now I could feel how high we were. I held my aimpoint and would not let it waver. I pulled the throttles back, clicked the trim, and drove the plane down. I sensed when to begin the roundout, and gently pulled back, making sure to hold back the yoke rather than "give up" on the landing and let the nose drop too soon, as I tended to do. The rear wheels touched; I held on to the yoke; the front wheels touched. Carefully, I kept the wings level and the BUFF on centerline. My evaluation would soon be over. I did not want to screw up in the last thirty seconds of the flight. My instructor didn't want me to screw up either. After this landing, he handed me the seat pins even before I had a chance to reach for them. If you didn't insert the pins before unstrapping, you could activate the ejection seat and send yourself flying out of the plane. An instant hook.

Neither of us should have worried. The landing was the best I'd ever flown. I had felt the thrill of it through my body—that physical sense of something perfectly executed.

The next day, I found out that the evaluator had agreed. Usually, you earned one of three grades for a check ride: Q1, Q2, or Q3. Q3 meant you had hooked; Q2 meant that you had qualified, but with one or two deficiencies that needed watching; Q1 meant that you had qualified with no problems. I received a final grade of EQ, "Exceptionally Qualified," a score that's very rarely given. Because of this grade and my academic scores, I graduated from B-52 school as the Distinguished Graduate, first in my class. Best of all, I knew I'd earned it. I got no special treatment in the classroom and none on the check ride. I'd performed and been judged on my merits just like everybody else. No one will ever be able to take that away from me.

I HAD RECEIVED some surprising mail at Barksdale. A prisoner had seen me on television and wanted to communicate. No, thanks. The other letter was from a woman at Minot, the wife of a navigator. She wanted to welcome me and wish me luck. She was excited, she said, that a woman was finally flying a B-52. She said she suspected that I was lonely and wanted to offer any support that she could. This letter I tucked carefully away. I was happy to know that I'd have a friend in Minot, particularly a female friend.

Of course, I'd been completely surrounded by men at Barksdale. I'd become friendly with some of them. I'd dated a bit, but as always, I didn't form any long-term attachments. My only female friend was the wife of another student copilot. We used to people-watch together at a local bar, and she often invited me over for dinner with her and her husband. But the friendship only went so far. The only thing we had in common was the fact that we'd eventually be moving to Minot. I never shared any of my deeper feelings with her. I couldn't have told her, for example, that spending time with her and her husband made me lonely. They were such a happy couple, deeply connected and in love. Being with them confronted me with everything I wanted and didn't have.

I figured I'd make a home for myself in Minot. For the first time ever, I would have a job, instead of being in training for a job. I'd have a real apartment. I'd put down roots. I'd been told Minot was a nice place to raise a family. Who knew? I thought. Maybe I'd start one there. Or at least meet a man I would date seriously. I climbed into my black Honda and began the twenty-six-hour drive to North Dakota feeling hopeful.

And then I looked around.

I arrived in Minot in early October. Winter had already begun, and I could see the remnants of a snowstorm. To my right, to my left, for miles, I could see only farmland. It was flat. Extremely flat. No hills, no mountains; just plains. The ground was yellow and brown and the crops looked dead. The main road through town was only about five miles long. I passed one McDonald's, one Wendy's, four Dairy Queens (all closed for the winter), and a tractor store. I saw a small college, a big red brick factory called the Sweetheart Bakery, and a large number of railroad tracks. It was the railroad that had brought Minot into being—overnight, the story went—in 1907. The city still had the feeling of something half-finished. Despite all the wide-open spaces around it, it felt very claustrophobic.

The wind blowing across the plains rocked my car as I drove the last ten miles north to the Air Force base. The entrance looked like a deserted toll booth, with a huge, dreary sign over the main gate: "Only the Best Come North." "When do they get to leave?" I wondered.

My impressions of Minot only worsened with time. There was absolutely nothing to do. Nowhere to shop, no cultural events, no nice sports centers. North Dakota winters last from October to April, and temperatures regularly reach 30 below zero. Wind chill can bring that down to minus 80 or 90. I had even felt minus 103 degrees one day. When it was cold like that, people never went outside. They went to and from their cars to bars, got drunk and went home. It was too cold to go skiing. There were no good indoor sports facilities on base. There was an *outdoor* swimming pool, which was open exactly two months out of the year. There was a mediocre gym. Those who could afford to join the YMCA downtown at least had a place to work out. But most of the enlisted personnel didn't even have that much of an escape. They were earning between $600 and $700 a month; not only could they not afford private gyms, some couldn't even pay for their groceries without food stamps. That was a shock for me. But it was just typical of the dreariness of life in Minot.

People struggled daily with boredom and frustration, and the Air Force turned a blind eye, doing nothing to make its members' lives easier or more pleasant. It let their frustrations simmer, and when the dissatisfaction turned to heavy drinking, or drunk driving, or violence, or illicit sex, it acted shocked and came down hard and heavy with punishment.

Minot wasn't exceptional in this way. On a national level, Air Force leaders started talking a good game about integrity and family values. And the louder they talked, the more things fell apart in the ranks. The brass was impotent. The generals didn't have the power to stop the political and social forces undercutting morale and good behavior. They couldn't stop Congress from voting for force reductions and base closings. Minot's base population was swollen with people who'd been transferred from closed bases. People who had never signed on to live their lives buried in snow were now stuck in it—and for tours of duty that were often twice as long as those they'd first agreed to. Aircrews had to fly more, longer missions. Personnel had to do more with less, so people were sent abroad to places like Saudi Arabia for eighteen months at a time. What did they do to vent their frustration? They drank. What did their wives or husbands do in the meantime while they were alone? They had affairs.

The truth about Air Force social life in Minot is quite simple: Everybody was sleeping with everybody. Every weekend brought the same mating rituals. On Friday and Saturday nights, officers and enlisted would file into Minot's three main bars—Cats, the Landing, and Peyton Place—and spend the evening drinking, dancing, smoking, and playing pool. At 12:45, the lights would come on and the bouncers would scream, "Get the fuck out!" Then everybody would scramble to find someone to bring home. And the next weekend take off with someone else.

I was twenty-four years old when I arrived in Minot. I was the only female officer in a squadron of 450 personnel. I was tired of hanging out with married couples, or spending my weekend nights drinking beer and getting slaps on the back from my male colleagues. I quickly became close friends with the woman who'd written to me at Barksdale. We were an odd pair, to say the least. She was the most feminine and flirtatious person that I'd ever seen. In tight clothing that showed off her great body, she turned heads every time she entered a room. Seeing her enjoying all the attention, I started to think that being one of the guys *all* the time wasn't necessarily such a great thing. I wanted to be able to change out of my flight suit and into a skirt and feel sexy, too. I started losing weight and wearing makeup. I grew my hair out and started dressing up on the weekends. I learned to flirt. But picking up men in bars and having one-night stands had never been my style. I still couldn't bring myself to do it. When the weekend was over, I'd have to return to base and look men in the eye. And I knew that, if I couldn't look them in the eye, they'd never take me seriously as a pilot. So I barely dated, and I didn't sleep with anyone for close to a year. I went out and partied every weekend, then went home alone to my apartment downtown and stared at the paper-thin walls.

I had been warned, before making my aircraft selection, that life in Minot could be rough. But I hadn't worried. So long as I was happy with my job, I had said, I could be happy anywhere. And I couldn't imagine being unhappy flying the B-52. Flying the plane, however, was only part of my job. The rest involved being part of a squadron and living my life on base. And it wasn't at all clear, when I came to Minot, that there was a place on base for me. The walls were painted with old B-52 nose art and busty women astride planes, captioned: "About Average." News of my imminent arrival had left many of the men in my squadron simmering with resentment. "So help me, if she has to get up and change her tampon in flight or has any female problems, I am going to throw a fit," one senior pilot told a group of people before I arrived on base. He wasn't alone in his feelings. At the annual Electronic Warfare Officers party, held a few months before I arrived, a whole video was devoted to my expected arrival on base. In it, an electronic warfare officer, speaking in effeminate tones clearly meant to be those of a gay man, gave a tour of the "new" B-52 that had been outfitted especially for me. He showed the flowered seat cushions that now covered the ejection seats and pointed out the curtains around the bucket; he pulled out a vanity mirror meant to allow me to check my appearance during flights, a hair dryer, and a curling iron. Then came the requisite Kotex dispenser. It was hanging in the spot belonging to the Mode 4—the apparatus we use in flight to allow other aircraft to determine whether we are friend or foe, and also used by air traffic controllers to verify position and altitude so as to avoid midair collisions.

The commanders, who ordered my colleagues to spend a couple of hours in sensitivity training before meeting me, were hardly any better at making me feel at home in Minot. They talked to me about more media appearances. They assigned me to the handpicked "Show Crew": the best in the squadron. They refused to simply let me fit in and be like everyone else. The operations officer, or second in command of the squadron, used to stop me in the hallway in front of all my peers and ask, "Hey, Token, want a kiss? How about a hug?" Then he'd chuckle, walk into his office, and dig out some Hershey chocolate.

After arriving at Minot, I had taken special classes on weapons and flying with night vision goggles, which I needed to become fully combat qualified. I had passed the program and qualified to fly combat missions in record time. But my actual flying just couldn't seem to get under way. Instead of being assigned to a regular crew, with a regular pilot with whom I could establish a productive rapport, I was bounced around from colonel to colonel until, after three months in Minot, I had flown with over two dozen different pilots and instructors. Each new instructor wanted to impart some special knowledge. Each time I flew, every move I made was critiqued. If I sneezed wrong, somebody wrote it down. My flying suffered, of course. I was losing self-confidence, and I was having problems landing. I'd had so much "instruction" that I was confusing different techniques. I asked my flight commander for help time and again. I asked to be assigned to just one pilot, with whom I could work out the new kinks in my techniques. If I had a bit of consistency in my practice, I said, I could work my problems out in just two weeks.

The whole point was to get help before news of my landing problem reached my superiors and became official. But nobody listened. Instead, the schedulers and the colonels sent me to fly with my squadron commander, Lieutenant Colonel Steven Schmidt, who decided that, until my flying improved, I had to fly with an instructor. Then, Schmidt sent me to fly with his second in command, Lieutenant Colonel Brian C. Rogers. It was a horrible flight. I had not flown at night in over six months, was not current for my night landings, and was now evaluated on my night landing proficiency. We hit the ground hard.

Once we were back in the air the colonel asked me what I had done wrong. I just looked at him and replied, "I have no idea." I felt completely hopeless. Usually, I knew what I had done wrong and could correct it. Now, nothing was registering. I felt as if all my landing lessons had simply been erased from my mind.

The next morning, the squadron commander called me in to his office. He said that my landing problems would remain in the strictest confidence. No one outside my squadron, no one high up in the Air Force brass, would ever know about it. He told me to practice in the simulator for a few weeks to improve my landings.

"The simulator can't help me," I said, as I had said to so many of my superiors in the past few weeks. "I need to practice my flare. You can't do that in the simulator." There are no peripheral references available in the simulator so that you can sense your height above the runway. All the pilots knew you could not practice the flare in the simulator.

He didn't listen. And two days later, I learned that he had lied to me. A friend of mine worked for the squadron commander and in screening his e-mail found a letter about me. It had circulated among the wing commander, the vice wing commander, the group commander, the deputy group commander, and my squadron commander. "What are we going to do about Flinn's problem?" it read.

The truth was, my superiors' agenda did not include helping me solve my problem for *my* sake. What they cared about was shining me up well enough to fly Secretary of the Air Force Sheila Widnall on a mission she had planned for that June. Coincidence of coincidences, I'd been picked to be her copilot: the first female bomber pilot would chauffeur around the first female secretary of the Air Force. That flight was five weeks away. The base commanders absolutely had to be sure that I wouldn't let them down and fly poorly. Finally, one of the instructors decided to take me under his wing. He laid down the law: I wouldn't be scheduled to fly with any colonels. I'd stick with him. And sure enough, after just two flights with this instructor, my landings were as good as that wonderful check ride had been.

With my confidence rushing back, I allowed myself to relax. Things were starting to go better with my crew, who'd gotten over their panic at the idea of my urinating on board. It had all become routine; I'd even done the Air Force one better in finding a discreet way to pee. The bucket hadn't worked out; no one ever remembered to put a plastic liner in, and the space where I had to sit was so cramped and dark, I couldn't get out of my flight suit. From a flying magazine, I purchased a "Lady J" funnel and plastic container to catch the urine, which I'd dump into the men's urinal. This way, I didn't have to undress. I didn't have to mess with the curtain or carry a Hefty bag of urine around with me after the flight. "Copilot clearing for relief," I would announce, crawl to the back of the plane, and then just unzip my flight suit like the men.

The crew had started joking with me and teasing me, treating me like a little sister. When there wasn't too much to do in the air, we'd listen to a portable CD player that someone had figured out how to plug into the airplane's interphone system. We'd sing along with the B-52s. We'd crank AC/DC just before some low-level flying. Sometimes we'd see the radar navigator, "Pins," doing a seventies-style disco step in the stairwell to the tune of ABBA's "Dancing Queen."

For a couple of good weeks, I felt as if I belonged. In late May, my crew flew down to Washington, D.C., to represent the 5th Bomb Wing at the Andrews Air Force Base Airshow, the largest air show in the United States. We were all so happy to get out of Minot and visit a big city that, for once, nobody minded that they'd gotten special treatment because the Poster Girl was on board their plane. My call sign, until the air show, had been Token—somebody's idea of an icebreaker. In Washington, it changed to "Scoper." I went out drinking in the Georgetown bars at night with my crew. I couldn't stop staring at the men—nonmilitary men, non-Minot men. I wasn't looking for someone to spend the night with—just "window-shopping," as someone on the crew put it. I was looking into another world where, I imagined, relationships with men could be completely different. Flying back to Minot afterward was more depressing than ever.

Preparing to fly with Secretary Widnall was demoralizing, too. It was my first vision of the worst aspect of the military: reams of paperwork and red tape. Preparations for the flight had begun in January. Secretary Widnall's office had contacted the Minot command with a request to do a Global Power mission in a B-52 with her on board. A Global Power mission is an extended flight, usually over eighteen hours long, during which the plane leaves the continental United States and performs a bombing mission on a practice bombing range. This was a very big deal, a major exercise, which was why my being chosen to participate just three months after I'd arrived on base and only weeks after I'd earned my combat-qualified status was such a blatant case of favoritism. I was one of the youngest and least experienced copilots in the squadron. But I was the right gender.

The mission, of course, got much easier once it became clear that the secretary was actually going through with it. From eighteen hours, it shrank to just over seven, less than most of our training missions. Nevertheless, the planning and preparation were monumental. The resulting stack of paper was more than three inches thick.

One of the biggest problems we faced was going to pick up Secretary Widnall at Andrews Air Force Base. She wanted to see a demonstration of our firepower, so we were flying loaded with MK-82s, 500-pound dumb bombs of the kind used during the Vietnam War and Desert Storm. Safety rules barred us from the usual parking ramp at the Air Force Base in Washington when we were loaded up like this, but the other spot we found gave the Secret Service palpitations because our plane would be parked too close to Air Force One. The Secret Service suggested we carry slabs of concrete in the shape of bombs. This wasn't acceptable to the secretary's office. Then the Secret Service and the secretary agreed upon another solution, but this one *we* rejected. All this took up tremendous amounts of time—crew time, as all the paperwork had been entrusted to us. We were all getting sick of being yelled at for not having the trip planned already. We were also getting sick of being called the Show Crew and getting static from the others in our squadron, who saw us as do-nothings flitting from big city to big city.

The flight finally came together. Just one day before we left Minot, we found acceptable solutions to the parking problem. We flew to Washington and met our guests at an ungodly 0500 hours because the secretary had a dinner party that evening. We briefed her and her associates, and I pulled aside the three women who would be onboard and explained the bathrooms, giving each her own individual Lady J souvenir. A photographer took some publicity shots; then I climbed into the cockpit to work. I was called back down for more photos, and one of the extra pilots on board volunteered to finish my job. I felt like an idiot, smiling for the camera while someone else finished my tedious work.

Finally, we took off. The secretary sat in the instructor pilot's seat, between the pilot and me. Once, during refueling, we changed places and she tried her hand at flying. She did get up once to relieve herself. On the way to the "privacy area," she passed by the navigators' station. She did not say hello to them or ask them about their duty on board. She just smacked their helmets and told them not to turn around.

The crew was extremely offended by the secretary's behavior. She had spoken only to the pilot and me. She had not asked the electronic warfare officer about his job, or even said hello to him, during the over seven hours we had spent in the air. She didn't seem to care about anything having to do with the nuts-and-bolts work of the plane, even though the B-52 was currently one of the planes most hotly debated by Congress. We'd expected her to ask us about our weapons and equipment. We had considered what needed to be upgraded or replaced. Waste of time. The preparation was all for nothing. It seemed she had just been along for the ride. And she didn't even thank us for it.

After Secretary Widnall's visit, I felt a more profound disappointment with the Air Force than ever before. And since I'd identified myself with the Air Force for so many years, that translated into dissatisfaction with myself. My life suddenly seemed incredibly empty. I was so terribly lonely. My best female friends, all officers in the Air Force, were scattered around the world. My friendships in Minot were really acquaintanceships. No other woman shared all my interests or experiences. I was even feeling alienated from my crew. They'd come up with the idea of having special name tags printed up that would say, "Kelly's Pilot," "Kelly's Nav," "Kelly's Bombardier," and "Kelly's EW." I was to be just "The Kelly." The idea was to poke some fun at our unique situation, but I was too worn out to find it funny. I suggested that my name tag read, "Who the Hell Is Kelly?" But the crew voted me down. As "The Kelly" I felt more isolated than ever, as if the Air Force had succeeded in turning me into a thing.

At last I began to feel that if I didn't have some normal human contact something inside me was just going to shrivel up and die. It was one thing to have spent my teens and early twenties as a high-performance machine, but I was tired of that now. A life with no love, no sex, and no real friendship was taking its toll. I had to *connect*. And finally, one evening, I took a break. I made a mistake. It sent me on a downward spiral that wouldn't end until my career was ruined and my life in a shambles. The mistake was a one-night stand.

It happened during an early May night of drinking. The owner of the place I was subletting in Minot had stocked up cases of wine in his basement. Now he was moving, and he didn't want to take it with him, so I held a wine-tasting party. I had about fifty people over and we went through twenty to thirty bottles of wine, plus several cases of beer. People were staggering around the house drunk and were flopped out all over the lawn. I was one of the most sober people present. Colin Thompson, a muscular, dark-haired airman, was one of the least. He spent the party kissing and fooling around with any willing woman who crossed his path. Afterward, he couldn't remember what he had done and with whom. Late in the evening, I found him in the hallway, and after a few drinks he looked pretty good. I had sex with him. He spent the night and left in the morning.

It would have been utterly forgettable had Colin not been an enlisted man. But though I was aware of that at the time, I didn't think I was committing fraternization. Colin, a senior airman, worked with missiles in the Space Command. Since I was a pilot in the Bomb Wing and worked under Air Combat Command, we weren't in the same chain of command and never would be. The "good order and discipline" of our respective units were not—could not be—affected by our one-night stand. I didn't use rank to get him into bed. He was so drunk, he just sort of oozed in. Under what I understood to be the Air Force rules, this was not fraternization.

My understanding, it turned out, was wrong. Unbeknownst to me, the rules had changed. As of May 1, 1996, it was against the rules to have a relationship—any kind of relationship— with any enlisted person, even if he was outside your chain of command. I happened not to see the base newspaper article concerning the regulation changes; they hadn't yet made it to the squadron bulletin board; and they wouldn't make it to the squadron library until almost a year later. Ignorance is not a defense, I know. The thing is, even if I had been aware of the rules, I don't think I would ever have dreamed that anyone would care about this episode. Fraternization was utterly commonplace, as was adultery. I once went through the squadron list and counted up the people who I *knew* had either fraternized or committed adultery. I left out the people I only suspected. I came up with 20 percent guilty, one in every aircrew. If this kind of thing had been prosecuted there would have been no one to fly the planes. The base newspaper published a monthly list of Article 15s punishments (nonjudicial administrative punishments). Each month at least two of the ten or so were for adultery or fraternization.

Colin, of course, bragged to some of his friends about having slept with me. "You've got to cut it out," I told him during soccer practice, after word got back to me. "It won't do either of us any good to have people talking."

He looked at me sheepishly, nodded, and apologized. I didn't have much faith that he'd really keep his mouth shut, but I didn't worry that much, either. I was tired of worrying about what other people thought of me. Idle gossip, I thought, wouldn't hurt me. And it wouldn't have—had not someone been listening very closely. Someone heard the Colin Thompson story and knew he'd struck gold. He'd been looking to collect dirt on me, and now he had something to file away for a rainy day.

That someone was a lieutenant named Brian Mudery, a tall, pretty-faced helicopter pilot who had come on to me a couple of times and struck out. He had better luck when he went after a married friend of mine. He'd basically raped her one night while she was nearly passed out drunk, and after that they started an affair. The drunken sex, I think, made my friend feel she was off the hook for having been attracted to Brian in the first place. Whenever my friend tried to break it off, Brian would threaten to tell her husband. Meanwhile, though, he put the moves on the wives of other officers on base. If they rejected him, he exposed himself and masturbated in front of them.

Finally, my friend broke down and told her husband everything. Then she went to end the relationship with Brian and
found him at home, in bed with another woman. He started to
choke her, even pushed her backward over his balcony. Fortunately, her husband had followed her and brought her home
safely. The next day, Brian saw the husband and muttered
some crude insult about my friend. Her husband retaliated
and beat Brian up pretty badly. The neighbors were terrified;
the security police were brought in, and the whole story of
Brian and his sexual practices blew wide open. The security
police started a full-blown investigation. I was called in to give
a statement corroborating my friend's side of the story. Brian
eventually pleaded guilty to reduced charges and was sentenced to dismissal and nine months in jail. My friend and her
husband reconciled.

I thought I had done the right thing; I didn't realize the
Brian Mudery story would come back to haunt me. But then,
so many things I did in that long, lonely period in Minot now
haunt me. It was probably the weakest point in my life. It was
the first time I'd tried to *have* a life. It was the first time I'd ever
lived anywhere for more than a year. I wanted friendships, relationships, a home. I wanted to fall in love. I was a prime target for a predator.

CHAPTER 6

The Wrong Man

Work is not an end in itself; there must always be
time enough for love.

—ROBERT HEINLEIN

A FEW DAYS AFTER THE FLIGHT WITH SECRETARY WIDNALL, I drove up to the base for a soccer game. Because there was no women's soccer team in Minot, I was playing on an all-male team. That meant that I didn't really get to play much—I wasn't fast enough to keep up—but it was better than getting no exercise at all or trying to work out at the tiny, cramped base gym.

While I was stretching and warming up, I overheard a couple of guys from the team talking about a new player who'd just moved to town. He was a professional, they said. He'd played for the Navy and for the Seattle Sounders. Great, I thought. Maybe we'd all learn something new. I went up to the new player and introduced myself. "Hey," he said smiling, "I'm Marc Zigo." They'd come to Minot because his wife, Gayla, was an airman stationed here. We shook hands all around, and then we played soccer.

A few days later, on July 3, I went out with some single guys from my squadron to the Ground Round, one of the few halfway decent restaurants in Minot. We were standing at the bar and talking when the bartender came up and set a drink in front of me. It was a B-52 shot: Kahlúa, Grand Marnier, and Bailey's Irish Cream. I looked over and saw three guys from the soccer team—Colin, Mark Munsey, and Marc—grinning at me. I walked over, thanked them, and did the shot, then rejoined my group. After a few hours, the guys I'd come with decided to go home. Marc and his friends invited me to go play pool. Since it was still pretty early, I said yes. We drove over to the Dakota Lounge, which is pretty much what it sounds like: a dive bar, with a jukebox and a couple of pool tables. Not long after we started to play, Marc sidled up to me. "I think you're great," he whispered in my ear.

I laughed and shrugged.

"I think you're sexy," he continued. "You know, we could be really good together."

I didn't know what to say. Or what to do. On the one hand, I knew he was married. Off limits. But on the other hand, I'd be lying if I said I wasn't attracted to him. He had the perfect soccer player's body: thin, but very muscular. He had light brown hair and darker eyebrows, and his eyes—depending on the light and his mood, I would learn—were a changeable brown and green. His features weren't necessarily perfect, but they somehow fit very well together. And he had such a powerful magnetism. It was the way he carried himself, the way he moved. The way he sauntered into a room, flashed a smile just when it was needed, caught your eye and twinkled back. Women from all over the bar were watching him that night. He was in prime form: smiling, charming me, acting sincere. It was all very flattering. No one had ever come on to me quite like *that* before. He knew just what I needed: to feel desired.

I kept on shaking my head and trying to act like it was all a big joke. "Whatever," I kept repeating. "Whatever you say."

But he didn't let up. "I'm telling you," he whispered, "we could be great together."

"What do you mean—together for one night?" I asked.

"No," he said. "No—for a lifetime."

Wow, I thought to myself, and wondered if he was at all serious.

Many hours went by. The guys had been doing some pretty heavy drinking. I didn't want them driving back to the base, where they were very likely to be stopped for DWI. Since my house was halfway between the base and town, I invited them to come over to sober up. We sat around my living room, listening to music and drinking lots of water. After about an hour, they all left, and I got ready for bed. Then Marc called a half hour later. "I just got into a huge fight with Gayla," he said. "She's kicked me out and I don't have a place to go."

I had a four-bedroom house, but I didn't say anything.

"Please," he said. "Can I come down for the night?"

He had a way of asking for things. You couldn't find it within yourself to say no. And I didn't. Not then, and not for a long time afterward. "I have plenty of extra rooms," I said. "It's no problem if you want to come and crash."

That night, he told me he was falling in love with me. "Wow," I thought, "that's fast." Somewhere in my head an alarm bell went off. There was something overintense about this guy. But I *did* believe in love at first sight—or at least, I wanted to believe in it. Particularly if it meant someone was falling in love with *me*. "Listen," I said, "you're married."

Only on paper, he explained. It was only a matter of time before he and Gayla broke up, he said; their marriage was a nightmare. They'd met in Japan, where he was stationed with the Navy. She was a military brat, still living with her family. She'd never gone to college. She'd married him instead. And he'd followed her here, to the hellhole called Minot, after she'd joined the Air Force. The marriage had been a mistake, he went on. Gayla was immature and didn't understand him. They fought all the time: he showed me scratches on his face and his arms where, he said, she'd clawed him with her nails. They'd been separated once before. Now things were definitely falling apart.

I saw that for myself a few weeks later, when Marc and Gayla asked some of us on the soccer team to come and help them move from their temporary living quarters into their new house. I showed up after work, expecting to be part of a crowd, and found myself alone with them. I knew right away that I should not be there. It was bad enough that I was socializing with Gayla—she was an enlisted airman, albeit in the Missile Wing, not my Bomb Wing—and hanging out with her amounted to fraternization. Worse, there I was in her kitchen, helping her unpack her wedding china and wondering if I should tell her that her husband was hitting on me. This was tap dancing on thin ice. I didn't have the guts to say anything. I just listened to them bicker constantly, the fights moving from room to room as they worked. I waited around, half listening, half pretending not to. "One way or the other," Marc hissed to me while Gayla worked downstairs, "with or without you, I'm leaving her."

Marc always knew how to say exactly what you needed or wanted to hear. It was almost as if he could see into your soul, find your deepest wishes, and make them come true. He told me that I was beautiful, that he would follow me anywhere, that my dreams were more important than his, because he didn't really have any except to attend law school. He was willing to cook dinner. He was willing to raise the kids. Anything, just to be with me, because I was the most wonderful, most caring person who had ever lived. He was even, he pointed out, Irish.

That was the icing on the cake. I'd always been proud of my own Irish heritage and had joked with my family about marrying a "nice Irish boy." Marc wasn't just of Irish heritage. He'd been born in Ireland, he told me; had lived there until the age of twelve and then moved to the United States, where he'd worked with a speech pathologist to lose his Irish accent. He even loved Notre Dame—just like my mother.

I believed him. The entire soccer team—the entire base—believed him. The group commander and wing commander who eventually hired him believed him, and even published an article about him in the base newspaper. We all believed that he had played soccer for the University of Virginia for three years—precisely the three years when they were going through all the national championships and winning them. We believed that he had flunked out of UVA, joined the Navy, and been part of the Explosive Ordnance Disposal unit, which sometimes collaborated with SEAL teams. We believed that he'd played soccer for the Navy. That he broke his leg playing soccer for the Navy; that the Navy doctors had fixed it wrong, leaving him with persistent problems. That the problems were bad enough to earn him medical disability pay amounting to almost half his former Navy salary, though they didn't keep him from playing soccer. No one questioned this. Nor did they question his story about having worked as a paralegal for the Navy while his leg healed. Certainly, no one doubted him once he got a job on base, as the director of the Youth Sports Center. After all, the Air Force would run a background check on its employees, wouldn't it? Particularly if they were working on a base where there were nuclear weapons. Particularly if they were working with children.

The real Marc, I discovered months later, once my life with him had turned from dream to nightmare, was born in Long Branch, New Jersey. He never went to UVA. He was in the Navy, but not in the EOD. He'd never played soccer professionally. And he wasn't, that summer, anywhere near a divorce.

Why did I fall so completely and blindly for a man whose own mother says he's a pathological liar? Who knows? I was unhappy at work. I was tired of being alone. I was tired of hearing everyone in my flight crew—everyone in the squadron, it seemed—talking about their wives and girlfriends. It seemed as if everyone in that dreadful, miserable town but me had someone to go home to on Friday nights. All I had were brief, long-distance relationships. I was also tired of constantly listening to another pilot's pick-up lines and his attempts to get me into his bed: "Come on, Kel, let's just get this over with. The winter is long and cold. Come on, let's just do it." He would also discuss his fantasies with other members of my squadron, picturing me running around the kitchen barefoot and pregnant. My best friends, my support group, were all far away. One of them, Lazarus, was living in the Khobar Towers complex in Saudi Arabia on June 25 when a bomb went off, killing nineteen servicemen and wounding 150 more. At the time when I met Marc, I didn't know what had happened to him. I was frustrated with my flying performance and growing disgusted with the role I was playing, on display like a freak. I was on the edge and vulnerable—and all the more eager to have someone nearby to love.

So I fell, and I fell hard. I felt that fate had led me to Marc. The night of July 3 had been magical. We'd talked and talked, and he had said all the things I wanted to hear. When he left early in the morning, I took a picture of the sunrise because I felt like a new person. Something had happened that made me feel entirely differently about myself. Marc had entered my life, and the whole world had changed. I would discover months later just how much.

Time seemed to slow down. My crew was preparing for a Nuclear Operational Readiness Inspection, the most intense kind of inspection a base ever went through, basically the Air Force's way of practicing for nuclear war. We were on "six-ring standby" for an entire weekend, meaning that we always had to be physically within six rings of answering our phones. We could be called to duty at any time. Three or four in the morning was a popular hour. We'd head up to base, where an intelligence officer would brief everyone on a fictitious scenario: a rebel leader in some Third World country, for example, had taken over and was going crazy invading his neighbors, so it was time for the United States to begin posturing in preparation for all-out nuclear war. After the briefing, those of us on the first few crews to launch would spend the wee hours of the morning preflighting our jets, checking our instruments and configuration, preparing them to launch at a moment's notice. Then we'd hole up in dormitories and wait—for the simulated war to advance, and for the crews who were at home with their families to be called in to work. Once they'd prepared their jets, they would join us in the dormitories. Then we'd all sit around and wait some more, often nearly a week, for the alert call to sound. Until the early 1990s, the B-52s had been on twenty-four-hour alert. Back then, the dormitories had been well outfitted, with kitchens and at least a minimum of creature comforts. Now, they're stripped down and pretty miserable: a grim reminder of the Cold War.

While we waited around, all the technicians, weapons loaders, mechanics, and crew chiefs would configure the planes for war and load the weapons. When the alert call finally came, we'd race to the flight line in our government-issued trucks, following all the speed limits as a safety precaution, and pile into our jets, where we waited patiently some more to be told the exercise was over. We weren't supposed to actually fly. We never, ever started engines once our aircraft were configured for war. Any minor action done wrong, once nuclear weapons were involved, might be taken by other nations as an act of war. We knew that if we were really flying with the ultimate weapons of mass destruction that was because it was all over for everyone.

Marc phoned me constantly while I waited for my call to come to the base. "I've fallen in love with you," he would say. "We've got to go for it. This kind of feeling only comes around once in a lifetime." One day, he came by with an Irish wedding ring, a Claddagh ring, as a symbol of his feelings for me and a promise for the future. I adored the ring. I was falling in love with him. But I still held back. For one thing, I wouldn't sleep with him. "For now," I said, "as far as I'm concerned, you're still married."

It was only a matter of paperwork, Marc assured me, only a matter of time. But I think my refusal to have sex with him made him nervous. He needed more from me, he said: some kind of commitment. "Just saying you love me doesn't mean anything," he said. "You have to show me what you mean. I need proof." So I made the fool-in-love mistake of sending him letters. Gayla found one of them under the seat of their car, and dug out the rest.

I came home from work in mid-July, after spending almost a week on alert, and found a note on my door: "Kelly, your [*sic*] busted." Gayla had handed the letters over to her first sergeant, who oversees discipline for the enlisted members of a squadron. First sergeant is an enlisted rank—so it was lower than mine—and Gayla's first sergeant wasn't in my chain of command, or even in my squadron. Gayla said she didn't want to get me in trouble; she just wanted me to go away. Her first sergeant called me in for a "secret" meeting in the parking lot next to the commissary. "You need to knock this off," she said. "You're making a mistake."

I agreed right away. I was under stress, I said; I suspected that in a kind of anticipatory grief, I was transferring my feelings for Lazarus, my friend in Saudi Arabia, to Marc. It was stupid, she said; it showed poor judgment.

I agreed, and I really tried to take her words to heart. I called Gayla up and apologized, telling her it was all a misunderstanding. I took two weeks' leave and went to visit my parents in Atlanta during the Olympics, fully intending never to see Marc anywhere but the soccer field again. But I just couldn't get him out of my mind. Being home meant being surrounded by couples: brothers-in-law and sisters-in-law, nieces and nephews, my best friend and her boyfriend. As always, I was the odd one out, and I felt I was getting a bit old for that. I thought of how nice it would be to show up for a family holiday with Marc. To arrive and leave *with* someone, rather than always being on my own or the fifth wheel.

Marc, it seemed, had been thinking of me, too. He called a few hours after my car pulled into the driveway. It was a mid-morning in August. I was at home resting in preparation for a night flight. He told me he had good news: he'd filed for divorce while I was away, and was now legally separated. The divorce, he said, would be final on December 20, whether or not Gayla signed the papers. The date was like a magic number: it gave weight and credibility to everything else he told me. Until the twentieth, he said, he and Gayla would be sleeping in separate bedrooms. "I am now, for all legal purposes, single," he said. "That means that, as far as the military is concerned, I can be with whomever I like." He said he'd dealt with cases like this before, as a paralegal in the Navy, and he quoted rules and regulations that sounded very official. Then he asked if he could come over and do some laundry.

Of course I said yes. By the end of the morning, six weeks after our first meeting, we were in bed. And for the first time, I made love with someone I truly cared for.

Once we'd slept together, there was no turning back. I let myself fall head over heels in love with Marc. We spent more and more time together. We'd sit at my kitchen table and plan our wedding—a big, Irish Catholic family wedding with all our close relatives and friends, plus his Irish family that I'd heard so much about. Lots of laughter, lots of drinking and dancing, just like the Irish do.

It was an idyllic time, and it lasted for just about two weeks. By the end of August we had started bickering. We had petty fights at first, over stupid things. But then the fights started to have a theme. Marc became obsessed with the men I worked with. "Do you realize," he said, "that you're *always* around men?"

"Wake up," I replied. "I'm in the *Air Force.* I'm the only woman in my job."

That explanation just didn't work for him. "Well," he said, "I just see you hanging out with all these guys all the time. It makes me start to wonder."

He wondered all the time: Was I looking for another boyfriend? Was I flirting? Was I going out with someone else? It made no difference what I told him. He could never be reassured. "Actions speak louder than words," he said. One day, at the youth center, he called me a whore. I kept myself in check in front of the kids. But when we got home, we had a huge fight.

And then we had more and more fights. He called me a whore again, a slut, a sleaze. All because I worked with men and was around men all the time. Short of quitting my job, I couldn't imagine how to solve the problem. So I did what seemed the second best thing: I started isolating myself from my friends. I stopped calling people, stopped going out for drinks, stopped talking to the guys in the squadron—all to prove to Marc, once and for all, that I loved him. I was hardly aware of doing it. Love is blind, so I've heard, and I could not see the warning signs. Only when things started coming apart did I realize how isolated I'd become.

For a while, things seemed to improve; we reconciled, and Marc called me nonstop, leaving one message after another

on my answering machine: "I love you. I love you. I love you."
But the peace didn't last very long. The storm clouds always
seemed to gather again, no matter what I said or did. And
then, within minutes, we were back to square one.

The pattern repeated itself over and over all through the late
summer and fall. I didn't know it then, but I had fallen into the
classic pattern of an abusive relationship. Such relationships
operate in a constantly repeating cycle: there's the tension
buildup phase; the release-of-tension phase, when there's an
eruption of emotional or physical violence; and then the loving and forgiveness phase. All this happens in increasing isolation. To run its full destructive course, the relationship
pretty much has to function in its own little world.

Despite the upheaval in my personal life, my career was
going wonderfully. In September, I was presented with the
Group Company Grade Officer of the Quarter Award. There
was also talk of me going to the Standardizations and Evaluations Crew, the top crew in the squadron. Plus, in October, my
crew was told we had planned and executed the best war-
fighting scenario in a two-week exercise called Red Flag. My
officer performance reports were outstanding and full of
praise for my work. I was on top of the world with my flying
and my professional career. Lieutenant Colonel La Plante, my
squadron commander, said I showed "maturity and responsibility above her peers. . . . Lt. Flinn is an outstanding officer
and aviator—her performance stands head and shoulders
above her peers . . . one of the best in the squadron."

It wasn't until October that I figured out I needed help with
my private life. I was in Las Vegas, on the Red Flag exercise I
mentioned, and though I was doing extremely well in the air, I
was moody on the ground. During my first week away, Marc
and I spoke on the phone every day. Our conversations were
perfectly normal. Then, after a break of a few days, Marc
called and his voice sounded like nothing I'd ever heard be-

fore. It was a kind of growl, low and sinister: "I don't ever want to talk to you again," he said. "I don't want to see you. I don't want to hear from you." I was dumbfounded. Nothing had happened since we had last spoken, earlier in the week. We'd ended that conversation by saying we loved each other. This made no sense. "What's going on?" I asked.

"What's going on," he said, "is that you're a slut."

He was off again. It was terrifying how this could happen, right out of the blue. I didn't even have to be present. Months later, I learned that Marc had just been served with court papers announcing his sentence for having assaulted Gayla. That had probably set him off. But I didn't know about it at the time. (I didn't even know about the assault.) It just seemed that Marc could go wild anytime, for no reason. That meant there was nothing I could do to get things under control.

It was easier to resist Marc when he wasn't right in front of me. "Fine," I snapped. "It's over. Your ring is in the mail." And that, I told myself, was that.

Determined to get Marc out of my system, I went to the officers' club on Friday night with the rest of the squadron and began to drink and party with all the visiting pilots and aircrews. Later in the evening, I went home, changed into civilian clothes, and hit the local bars with some old friends and their fighter pilot buddies. We all got drunk, and later that evening, I kissed one of them good night. Marc had pushed hard enough, and it was over between us. There were definitely other fish in the sea.

True to form, Marc called again two days later, as if nothing had gone wrong. Then, abruptly, he changed his tune again. "I know something happened," he said. "I'm having you watched. You may as well tell me the truth now." I didn't know whether he knew anything, but I decided to come clean. I told him I had kissed someone in Las Vegas. I tried to explain: a few days ago, we'd both said we never wanted to see each other again. But you can't reason with Marc. "You really are a slut," he said. He got more worked up than I'd ever heard him before. There was a new kind of darkness in his voice. He sounded destructive, purely evil. "I'm going right to your colonels right now and telling them about the behavior of their nice little lieutenant," he said. "I'm going to destroy you and your career."

I screamed into the phone, "*Nooooo!*"

"Oh, yes," he said. "I'm going to find your commander and tell him about how his sweet, innocent little lieutenant goes out and has sex, sleeps with all kinds of different men, and about how she slept with me, and my divorce isn't final yet."

"Please, no, don't do that," I begged.

"Yes—I'm going to destroy your career. I'm going to destroy your life."

I started to whimper. I pleaded with him not to do this. But I was now face-to-face with his threats.

I believed him. I already knew that Marc liked to see people squirm in pain. When his temper blazed out of control, he could be physically violent. He was always getting reprimanded on the soccer field for fighting. I saw him attack a referee once, over what he thought was a bad call. And break a guy's nose with the cue ball one night in a bar. At work, he once got a friend to hold another man's arms back and then sucker-punched him. He'd head-butted Gayla in the course of an argument and left her with a bump on her head the size of a lemon. He'd even told me that he once knocked down his mother during an argument. He said he had "anger management problems." But until now, he'd never frankly assaulted me, the female pilot. With me, he was more subtle. He'd run and knock me down during soccer games, just for "fun." He'd inflict ever more exquisite forms of emotional pain.

I had no idea how to protect myself. From past experience, I knew just how dangerous it could be to ask for help in the Air Force. And I'd heard a story about an officer who, remorseful about an affair, confessed it to his commander. He'd ended up being court-martialed. His guilty conscience just about destroyed his life.

Like most victims of abusive relationships, I conned myself into believing that I was managing things. Not knowing whom to ask for help, or even how, I tried to handle it on my own, as I always did. I started reading books and questioning folks about relationships.

My sister Gail said, "That man is dangerous. Stay on his good side." So I started doing and saying whatever I thought might pacify Marc. I also talked to a member of my squadron whom we all called the Doc. He said that he and his wife had fought constantly during the first six months of their relationship. Well, maybe everything happening between Marc and me was normal, I thought. He'd returned to calling me all day on my cell phone, telling me that he loved me and everything was going to be all right. I wanted things to be all right. And I *didn't* want him running to the colonel. So I agreed to another chance. The "I love you"s kept on coming, and we were reconciled.

In early November, Minot began clouding over, the start of another interminable winter, and there was a major Conventional Operational Readiness Inspection. Then I left town with the soccer team for a tournament at Offutt Air Force Base in Nebraska. It felt good to jump in my car and leave Minot.

Marc had gone a day earlier with another team member, Martin. Martin was married but, according to Marc, was out to have a fling. They'd stopped at Grand Forks on the way and had both—I heard this later—picked up women for the night, à la the movie *Fargo*. I had a happy reunion with Marc at the Air Force base. But after the game, Sunday night, we had the worst fight of my life.

A group of us from the team had gone out to an Irish pub. I was the designated driver, so I wasn't drinking. Everyone else was pounding back Guinness. We were standing at the bar when I noticed an older man, maybe in his fifties, sitting next to the jukebox with a book in one hand and a Guinness in the other, totally relaxed, his feet propped up on a chair. I said, to no one in particular, "Now, that's the way to spend a Sunday evening."

Marc went crazy. "If you want to sleep with him, just say so."

"I didn't say that," I said.

"If you want another boyfriend, that's fine. It's over."

I couldn't believe he was doing this in front of everyone. I kept silent, staring at him. "Get the fuck out of my face!" he yelled.

I got up and left, just drove away. But I was worried about the other guys, who were stranded, so I came back to pick them up. Marc was waiting for me outside the bar. "What the fuck are you doing?" he screamed at me.

"You told me to get out of your face, so I did," I replied.

I tried to get out of my car, but he blocked the door. I half opened it, and he pushed it back on me. I was shaking with rage. I finally got out of the car and said, "I'm going to get the guys, and I'm leaving." As I started to walk around him, he stepped into me, put both hands on my chest, and slammed me back against the car. "Don't ever get in my face again, or you're fucked," he said. "That was only a taste." Shaking, I walked into the bar and told the guys to finish up their drinks. I was leaving.

The fight started up again once we got back to Offutt. Marc came pounding on my door, yelling in the hallway. Once again, I was a slut, I was a whore. Only now we were on an Air Force base, and the walls weren't very thick. I had to get Marc to shut up, and the only way to do it was to agree to spend the night in his room. Too scared to sleep at all, I waited for my alarm clock to go off; then I grabbed it and went downstairs to my room and changed.

Marc came by while I was packing my car to leave. "What, no good-morning kiss?" he said, as if the night before hadn't happened.

We drove back to Minot in separate cars, Marc pulling his car up beside mine and mouthing "I love you" through the window. Whenever we stopped our convoy to get gas, he'd come up and whisper, "Please forgive me. I'm so sorry." It was a very long fourteen-hour ride.

In Minot, absolutely exhausted, I swore to myself that Marc and I were through. He left town for the week and I refused to call him. It was over. I finally saw the destructive power of the relationship. I wanted my life back, and now I started to take it back.

But neither the Air Force nor Marc, it seems, was going to let me. On the morning of November 24, after I'd been away from Marc, rebuilding my life, for almost ten days, the phone rang. "They're investigating us," he said.

"Who is?"

"The security police."

My stomach hardened up into a ball.

"Just tell them nothing happened," Marc said. "That's what I did. If I don't confess, and you don't confess, they won't be able to prove it. And by law they have to prove it."

I should have been more on my guard. But I felt protected. Marc was, after all, a civilian. He was legally separated. He was covering for me. And no one, I knew, really went after adultery anyway. If they had, 20 percent of the base would have been court-martialed years before.

But that afternoon, a Monday, the security police called. "We have some more questions for you concerning Lieutenant Mudery," I heard. "Can you come in this afternoon?" I was studying at home for the final in a course on remote sensing for my master's degree in space studies at the University of

North Dakota. I figured the interview would take about an hour, and afterward I'd come back and finish my work.

I dressed in my flight suit, drove up to the base, and walked into the security police squadron. I was shown into a small room with a big window on one side, a small desk, and two or three uncomfortable chairs. A man in civilian clothes was there waiting for me. He turned out to be a sergeant. With him was First Lieutenant Tamara Kieffer, looking prim and proper with a huge wedding ring and hair pulled back into a ponytail.

They thanked me for coming in. Then they read me my rights. They said I was suspected of adultery, fraternization, and conduct unbecoming to an officer. I tried to focus and breathe slowly. It was as if the earth had opened at my feet. The friendly interview was nothing of the sort. I had walked, unawares, into enemy territory.

"How do you know Amy Rice?" they asked.

I said that she was my friend.

"Have you ever had sex with her?"

"Excuse me?"

"Have you ever had a homosexual relationship with her?"

"No!" I was completely taken aback. This was appalling.

"Have you had sex with her husband?"

"No!"

"We have a report that you did."

When charges were pressed against him, Brian Mudery had said, "If I'm going down, then I'm taking everyone down with me, including the female bomber pilot." He'd made good on his promise, particularly where Amy Rice and I were concerned, since we had both testified against him. During his pretrial plea-bargaining in mid-November, he made a false, ridiculous, hateful statement to base investigators in which he accused almost all the witnesses against him of some type of wrongful activity. He accused Amy and her husband, Justin, of frequent "wife-swapping." He accused me of having had sex with both Justin *and* Amy during a party at their house the previous summer. I remembered the party; I'd gotten drunk, too drunk to drive home, and had stayed overnight in a guest bedroom. Alone. Mudery had reported an orgy, complete with "headboard banging and sexual moans." He'd provided every intimate detail that his fevered mind could imagine. Anyone other than the Minot Air Force Base security police would have recognized this as a personal attack against two witnesses and not worthy of precious Air Force investigation time and money. Brian Mudery pleaded guilty to several charges and was sentenced to nine months in prison.

The security police named three or four other men, single and married, and asked me if I'd slept with them. I said no. My shock was quickly changing to a feeling of deep and utter humiliation. What kind of person did they think I was? A part of me just wanted to get up and leave the room. My sex life was none of their damned business. But that would make me look guilty. When they asked me if I'd slept with Marc, I denied it, denied everything.

"What about the evening of July third?" they said.

"Nothing happened July third," I answered.

"What about the letters?"

They had a Hallmark card I'd sent Marc, and two love letters—the "proof" he'd asked for. Plus a key to my house that I'd given him in case he fought with Gayla again while I was away on leave.

"That was stupid."

I wrote and signed a statement admitting that I had made an "extreme error in judgment" in writing love letters to Marc and giving him my key. As Marc and I had agreed I would do should the letters come into play, I said that I had pursued him without encouragement, having mistaken his complaints about his marriage for interest in me. I wrote: "Marc Zigo and I have had a strictly platonic relationship since we first met." I still didn't understand what was going on.

"What are you going to do with all this?" I asked.

"We'll write up a summary of the investigation, and then it'll be up to your squadron commander to administer punishment," the investigators said. They told me the meeting was over.

I got up to leave.

"No," they said, "you can't leave by yourself. You have to have a representative from your squadron pick you up."

"Look," I said, "I came in here freely. I want to leave on my own."

"Sorry. Once you've been read your rights you can't leave on your own."

"Am I under arrest?" I asked.

"We're just following regulations" was the reply.

Now the reality dawned on me: *I* was the subject of this investigation. But I still did not understand that it was a criminal investigation; I thought my case would be handled administratively. I'd seen this done on many occasions. I might get a letter of reprimand, or at worst an Article 15. The idea of a criminal case—I couldn't believe it. I couldn't see how my sex life, such as it was, was anyone's business. I'd never read the military's justice code, or even seen the published book. I thought the kinds of crimes that could lead to court-martial were things like murder, rape, treason—not consensual sex. I was wrong.

The investigators called in Section Commander Jackie Bieker, a second lieutenant who'd arrived at Minot recently and was in charge of punishment for the enlisted men and women in the squadron. She was tall and solidly built, with a lazy eye. She was also younger than me, and lower ranking. I avoided her gaze and silently left the room. As we passed through the front office and out onto the base, I knew that soon all of Minot would be talking about me and my sex life. The security police weren't supposed to talk about official investigations, but someone always did.

THAT WAS MONDAY. On Tuesday morning, I slept late, working on my twelve hours of mandatory crew rest in preparation for a flight that evening. Crew rest is a safety measure, intended to make sure that pilots can sustain their concentration and energy during flight. If you didn't rest, you couldn't fly. At ten o'clock the phone rang. "I have some more questions for you," Lieutenant Kieffer said. "I need you to come in."

"Thanks for calling me at home," I answered. "You just broke my crew rest."

"This is an official investigation," she said. "I don't care about your crew rest."

I called my duty officer and reported that I wouldn't be able to fly that night. By the time I'd dressed and returned to the base, I was furious. The interview made me even angrier. All the investigators wanted to talk about was my letters. They wanted explanations of a few lines: What did I mean when I wrote, "You make me complete. You make me whole." The meaning, I thought, should have been clear to anyone reading at or beyond a fifth-grade level. It seemed the whole point of the questions was to mortify me. When they asked what it meant that Marc was "coming to get me" I said it referred to soccer games, during which he'd tease me to get me to run faster. A reference to arms, I said, also had to do with soccer. I still thought that if I played my cards right, they'd let the whole thing drop. But midway through the interview, the investigators read me my rights again. Then I had to write another statement. Not only was I angry, I was becoming desperate. I just wanted this to end so I could get on with my life. So I said, again, that we'd had a platonic relationship. "Nothing intimate or sexual has ever occurred between Marc Zigo and myself," I wrote.

At the Academy, it sometimes happened that you would lie, unthinkingly, under stress. An upperclassman might be training you and yell, "Were you in your room at ten-thirty last night?" You'd scream "Yes, sir!" and then, a moment later, realize that you were lying. It wasn't a willful lie. It was just that, in the heat of the moment, you'd said the wrong thing—popping off, we called it. To fix it, you'd go right back to the upperclassman and tell him of your mistake. I was on my way to the parking lot, thinking about what had happened, when I realized that I'd just popped off. I had wanted to get the hell out of there. I wanted the questioning to end. I wanted the investigation into my private life to end. I wanted to pacify the investigators and get them off my back. Most of all, I wanted this humiliating experience to be over.

I rushed across base to the office of my commander, Lieutenant Colonel Ted La Plante. I wanted to correct my statement immediately, and La Plante, I thought, could help. As squadron commander, he was supposed to oversee both the discipline and the well-being of his troops, and he would be responsible for handling my case. I had no reason to expect that he wouldn't stand by me, or at least give me a fair hearing. He was always talking to the squadron about teamwork and family, esprit de corps and solidarity. And apart from a tendency to produce bad metaphors, and a waddling walk that made him the butt of a good number of jokes, he was well enough respected on base. His most important command decision to date had been changing our uniform policy so that we were required to wear the battle dress uniform (camouflage fatigues) every so often. He had also assigned a bugler to the squadron and had us begin chanting a "war cry" before we went out on exercises: "Fight's on!" a lieutenant would shout. "Fight's on!"

the room would echo. The lieutenant, again: "Fight's on!" Again, we echoed. Then, in unison, "Bomber Barons *fly, fight, win!*" It was ridiculous, but benign. It was no secret that La Plante was a man with his eye on his next promotion. He really wasn't looking to make waves.

This situation was so ironic, I thought as I crossed the base; I'd always been such a straight arrow. Apart from my one-night stand with Colin, my biggest bending of the rules in the military had been sending myself chocolate bars at the Academy. That was part of the problem. I didn't know how to deal with trouble. And I was in for so very much more.

La Plante waved me into his office.

"I need to talk to you," I said. "I think I've made a mistake."

La Plante said nothing.

"It's these outrageous charges," I began again. "It's all so crazy. I think I made a mistake."

La Plante did not know I was under investigation. My own commander had not been informed by the security police that they were investigating several members of his squadron. I began to tell him I was under investigation and wanted to correct something I had just said to the investigators.

"Don't tell me anything," he said. "Go talk to the base defense attorney." There was only one.

"I can't talk to the defense attorney," I said. "He's representing Brian Mudery, he has a conflict of interest." I did not know how to get other legal representation. This was not in any of our in-processing briefings.

"Well," La Plante repeated, "don't talk to me. I may be the ultimate hammer."

I stared at him blankly. He was a square, muscular man with a cleft chin. His face now was utterly impassive. "Just keep this in mind," he said, citing one of his "war" quotes. "During times of adversity, your true character shows through."

I left the office devastated. *Now* where did I go for help?

He was clearly washing his hands of me. Ultimately, he'd pass the buck altogether—proving the truth of his adage.

The next day, Marc Zigo made his own statement. It was completely gratuitous: as a civilian, Marc didn't have to cooperate with the security police at all. They had no jurisdiction over him. Of his own free will, he chose to tell the investigators that we'd had sex. For some bizarre reason, he said we'd done so twice. He told them all kinds of sexual details, mixing up truth and lies. I think he enjoyed the attention. The investigators asked him to draw a diagram of where in the house the sexual intercourse occurred, and he obliged. He even gave the investigators Colin Thompson's name. This was the first they'd heard of Colin.

When he told me what he'd done, he seemed very proud. I felt as if I'd been kicked in the stomach. Denying the relationship had been his idea. Now I was the only one coming across as a liar. And I was the one who had everything to lose.

"Why did you say we had sex *twice*?" I asked weakly.

"I thought it would be better for you."

We were standing in the parking lot of a Kentucky Fried Chicken in downtown Minot—Marc's choice of location. When I'd arrived, he'd patted me down to see if I was wired. He started screaming at me when I told him that he'd put me in an impossible position. "I did you a favor," he said. "They said you were a husband-chaser and a whore! They said you'd slept with all kinds of men!"

Now I understood what must have happened. In going over Brian Mudery's complaint, the investigators had read Marc the list of men with whom I'd allegedly had sex. And he'd gone nuts. He'd lost his temper and decided just to screw me over. (He claimed later, at least to my attorneys, that the investigators had threatened to have him fired and kicked off base if he didn't talk. I doubt this: Marc would always say or do anything to remove the blame from himself.) And then, talking to me, he'd tried to put a good face on the damage. At this point, I wanted nothing to do with him.

I left the Kentucky Fried Chicken, devastated and not knowing where to turn. It was Thanksgiving weekend, and I had to get the hell away from Minot and its rumors. I went to see my friend Lazarus. Back from Saudi Arabia safe and sound, he'd offered to help me out. He, too, had once been investigated by the security police, after a one-night stand with a woman in Panama City, Florida. In the heat of the moment, she'd neglected to tell him that she was married, enlisted, and in his squadron—a triple whammy. The case would probably have died, had her husband's lawyer not dug it up and ignited it when the couple divorced. Despite his prodding, the security police had been willing to let things lie. But Lazarus's commanders had refused, saying they didn't like his morals, and Lazarus got this letter of reprimand: "Your failure to determine even the slightest information on [the enlisted person's] background before engaging in a very public display of intimacy weakened your authority and damaged your squadron's professional climate. . . . Furthermore, you engaged in sexual relations with your door unlocked and your light on. . . . Your actions show a serious lack of judgment, restraint, and discretion. . . . You need to develop a far more disciplined and discreet approach to socializing with members of the opposite sex." With the letter of reprimand, Lazarus also received the unsolicited advice that he should join a church group to meet women. He'd saluted smartly and walked off wondering whatever happened to separation of church and state.

I spent Thanksgiving weekend crying on his shoulder—and despite the mess my life had become, despite my humiliation, all I could think about was Marc. I was beginning to realize that no one in the AF who could possibly help me *wanted* to help me. What hurt the most was Marc's betrayal. If he had just kept his mouth closed, as he had said he would, the investigation would have died. I cried for the loss of "love." Only something drastic, I still somehow believed, could salvage this relationship now. As far as I knew, he and Gayla were less than a month away from a divorce. I had the big date circled in my pocket calendar. And I had numbered all the days leading up to it. The countdown was about to begin. That meant that my chance was coming. My chance to have a real relationship, be part of a couple, live my life with a soul mate whom I really and truly loved. After all, I thought, what was the point of being the first female bomber pilot if you had no one with whom to share it?

I never thought that the investigation—which started as Brian Mudery's revenge, and not on account of a complaint by Gayla, as the Air Force liked to report—could put me in jail. The worst thing that could happen, I thought, was that I wouldn't have a career in the Air Force. I'd accept my Article 15, and get out after my eight-year commitment. I never imagined that consensual sex might be a felony. I never imagined my commanders would refuse to command. They all passed my case to the next higher decision-making level, and let the train leave the station without so much as a glance back or a thought of the consequences.

CHAPTER 7

———◆———

Falling
in Love

Actions in Response to Unprofessional Relationships.
If good professional judgment and common sense indicate
that a relationship is causing, or may reasonably result in, a
degradation of morale, good order, or discipline, corrective
action is required. Action should normally be the least severe
necessary to correct the relationship, giving full consideration
to the impact the relationship has had on the organization.
Counseling, alone or in conjunction with other options, may
be an appropriate first step. . . . One or more administrative
actions may be appropriate.

—AIR FORCE INSTRUCTION 36-2909,
"Professional and Unprofessional Relationships"

I RETURNED HOME AFTER THANKSGIVING WEEKEND AND TOOK
stock. On balance, things were looking pretty grim. The love of
my life was a jealous madman. My sex life was being dissected
up and down the military command structure. I had made a
false official statement. I had no legal representation. My commander would not talk to me. And—just so I couldn't take my
mind off things—I wasn't flying anymore.

Initially, that had been my own decision. In mid-November,
just days before the terrible fight with Marc at Offutt and the
beginning of the investigation, my gynecologist had called to
tell me my Pap smear was abnormal. What that meant wasn't
clear, but the likely causes were, he said, "infection, inflamma-

tion . . . or cancer." The word "cancer" flew around crazily in my head like a bat caught in a brightly lit room. I was twenty-five—too young to have *cancer*. But I couldn't get the thought out of my mind. It batted around, knocking up against all my worst fears about Marc.

This wasn't, I knew, an acceptable state of mind for someone entrusted with flying nuclear weapons. So I decided to remove myself from the Personnel Reliability Program, by which the Air Force allowed its personnel to temporarily recuse themselves from contact with nuclear weapons in times of extreme personal stress, without being grounded. On the advice of one of my crewmates, though, I waited until my squadron had completed a major nuclear exercise. "If you don't," he'd said, "people will talk about you. They'll say you got out of it because of a 'female problem.' " I didn't need the stigma.

I could still fly conventional missions; PRP was only for dealing with nuclear weapons. And flying had always been my way to take my mind off things. Like every other pilot in the Air Force, I could leave all my problems on the ground and just concentrate on flying. When you're soaring at 30,000 feet, the problems of everyday life look, temporarily, too small to be worth noticing. But Lieutenant Colonel La Plante grounded me completely until the investigation and administrative process were over. Now I'd lost the escape of flight, with nothing but problems all around.

Marc had a unique way of calling me. He'd call my home number (my caller-ID unit identified the number), let it ring until the answering machine picked up, then hang up and immediately call my cell phone, letting it ring fifteen times. When we were in the making-up phase of our crazy cycles, he'd do this about twenty times a day. The familiar process started up again as soon as I returned to Minot after Thanksgiving. I ignored them for the first day. By the second, Monday morning,

December 2, I couldn't take it anymore. I picked up the receiver and said, "What the hell do you want?"

"I'm in the hospital," I heard Mark say meekly. "I tried to kill myself." His voice was dry and raspy. "I need to know if I still have a chance with you. Because if I don't, I don't think I can go on." He implored me to come see him. He said Gayla had deserted him and even his own mother and father would not visit him in the hospital.

Angry though I was, and sure there was something terribly, terribly wrong with our relationship, I couldn't let Marc drop now. I felt manipulated, I felt mistrustful . . . but there was always that chance that he was serious. I couldn't go through the rest of my life being responsible for his suicide. I believed truly in forgiving mistakes, learning from them, and allowing second chances.

I drove up to the base hospital. Marc's boss, Melody Brown, was standing outside his room. She pulled me aside before I could go in to see him. "Don't say anything to upset him. He's still in a very fragile state," she told me. She also confirmed that he had come extremely close to dying that night. Melody Brown left that evening and the next day intended to retract the previous condemning statement she had written about me. The investigators would not let her.

She didn't have to worry about me upsetting Marc—he did all the talking that day. I found him lying in bed, his arms sticking out pitifully from his hospital gown and resting on top of the sheet. He was pale and ashy; his cheeks were swollen, and the skin around his mouth was gray. He'd been given charcoal to empty his stomach, and the vomiting had left his throat parched.

"I've lied to you," he said. "I've lied to you from the start." He wasn't from Ireland. He wasn't a professional soccer player. It was all lies. He'd made a mess of things, he said. His family was disowning him. Gayla was divorcing him and would not visit him in the hospital; she'd moved into the dorms, canceling the phone and cable while he sat in his hospital bed recovering. And he never had filed for divorce.

I was caught between the pain of knowing how much I'd been lied to and the pleasure of hearing Marc beg me for another chance. There was something cathartic about putting all the lies on the table, as though we were about to start our relationship over and could now give it a firm grounding. And Marc was finally free. I listened to him beg me for another chance, and I heard myself say he could come to Georgia with me for Christmas. I could not let someone who had just tried to kill himself over Thanksgiving remain alone for the Christmas season.

I left the hospital with my head reeling. Marc was mine—if I still wanted him. But I simply did not know anymore what I wanted. There was every reason in the world not to help him. I decided that I would at least give him a chance, as a friend, to get on his feet again.

Gayla had taken the decisive step Thanksgiving weekend. She'd gone to a promotion party for a friend in downtown Minot. There, a pretty civilian girl named Ellen was talking about how she was going out with a professional soccer player named Marc Zigo. What a great guy he was! Someone said, He's married, and his wife is right over there. Why don't you introduce yourself to her? So Ellen did just that. Right in front of everyone at the table, she asked: "Do you have any idea of what your husband's been doing?" She told Gayla everything about her and Marc. He'd told her the same story he'd told me: the marriage was over, he'd filed for divorce, it was only a marriage on paper. Turns out Gayla had heard it all before: she'd discovered Marc had slept with another woman just weeks after the wedding. This time was once too many. She called him up from the party and said, "Get out of the house. It's over."

He couldn't let her just end things that way. So he took about a dozen sleeping pills, wrote a note, went into the garage, stuffed a rag in the car's exhaust pipe, and sat in his car with the motor running. (But, we discovered later, he neglected to close the garage door.) He waited. And when no one came by to save him, he called Gayla from his cell phone. "I need help," he said, choking on the fumes.

"I hope you fucking die," she answered. She did call for help, though, a few minutes later.

Marc was slipping in and out of consciousness when the security police found him.

Bright and early Monday morning, when Gayla was still in the dark about the extent of my relationship with Marc, she filed for divorce. They were formally separated as of December 1. She moved out of their house and gave Marc thirty days to vacate the premises. Finally, after moving out and starting the divorce proceedings, she came to visit him for the first time in the hospital, after he had been there alone all weekend long, a few hours after my visit. She arrived just after I left. And that's when he told her about me.

After my visit to Marc in the hospital, I was utterly confused. Seeing him, I'd once again fallen under his spell. And he looked so helpless and hopeless. But once I was away from him, I started to question things once more. It was all such a mess in my head. I needed guidance, but didn't know whom to confide in. Finally I went to see the Catholic priest on base, Father Kerry, who suggested that I take a break from Marc to get myself back together. His parting words to me remained in my mind: "You have to find peace within yourself. You have to do whatever will bring you that peace."

A break; peace. That seemed like a good idea. Gayla had cut off Marc's phone, which made it easier to stay away. Then he called me from the base one night. "I love you," he said. "I miss you. When can we see each other?"

I told him about my conversation with Father Kerry.

"I have no place to go," he whined. "I have no one to go home to. I have no reason to live." He started sounding more and more desperate, started threatening to kill himself again, and finally hung up on me. I sank into the big blue chair in my living room and cried until I had no tears left—cried for all the weeks, all the months gone by.

I called Father Kerry again and asked him to check up on Marc. He said he would.

I didn't hear from Marc or Father Kerry again that evening. I felt that what would bring me peace was being able to love someone unconditionally and forgive him all his past sins. And that seemed to be the morally correct thing to do. I couldn't turn my back on Marc. Yet I was being investigated for loving him to begin with. I cried all evening long.

Amy and Justin stopped by on the way home from their Thanksgiving holiday and saw the pathetic state I was in. Amy stayed for a while, trying to comfort me. She later described me as almost hysterical. I just sat in the big blue chair, hugging myself, and alternated between crying and laughing. I was in hell. The man I had loved, the man who had put me through so much torture, so many threats, was begging for my help, asking for one more chance, and threatening to try suicide again. The Air Force, I knew, wasn't likely to help me, but I had to find some guidance. So I again tried to ask my commander for help. "One of my very closest friends has tried to commit suicide and has asked me for his help," I told Lieutenant Colonel La Plante. "I can't turn my back on him. I can't go through the rest of my life with the guilt of having someone kill himself on my conscience, knowing that I may be able to help." I suppose I still thought it could be possible to appeal to his human sympathies. But once again, he just wasn't interested.

"Thanks for your time," he said. "Don't say anything more about it. We'll handle it all when the report is finished. Perhaps you should talk with Father Kerry."

IN THE DAYS following his suicide attempt, Marc seemed like a changed man. He was caring, concerned, apologetic, understanding. His temper subsided and his violent streak seemed to disappear. Perhaps, I thought, his near-death experience had given him a new take on life. We had our best reconciliation ever, and I was confident that my future lay with him. He moved in with me on December 11. I heard from La Plante on Friday the thirteenth.

"Flinn," he said, "I need to talk to you. Come on up to base. Whatever you're wearing's okay."

I had just come back from work and was still in my flight suit, so I just put on my boots and drove up to the base. Then I cooled my heels outside La Plante's office for forty-five minutes. I had no idea what was going on. I now had legal counsel. But my lawyer, Captain Karen Hecker, was in Colorado and it was nearly six o'clock on a Friday evening; I had no way to reach her. I thought perhaps this was the formal counseling described in the regulation. I was told that I needed to report to Colonel La Plante formally. I'd thought he just wanted to talk to me; so he'd led me to believe. So I walked in, stood in a position of attention, squared my corner, and saluted. Good thing I was still wearing my flight suit. Colonel La Plante saluted back.

"Lieutenant," he began, "you have the right to remain silent. You have the right to an attorney. . . ."

Not a casual conversation, then.

"Do you understand these rights?" he asked me.

I said yes.

"Do you waive your rights?"

"No, sir."

"Fine," he said. "I have an order for you to sign." He read it: I was to cease and desist from all contact with Marc Zigo and Colin Thompson, "all contact" being "defined to include any physical, verbal, or written communication with either individual. Specifically, you will not be found within 100 feet of either individual, their family members, nor their residences or workplaces. In addition, any attempt to contact either individual by calling their home, workplace, or by leaving a message with a third party or answering machine/device will also constitute a violation of this order."

"Do you understand the order?"

"Yes, sir," I said.

"Do you have anything to say?"

"Not without my attorney present." It was now well after six. Too late to reach Captain Hecker, for sure.

"Then sign here," said La Plante.

I understood the order, but I didn't understand how I was to obey it. The Colin part was no problem; I never so much as saw him. But Marc was a problem. He was already living in my home. I couldn't even tell him to leave without violating La Plante's order. I could not tell my attorney to tell him to leave—that would have been communicating through a third party. I could not even tell my commander any of this, because anything I said could "be used against me in a court of law." La Plante had just severed the lines of communication that might enable the Air Force and me to correct this situation civilly. What was I going to do—move to a hotel, start a new life, leave all my things behind, without ever telling Marc what I was doing? The order was impossible to obey.

And the Air Force, it turned out, already knew that. It was a setup. The security police had my home under surveillance. So they knew that at 1532 hours, Marc had gotten into my car and we'd driven to his house to pick up the remainder of his clothes. They had followed me off base to my home and even noted when I passed one of them on the highway. At 1607 hours, Marc and I had walked back into my house. At 1630 hours, I'd received the phone call to come up to base. The Air Force knew perfectly well that it was issuing an order that I could not obey. La Plante himself had to know it. But he didn't care. "I'm sorry," he said, "I cannot help you."

I signed the order, acknowledging that I understood it. I did not know what to do. As of the moment La Plante read me the order, I was disobeying it. Marc was living in my home! I wanted to scream. I wanted to cry. I wanted to ask how on earth I could obey—but I could no longer talk to La Plante. I had just been ordered to stay away from the man I loved. Was this legal? I'd given up.

Later, the Air Force claimed that Gayla had filed a formal complaint against me to stay away from her husband. If this is so, my attorneys were not informed. Nor did the Air Force produce any formal complaint on her part during the discovery phase of the trial. Furthermore, if she was trying to reconcile with her husband, then why had she served Marc with divorce papers just that morning? Perhaps someone in the Air Force imagined this complaint and lied to members of my chain of command. Perhaps it was the prosecutor's way of setting me up to fail, since she dictated the no-contact order to La Plante and gave the Air Force more severe charges to assure a conviction.

There was nothing to do but go home. And celebrate the one Pyrrhic victory of the day: Gayla had served Marc with divorce papers.

A WEEK LATER, Marc and I flew to Atlanta, and for the first time ever I walked into my parents' home as part of a couple. The day after we arrived was my twenty-sixth birthday, December 23. I called my answering machine in Minot to check for messages, and what I heard sent chills down my spine. Captain Hecker had called from Colorado: the security police had completed their report, and the investigating officer had recommended a criminal court-martial. My knees were shaking. Court-martial had always been a distant threat, but I hadn't taken it seriously—the Air Force didn't court-martial people for having sex. And I certainly hadn't expected the news to come down before Christmas. Much less on my birthday. When I'd last asked La Plante about the progress of the investigation, he'd said the investigators' report would be on his desk when he returned from Christmas leave on January 3, and that he'd rule on it at that time. In fact, it had arrived the day after he left on vacation. His second in command, Lieutenant Colonel Brian Rogers, had grabbed it, panicked, and passed it up to La Plante's superior, 5th Operations Group commander Colonel John G. Miller. La Plante didn't even have to pass the buck; it had been passed for him. Colonel Miller was later to become my official accuser, while his superior, 5th Bomb Wing commander Colonel Robert J. Elder, requested the legal proceedings.

I reset my answering machine and stood there, holding the phone, for a moment. We'd just come back from Christmas shopping. My nieces and nephews were running noisily around the house. People were talking and laughing in the kitchen, preparing for my birthday dinner. Marc was charming everyone in sight: even Gail, who'd come home ready to hate him, had told me that within five minutes of meeting him, she really liked him. He was talking up a storm, telling everyone how much he loved me because, he said, I knew exactly what I wanted and where I was going in my life. They figured he was perfect for me, a man who wouldn't cause me to lose my focus.

I put on a happy face until the end of dinner. Then I told Gail and Marc what had happened. I couldn't tell the rest of my family. It was the first time that they were seeing me with a boyfriend. I couldn't let things fall apart.

We celebrated Christmas and went to the big post-Christmas sales. Marc didn't have any money. His separation from Gayla had left him with no credit cards, with only his Navy disability checks, he said. I'd started taking care of things for him. I had paid for his first semester of undergraduate classes at the University of North Dakota. This, I thought was only normal: after all, we were living together, starting a life together, planning to get married. Plus, he told me this money would be reimbursed by the Veterans Administration once he completed the necessary paperwork. I'd bought his plane ticket to Atlanta (well before the no-contact order). Now he wanted some clothes for school. So I took him shopping at all the Atlanta malls. Marc bought out the Gap and Abercrombie & Fitch: khaki pants, oxford shirts, whatever preppie things he could find. He had a great time checking himself out in all the mirrors, wiggling his butt for the world to see.

Everything, on the surface, was as I'd always dreamt it could be. I so badly wanted it to be that way in reality, I buried what was happening back in Minot as deeply as possible. *This* was real, I thought, *this* was the future: me and my family and Marc. I went to a local car dealer and picked up the Jeep I had ordered months before. I'd been saving up for one for some time. The Jeep felt like *our* car, just as my money now felt like *our* money. My family, I hoped, would soon be *our* family. It's incredible just how much amnesia you can be capable of when there's a relationship at stake. In the horrible roller-coaster ride of my life with Marc, I'd been able to switch gears from misery to bliss so many times. Now, though I was legally bound not to be with Marc, I could do nothing other than plan for our future. Deep down, I still hoped that someone in my chain of command would sit down and talk to me, counsel me, and try to work this out administratively. The contradictions just melted in my mind. And when Marc signed his divorce papers on December 31, I took it as a sign that the new year would be ours.

I should have known better. Being divorced left Marc wide open and vulnerable—not a condition he could tolerate for long. He had to get me into a chokehold again. He began to badger me incessantly about getting on the phone to my lawyers (I now had two of them) and forcing them to straighten things out. When my nieces, Erin and Melissa, mentioned that I'd once before brought a friend home to go shopping, Marc flew into a jealous rage. It didn't matter that the friend in question was named Elizabeth; he was off. He glared at me across the dinner table. Then he started pouting. Before long, he was up in my old bedroom, shouting his usual cruel, degrading comments. My family heard that. They noticed other odd behavior too. Marc could barely contain his irritation when my eleven-year-old nephews, Patrick and Danny, beat him at basketball. And he bragged constantly about women flirting with him. Waitresses and saleswomen, he was sure, just couldn't take their eyes off him. Once, at the Gap, he even carried on a flirtation with a salesman.

The vicious circle had begun again. We were fighting all the time. Marc hounded me to extend my leave so that we could drive my new Jeep back to North Dakota. I complied. Then we fought about who was going to drive it. I was rude to my best high school friend, Jennifer, when she called to see if we could get together. The prospect that I might see another friend created an evil tension between Marc and me. He did not want me spending time with anyone else. So I did not see Jennifer. I wanted to keep Marc calm and on my side. I was putting all my energy, once again, into trying to pacify him.

Yet when we finally jumped into the car and headed for Minot, I realized that something had changed. Maybe the presence of my family had grounded me in myself again, helping me realize that I had once lived without Marc and could do it again. Or maybe I had just grown tired—maybe the Coke can he'd thrown at me the day before was one thing too many. Whatever the reason, the cycle of obsession was breaking. Some little flame, some spark of self-preservation had come aglow. The flicker of doubt I'd felt since August was getting stronger. I realized, as we lurched from fight to fight, that this was no longer just a matter of playing out some sick drama with Marc. My entire future—my life—was on the line.

With this thought in my mind, we set out on what was to become the road trip from hell. We drove first to Gail's house in St. Louis. My second lawyer, Captain Barbara Shestko, was in town, I'd learned. I made an appointment to go see her, leaving Marc with Gail.

This was my first face-to-face conversation with an attorney since the investigation began. (North Dakota is a long way from Colorado and Texas, where my two attorneys were stationed; the Air Force thought phone calls would suffice.) Once I started talking, the floodgates opened. I told Captain Shestko almost everything. I described most of the relationship in detail. I told her about my love for Marc and our future together. I mentioned some of the fights, but downplayed them. I did not want the captain to see me as weak. I talked about the cancer scare, and how I was still waiting for the biopsy results. I told her about how I'd grown isolated from all my friends. But though I talked, I did not trust her fully: she was part of the system.

She shook her head. She said she was worried about me. "You'll have to try to obey that order until I can do something about it."

I bristled. I wished I'd kept my mouth shut. It was one thing for me to have my doubts about Marc; it was another to hear them voiced by someone else. Somehow, that made me feel as if I had failed. "It's not such a big deal," I protested, wiping away my tears. "I can handle it."

"No, you can't," she said. "That's obvious. And you're not thinking clearly about what all this means. If you don't get Marc Zigo out of your house, you will probably go to jail."

For the first time, I let that sink in. What had I been thinking all this time?

It was snowing when I left Shestko's office. I called Marc on my cell phone. "She said you have to move out," I said in a dull voice.

"Do you want me to go?" he asked.

"Yes and no."

He hung up. Gail told me afterward that he started crying: "She wants me to leave. I have nowhere to go. I have no home apart from her. No one can force me to move out!" But by the time I reached her house and we packed up the car, his mood had changed. I could tell there was trouble coming.

It was starting to snow hard, but I had to get back to Minot. As we started down the highway, Marc sat quiet and angry in the passenger seat. When he finally spoke, it was as if a conversation he'd had going in his head had just ended.

"Fine," he said. "Pull over. I'm out of here. I'm going to live with a friend of mine in Hawaii. It's over."

We were about an hour west of St. Louis. The highway was slick. The roadside was covered in white.

"You idiot," I said. "We're in the middle of a snowstorm."

"You've never loved me," he answered. "You only care about yourself."

"I don't want to go to jail."

"Well, where am *I* supposed to go now?" He was yelling and screaming. All the old insults were coming back again. I was a slut, I was a whore, I had never loved him.

I had never felt so low. For the first time in my life, I wanted to die. I wanted to end this misery, wanted to stop living in terror. I was tired of living under threat. I was holed up in a Jeep with a maniac while a blizzard swirled outside. He had no food and no money on him. The road grew more and more empty, and the snow was piling up outside. If he walked off into that weather he would probably not survive the evening. A subtle suicide threat.

I didn't think I could drive anymore, but the last thing I wanted on a dark, wet night was to be captive in a moving vehicle with Marc at the steering wheel. I stopped at a gas station and started to get out of the car, planning to call Gail and ask her to come pick me up. Marc, I thought, could take off however he pleased.

"Where do you think you're going?" Marc grabbed my shoulder, pulled me back into the car, and pinned my shoulder against the seat. "You're not leaving me." The fight continued. I kept trying to leave, and he would not let me. Finally, a calm came over us; I decided to keep driving west and look for a place to stop for the night. I wanted out of the car.

As we drove, Marc kept up his incessant insults. I wanted him the hell out of my life.

He yelled, "Drop me off, *now!*"

I pulled the car off to the side of the road and stopped. "Then let me drop you off near a phone," I said.

"You know where you can drop me off?" His voice was low and thoughtful, almost sinister, as though he was measuring every single word. "You can drop me off on the prosecutor's doorstep." (I learned later that Marc had been calling the prosecutor from my home in Georgia. Who knows what lies he told the Air Force then?)

I was terrified. Gail's parting words to me had been "Keep him on your side." Captain Shestko had agreed that he could make a dangerous enemy. So, once again, I tried to pacify him. If I could do it just this one time, I thought, it would be the last. I'd keep him on my side until the whole court nightmare had ended. Then—I'd get my life back.

The road got so snowy we had to stop. At a motel, we took a room with two separate beds, and he immediately headed for the shower. He came out with a happy look on his face, full of kind words and love. In the past, my heart would have lifted. We would have made love and drifted off again into the happy phase of our dreamworld. Now I just smiled at him peacefully and went to sleep. I had finally disengaged.

BACK IN MINOT, in the home that was ours and that I no longer wanted, I grew further and further away from Marc in my mind. As soon as the trial was over, I wanted him out of my life. Meanwhile I would tread water, to try to keep him sane and away from the Air Force's investigative team. I started to feel a bit stronger. I would fight the court-martial, I thought. The relationship with Marc was dead, no matter what; but the Air Force, I hoped, might give me a second chance.

In Minot, I could talk with my attorneys alone on the phone, without worrying that Marc could hear. To Captain Shestko, I finally revealed all: the threats, the fights, the terror. I needed to get out of the relationship, but could not risk Marc running back to the prosecutor. No matter what I did, I was in trouble. Captain Shestko was afraid for me. She feared for my personal safety and even asked her boss how best to help me. They both advised that I get Marc out of the house. I convinced them that I could keep him calm. Truly, though, I was too scared to tell him to leave. How would he react? Would he attack me? Would he go off in the other direction and try to kill himself again? He was extremely unstable. I did not want to risk either response. I settled for the middle ground: do nothing. So I sat back and waited, not knowing that at every moment I was being monitored by the security police.

My inner strength was rebuilding slowly.

Then the wind was kicked out of me once again. We'd been back less than two weeks when my mother called to say that my father had had a stroke. He was only sixty-six years old, and a very proud and strong man. Now his speech was slurred and he had a great deal of difficulty in making himself understood. When I talked to him on the phone, I could hear and feel his frustration; I wanted to help. He was recovering; he would, in fact, recover almost fully. But he had lost some of his power. He was growing older. I finally realized that my parents were not immortal. One day, they would be gone—my silent supporters and a source of my strength.

It was just too much to deal with all at once. And all alone. Most of my family still had no idea what was happening in Minot. I'd lost contact or fallen out with nearly all my friends because of Marc. I did not know whom to trust. I had no faith in Air Force counselors and couldn't confide in any of my higher-ups; when I told Lieutenant Colonel La Plante about my father, he more or less shrugged it off, telling me once again to talk to Father Kerry. Out of desperation, I'd started confiding in Marc's boss, Melody Brown. I'd gotten to know her during a few visits to the Youth Center for sports camps and when I met her in the hospital after Marc's suicide attempt. She was kind and, I thought, discreet: she always said that she didn't like getting involved in other people's affairs. She told me that Marc—he had always confided in her, too— still really loved me and wanted things to last. But he went wild when I began to grow close to her. "Stop talking about me behind my back," he snarled. So I stopped talking to anyone at all, instead withdrawing further and further into my shell.

Living together with La Plante's order hanging over our heads was like trying to work under a guillotine. In the third week of January, Marc snapped. "You have got to realize the seriousness of what's happening to you," he said to me when I returned home from work. "You have got to talk to your attorneys and get this order fixed."

"I've been talking to them every day," I said. "So far, there's nothing we can do." He was pacing and yelling. "It's all over. I can't live like this anymore, sneaking in and out the back door." This was the only entrance to the house from the garage.

"Look," I said, "I'm doing all I can do. It's in the attorneys' hands now!"

"Well," he replied, "do more." He punched the air in frustration and his face contorted with anger. He moved to within two feet of my face. He placed a hand on each armrest of the blue chair where I was sitting, and surrounded me. He glared at me and hissed: "If you think you're fucked now"—a pause— "I'll show you what it means to be fucked."

You're not supposed to look a wild animal in the eye, so I looked away. He grabbed his jacket and stormed out.

The security police were there to watch him drive off—and clock him, and document it, as I learned the next morning, when my attorney faxed the official Report of Investigation to me. I was at work and headed to the base defense attorney's office, to wait for the fax. I stood alone over the machine, reading, frozen in horror. There was the complaint, Brian Mudery's complaint, which set the whole case in motion . . . the witnesses' testimony . . . their characterization of me and my sex life. . . . It was filthy—pornographic, even—and it was packed with surprises. Marc had not only told the investigators that he'd had sex with me; he'd drawn them a picture of my house to show where it took place. Other people said that Marc told them I'd stolen his Claddagh ring. Marc talked about K-Y Jelly and what it was good for. He said that I was a "screamer" in bed. The investigators also asked witnesses to detail how

many times they'd heard I had oral sex or intercourse occurred, where, and in what position. I was mortified.

Everyone, it seemed, had something to add. Melody Brown,
it turned out, had told investigators that I'd pursued Marc,
forcing him to duck my incessant calls at the office. She'd
warned him I was bad news. He'd told her all kinds of things
about our sex life: what kind of birth control we used, what
kind of underwear I wore, what type of positions we did it in.
She was all too happy to pass that information on to the security police. Colin Thompson was pleased to cooperate, too.
Our "affair," as I remembered it, had been an all-too-brief
drunken encounter late one evening after a party; he'd partici-
pated between two episodes of blacking out. Colin, though, re-
lated five episodes of oral sex on my lawn, followed by four or
five command performances over the course of the night in my
bedroom. "Why didn't you hold on to him, Kelly?" my lawyer
Karen Hecker would joke. "This guy deserves a medal." I
wasn't in the frame of mind to have a sense of humor and
laugh at Hecker's comments. This was how people talked
about me on base. They lied to clear themselves ("I have not
committed adultery with anyone and never will," wrote one
officer, who was having an affair with one of my married
friends), and they dished the dirt on me. I was horrified to
think of the commanders reading this. None of the higher-ups
knew me; this would be their first and lasting impression.

After my defense team picked up the investigation where the
security police had left off, I learned that Colin Thompson had
been chasing another woman around while we were supposedly on the lawn together. He'd even attempted to kiss her in
the hallway outside the bathroom. This woman, an officer's
wife, had a build like mine, and blond hair. Perhaps, in his
drunken stupor, Colin had confused all of his women. The security police, investigating officer, and all my commanders

chose to believe him, and despite his admission of blacking out he kept his security clearance and PRP. Usually, people who have alcoholic blackouts lose their top secret clearances.

But once I came under investigation, it was the Marc Zigo story that led to my downfall. This may not have been totally accidental. Adultery and fraternization cases are hard to prove. My accuser, Mudery, was looking at jail time in Leavenworth. And Marc was a known liar. But the Air Force, I've just recently learned, had come up with a solution for guaranteeing a conviction in such messy cases: go for another offense. Try for "violation of a regulation" or "false official statement," advises the Air Force's *Courts-Martial Handbook*, which was written by Colonel Reed, the chief of Military Justice, and is distributed only to prosecutors. "Beat the bushes," it advises. "Often this is the simplest, surest basis for prosecution."

I couldn't go back to my house and play the game anymore, but I had no idea what Marc would do once I finally told him to leave. I told my attorneys that after the "I'll show you what it means to be fucked" comment, I didn't feel safe, physically or emotionally. Then I sat in my office alone for hours, crying, rocking back and forth, while the lawyers tried to decide how to help me. Finally, they had me sign a statement that I feared for my own safety and Marc's, and was asking the government's help in removing Marc Zigo from my house. I also understood that in light of this new information, the government could prefer an additional charge of failing to obey the lawful order. Captains Hecker and Shestko had asked the government not to do so, in view of the circumstances. All the colonels in my chain of command were informed of the crisis: my attorneys, wanting me safe and sound, had decided to worry about the charges later. Like me, they believed they could reason with the government. My lawyers and my superiors, all the way up to Colonel Elder, the wing commander, had agreed that I would be escorted to my house by two members of the squadron;

there, we'd meet the local Minot police. (The security police have no jurisdiction off base, which is why the local police were involved. Oddly, this regulation had not prevented them from setting up and performing surveillance on my house.) I would pack my bags and leave Minot for the weekend.

Marc was home. With the squadron members and police standing around us, I said: "I'm asking you to leave my house and I want you out by Monday morning." The first words out of his mouth were "Am I in trouble?" Then: "I don't have any place to go."

I was shaking as I packed up my things and took the keys to my Honda and Jeep. Marc followed me around the house, telling me he loved me, begging me to explain what had happened. I didn't reply.

I went back up to base, and stayed in one of the base hotel rooms. La Plante sent a message through Lieutenant Jackie Bieker, ordering me to talk to the chaplain. (Father Kerry was out of town for the evening.) I just wanted to sleep, but first I had to convince the chaplain I was okay. I sat next to the chaplain, wiped the tears away, and said, "At least I have my life back."

No one in my chain of command called to see if I was okay that weekend. According to Marc, Colonel Elder phoned Marc's father; I guess a civilian was more important than one of his pilots. And that Sunday, I went to mass. Both Colonel Miller, the group commander, and Colonel Elder, the wing commander, were there to hear Father Kerry preach about mistakes and forgiveness, but both officers refused to shake my hand during the sign of peace, or even to look at me. Nor, after the service, did either man ask me how I was doing. Perhaps they were not listening during the homily or were too busy planning their next move against me.

Marc left town almost immediately. But even with him far away in Florida, I stayed on base a few extra days, still too afraid to go home. Finally, a friend—just about my only re-maining friend—escorted me there. I had always kept it un-locked all the time; no more. I secured it, locking up all the doors and windows. I had already taken back my extra key.

Marc had left most of his things in the house, though he'd taken one of my suitcases with all the new clothes I'd bought him in Atlanta. I boxed up the rest of his possessions and put them in storage.

Until now, what was happening to me had seemed slow-moving and unreal. All of a sudden, the train left the station and started picking up steam. No one was willing to slow it down. None of my commanders were acting like commanders. Not a single one asked me what had happened. Nor would they talk with my attorneys. Soon I was having cryosurgery to remove the precancerous cells, and my Article 32 hearing was approaching fast. This was the military's equivalent of a grand jury: the charges and the findings of the investigation would be formally presented to an investigating officer who would decide whether there was enough evidence against me to war-rant a court-martial. If not, my case, like every other adultery case on base, would end with an Article 15: a nonjudicial pun-ishment that basically amounted to a letter of reprimand for my permanent file. Once you had an Article 15, your career in the Air Force was basically over. You wouldn't be kicked out, but you would never be promoted, either. At best, I would have been able to fly for my remaining Air Force commitment, then find a flying job in the civilian world. A court-martial, however, is a criminal trial, and conviction makes you a felon. I was being charged with adultery, fraternization, lying, disobeying an order, and conduct unbecoming an officer. If convicted, I faced nine and a half years in prison.

It was going to be ugly. The legal office forced me to cancel my surgery appointment because, in its view, the legal proceedings took precedence over my health concerns. Marc was voluntarily coming up from Florida to take the stand. He'd lied so many times already that it was impossible to predict what he'd say to the prosecutors. But before I faced him, I had to make a phone call that I'd long been dreading. To date, I'd told my family nothing about the Air Force's investigation of me. As far as they were concerned, I was now Marc's fiancée.

When my mother answered the phone, I didn't know where to begin. We had never shared personal problems before. There was so much ground to cover, so much to explain. And it was all so very embarrassing.

I started crying and told her everything, just as plainly and simply as possible. I'd gotten so used to telling my story to lawyers that I nearly knew it by heart. My mother simply said, "We love you, and are so proud of you. We'll help you through this." My father cried after we got off the phone. It was only weeks after his stroke, and like everyone else in my family, he felt stunned and powerless. "What will happen now?" my mother asked.

If the result of the Article 32 hearing was a decision to refer my case to court-martial, I would have seven days to state whether I wanted to resign or move ahead to trial. I had decided in advance not to resign. I knew that Secretary Widnall hardly ever accepted resignations—and if you asked to resign but were refused, your entire defense strategy was taken away before you saw the inside of a courtroom, since you had to include it in the resignation package. I also didn't want an "other than honorable" discharge. I had served honorably for eight years. I still believed that someone in the Air Force, someone in my chain of command would regain his senses and handle this nonjudicially. I should not become a convicted felon because I had had consensual sex. I could not quit. I had to fight. I could not just walk away and have my entire life trashed by the Air Force. I would stand up and fight for myself, my honor, my pride, and my dignity. I would show them what truly happened, since no one had bothered to ask.

My family gathered that evening in Atlanta and prepared for battle.

The next day, my brother Don flew to Minot. My family hired an experienced civilian attorney. The troops had started to rally behind their little sister. We were going into battle. And we were taking on the United States government. "Fight's on" became our battle cry.

CHAPTER 8

Falling Apart

[He] was guilty, of course, or he would not have been accused, and since the only way to prove it was to find him guilty, it was their patriotic duty to do so.

—JOSEPH HELLER, *Catch-22*

THE ARTICLE 32 WAS A HUMILIATING FIASCO. I SAT THERE IN my flight suit with a Velcro'd blank where my squadron patch belonged. Earlier in the month, Lieutenant Colonel La Plante had removed the patch from my sleeve because he thought I was unworthy of it. During the 32, I was accused of everything but flying over the base on a broomstick. Marc told one lie after another. He'd tell my attorney one thing during her interview with him, then say something else on the stand. Marc also claimed he was a victim and needed someone present during all interviews to protect him. The prosecution had advised him of this right. A victim of what, I had no idea, nor did my attorney. Marc said we'd had sex in his house. That we'd had sex on the base. That we'd had sex during our first evening together, on July 3. None of this was true. I wrote my attorney note after protesting note. Marc kept looking at me and shaking his head. He denied ever having been physically violent toward me. He admitted to having lied on his prior statements. I wondered if

the Air Force would prosecute *him* now for false official statements and obstruction of justice.

"Why should I believe you now?" the investigating officer
said.

"Because I'm telling the truth now," said Marc.

That was good enough. It was good enough, too, when Colin
Thompson said he knew he'd had sex with me here, there, and
everywhere but didn't remember when, since he'd had ten or
twelve beers on the night in question. It still has not ceased to
amaze me that someone's fantasy became the word of truth
and was taken as proof of an act. Colin openly admitted that
his memory was unclear, that he had been drinking, that he
had blacked out during the time in question. The outcome of
the hearing was no surprise: court-martial.

My brother Donald arrived two days after the Article 32 and
said he wasn't leaving Minot until we'd gotten a couple of
things straightened out. First of all, there was the question of
my Air Force legal representation. My senior lawyer, Captain
Shestko, hadn't shown up for my Article 32 because she was involved in another case. And Captain Hecker did not have a lot
of experience with consensual sex cases. In fact, I was one of
her first consensual sex cases. She was eager to do her best, and
she was energetic: she walked around with a thirty-two-ounce
cup of Coke all the time, as though the caffeine could pump her
up enough to take on the big guns of the Air Force. But she was
really out of her league. My parents hired me a top-notch civilian defense lawyer, Frank Spinner. Spinner had seen it all. His
most famous case was the court-martial of Delmar Simpson, a
drill sergeant at the Aberdeen Proving Grounds who was accused of rape in 1996. Spinner also represented Captain Wang,
an AWACS crewmember, who was being held solely responsible for the friendly-fire shoot-down of two American helicopters over Iraq. Wang was later acquitted. Spinner had also
represented a military heart surgeon convicted of adultery, and

a lieutenant colonel who'd been convicted of an "unprofessional relationship" with a colleague, a female officer, because he'd accompanied her to the gym.

Spinner immediately began to fight the move to court-martial and started preparing my defense. He recommended that I go see a psychologist he knew in St. Louis so that we could find out more about Marc's character and have her draw up a psychological profile of me to convey how someone so successful could get into such a mess. These were the questions we'd have to answer in order to make plain the extenuating circumstances of my actions. So, in the second week of February, I took leave and went to stay with Gail in St. Louis. The whole family gathered. It was the first time I'd seen my father since his stroke. Gearing up for a fight had given his life a focus again. It was good to see him with his spirit restored.

I made a series of appointments with a civilian psychologist, Dr. Ann Duncan. She was the kind of person you rarely encountered in the Air Force: Long brown hair mixed with gray and worn in a long braid over her right shoulder. Long skirts and big glasses. Understanding looks. In her office overlooking Clayton, Missouri, there were lots of green plants and tissues always within easy range. I trusted her. And I opened up to her with a real sense of relief.

Dr. Duncan put me through a full battery of psychological tests. Then she showed me a book by Lenore E. Walker, *The Battered Woman*, where I read about the symptoms of living in an abusive relationship. Walker discussed the cycles of violence and reconciliation, the jealousy, the isolation, the loss of control. Dr. Duncan added how suicide attempts were the batterer's last attempt to manipulate and control. Walker's book described Marc and me perfectly. It made some sense of the senseless mess of a life I'd lived over the past nine months. There was comfort in that. After I'd been cast for so long as a sexual predator, it felt nice to have someone tell me that I was, in fact, the victim, as were all the other women Marc preyed on. *Marc* was the predator. For the first time since August, I didn't feel totally alone. I started to gain some strength through this understanding.

Then the Air Force upped the ante. On February 21, Gail woke up early to get ready for work. I didn't have to see Dr. Duncan until later in the day, so I slept in. Gail went downstairs to pick up her newspaper and a few minutes later came into my room. "Kelly," she said, "I have some bad news. It's in the press."

It was on the last page of the front section of the *St. Louis Post-Dispatch:* "Female Bomber Pilot Faces Adultery Charges." I crawled out of bed and turned on the TV. There it was on *CNN Headline News,* and there I was, every single half hour. The charges were all wrong: CNN was saying that I'd had an affair with a married enlisted man. But the images were right on the money. It was a perfect TV story—Blonde Ambition: Sex, Lies, and the B-52. No one had told me that the story was being released to the press. No one, in fact, had told my squadron commander. The public affairs officer for Minot AFB, Captain Curtis, told me later that he wanted to tell me, but the base legal office told him not to. My squadron was in Nevada on an exercise when the news broke. A German officer saw it on CNN, walked into the squad room in Las Vegas, and said to Lieutenant Colonel La Plante, "What's going on with your pilots?"

The Pentagon must have known it had a great story on its hands, for the words of the press release made clear that this was to be milked for all the media attention it was worth: "Court-martial charges have been preferred against the Air Force's first female bomber pilot, 1st Lieutenant Kelly J. Flinn." The Air Force turned my case into a gender issue and a media circus with that phrase "first *female* bomber pilot."

I'm not sure what they thought they were going to accomplish by going public, but I have a few theories. It had been a bad couple of years for men in the armed forces. There was the Tailhook incident, during which Lieutenant Paula Coughlin and eighty other women were sexually assaulted and made to "walk the gauntlet" at a naval aviators' convention. There was the rape of a twelve-year-old girl by servicemen stationed in Okinawa. There was the Aberdeen trial: nineteen female trainees had filed rape and assault charges against twenty drill sergeants. And, most recently, there was Sergeant Major Gene McKinney, the most senior enlisted man in the Army, who had been charged with sexual misconduct by a woman who formerly worked for him. These cases had received enormous public attention. Maybe the military brass wanted to even the score, to show that women were every bit as capable of sexual peccadilloes as men are—a kind of perverse equal-opportunity project. Or maybe, as many women's advocates have suggested, this was a way of saying, without having to say it, that women have no place in the military: let them in and all hell breaks loose.

Knowing the military as I do, though, I think it's entirely possible that there was no "big idea" at all. I think it's very possible that someone in the press office at the Pentagon was just very, very stupid. Or perhaps the Air Force thought this would be the straw that broke my back; now, maybe, I'd leave quietly. Incidentally, as of the moment of the press release, the court-martial convening authority, Lieutenant General Phillip J. Ford, had not officially decided to court-martial me. The final decision, it seems, was made in the Pentagon.

It is impossible to describe what it feels like to be a private person and have your sex life displayed on the national news—incorrectly, I might add. I just stared at the television in shock. My family stared at me with pity. If there's one thing I can't stand, it's looks of pity. So, with my mother shouting that we had to get on the phone and *do something*, I left the room. I went upstairs to my sister's bathroom and I sat down on the carpeted stairs leading up to her tub, and I cried. I cried from the bottom of my soul, my whole body shaking. *How could they do this to me? Did they know what they were doing to me? Did they care?* I felt my whole world collapsing around me, my dreams destroyed. Why was there nothing in the news about Lieutenant Brian Mudery and his sexual exploits? After a little while, Gail came up and sat down next to me. In my family, we believe that things always happen for a reason. But neither of us could see a purpose to this. She held me and we sat there rocking back and forth for a long time.

I went to see Dr. Duncan later in the day and cried some more. I wouldn't have believed I had any tears left. Having surmised that I seemed "a little depressed," she did some diagnostic tests. I was asked to rate my mood on a scale of 0 to 5, with 5 being the happiest I'd ever been and 0 the saddest. I had never been lower in my entire life, but I said 2. I couldn't let the Air Force know how "officially" down I was. If a psychologist said I was depressed, I might be believed suicidal, and in that case I'd lose my flying job. For I still believed that if I played my cards right, I could keep it. Deep down, I truly believed and hoped that Lieutenant General Ford would recommend nonjudicial punishment.

I went back to Minot knowing that from here on in, everyone I passed would know everything about my private life. Unable to make eye contact with anyone, I shuffled off the plane, almost lifeless, put on my baseball cap, and handed myself over to a friend. A sergeant in my squadron, he was one of the few colleagues who showed concern for me. Extremely upset at my chain of command, he offered moral support.

I felt I'd lost everything. Marc had kept his word and destroyed the "perfect little bomber pilot." The Air Force had helped. My commander had taken away my squadron patch, my flying colors. I had lost my security access, so I couldn't deal with any classified materials—which basically meant I couldn't have anything to do with my regular job. In contrast to the civil justice system, the military considered me guilty unless I proved my innocence. General Fogelman, the chief of staff of the Air Force, even said so on the floor of Congress. I'd been taken out of my squadron and given a new assignment: writing letters of appreciation and congratulations. It was an hour of work a day that I had to stretch into a full eight-hour shift.

The Monday after the news broke, I walked into work with my head held high. That required all the strength and concentration I could muster. It was far harder than landing a plane. I sat down at my desk, waiting for something to do and trying to maintain some dignity. The desk was right next to the squadron commander's office. Everyone—including La Plante himself—had to see me every time they walked down the main hall.

La Plante went into his office, followed shortly afterward by his second and third in command. They shut the door behind them. I knew from the furtive glances they'd given me as they walked by that they were about to talk about me. A few minutes later, they came out again and asked another sergeant working near me to leave. Major Girard, La Plante's third in command, sat down across from me. "How's your father?" he said. He started to talk about how his own father had had a stroke and that he knew what a strain it was and that if I ever needed help, I shouldn't hesitate to come to him. I just looked at him blankly. The events of the weekend, the court-martial and public humiliation, just didn't seem to exist for him. Either that, or he just didn't have the courage to mention them to me.

After he left, La Plante said, "Flinn, come with me." I followed him all the way down the hallway to the other end of the building, through a door, around a corner, and finally into an office that was pretty much as far away from everyone as possible.

"Let's put you away from the crowd," he said. "You'll be protected here." He went on to describe my new job working with the Awards and Decorations program. I would now print medals for all the hard workers in the squadron.

"No one in the squadron has turned their back on you," he said.

I stood there in my flight suit, and then glanced at the blank spot on my right shoulder where my patch was supposed to be.

"Yes, sir," I replied.

Then he left. The eyesore had been removed. Now he no longer had to look at the female pilot and see the constant reminder of decisions he had chosen to pass along to others to make.

Carey La Plante, the lieutenant colonel's wife, stormed into my office later. I looked at her emptily. I was just a shell. She told me I had to fight, and fight dirty. She was preparing a letter to Sheila Widnall to complain about my treatment. She had also bragged that before she and La Plante were married, their relationship was adulterous: she had been married to one of her future husband's students during undergraduate pilot training at Columbus. (I learned about this admitted affair from the wives on base.) I was living in a truly hypocritical society. Like me, Carey's husband had committed adultery. Now he led the largest flying squadron in Air Combat Command, while I was about to be court-martialed. I had no words for her.

And despite her initial support, Carey La Plante quickly changed her tune after her husband was removed from his position as squadron commander in late April. Although no one in my squadron said anything to me, I could read in their eyes that they all blamed me for La Plante's lost job. Now I was even more ostracized by my peers.

EVER SINCE WE'D heard the result of the Article 32 hearing, Frank Spinner had been trying to persuade Lieutenant General

Ford, the commander of the 8th Air Force and the court-martial convening authority, to issue a nonjudicial punishment. This didn't seem unrealistic: according to official records, the Air Force was handing out Article 15s for adultery at the rate of four a month at Minot alone. Ford himself, I'd heard, had intervened recently when an officer in my squadron had been stopped for the life-threatening offense of driving under the influence, which is usually punished with an Article 15. General Ford sent La Plante a letter ordering him not to include any mention of the Article 15 in the officer's permanent record. At the same time, I read an article in the base newspaper about a lieutenant colonel who had an affair with his enlisted secretary during which the couple took trips together on government money. He received an Article 15 and was allowed to stay for three years, long enough to earn retirement benefits.

Clearly, there was much more leeway in handling punishable offenses than the Air Force was willing to admit. And my behavior had taken place under extenuating circumstances. If they were known, I believed—if someone would just sit down and *talk* to me, human to human—then I wouldn't have to go to trial. If only one of my commanders would just command, instead of watching from the sidelines!

In his letter to General Ford, Spinner pointed out that just a year earlier a male lieutenant from Minot had been charged with fraternization and other offenses and had been punished with an Article 15. He pointed out that La Plante had told him he wouldn't object to a nonjudicial punishment. "Lieutenant Flinn deserves an opportunity to be rehabilitated," he wrote. And: "If this case is referred to trial, intense public scrutiny is sure to follow. . . . The race to judgment and to the courtroom that I have observed in this case may damage not only Lieutenant Flinn, but the Air Force as well."

I don't think General Ford ever read that letter; even before he received it, he probably had signed the order to refer the charges to trial. The advice he took was that of his chief legal adviser, Colonel Charles G. Mangin, the chief judge advocate general for the entire 8th Air Force. Colonel Mangin later said to a group of new arrivals to Barksdale Air Force Base during an orientation briefing that "the Secretary of the Air Force caved in. [If Secretary Widnall had waited two more days before accepting the resignation,] the court-martial would have begun and we would have had the female lieutenant pilot." Apparently, Mangin had his own agenda.

I still hoped that Ford would change his mind. It was the last bit of hope I was to have. On Wednesday, February 26, just after I learned from Frank Spinner that the charges had officially been referred to court-martial, La Plante walked into my office and told me I had to pick up some paperwork from the legal office. I told him I already knew that, because my charges had just been referred to court-martial. La Plante said he did not know what that meant. I explained: Lieutenant General Ford had officially decided to send me to trial. He repeated that he did not know what any of that legal "mumbo-jumbo" meant. I stared at him in shock. He was my damned commander! He was in charge of punishments for squadron members. One of his own was going to trial and he did not know what that meant? I almost threw the *Manual for Courts-Martial* at him. This was the darkest and lowest day of my life.

NOW THE COUNTDOWN to court-martial began. My family teamed up with the lawyers to prepare our case. First, I was never to use my home phone to discuss the case. My family believed it was tapped by the Air Force. Whenever I wanted to talk about the case, I drove to the nearest pay phone. Second, they decided, it was time to learn everything we could about Marc Zigo. We hired a private investigator.

A few phone calls later, the entire personality Marc had constructed lay in ruins. We never were able to confirm his birth date, but we did learn that his mother wasn't a doctor, as he'd said; his education had been nothing more than a couple of years at a community college. He had not been a paralegal in the Navy. He'd been a claims officer, which was little more than a secretary; all he knew about military law was what he'd made up to serve his own purposes. He was also, we learned, supposed to be seeing a doctor regularly, to determine when he was no longer eligible to receive disability checks from the Navy. As far as I knew, he hadn't seen a doctor in two years.

In late April, two months after the Air Force's press release, I finally made a public statement to *The Washington Post*. That was followed by interviews with *The New York Times* and *60 Minutes*. And then we didn't have to dig any further. All of a sudden, we started receiving letters. Five or six women wrote from Washington State with their own Marc Zigo stories to tell—chillingly familiar ones. A teacher had met Marc in Japan and had fallen for him. They were engaged while at the same time he was courting Gayla. He told the teacher he would meet her family in the States over Thanksgiving. "Thanksgiving came and went, and Marc never came," she wrote. Within a week of Gayla's departure for basic training, Marc had started coming on to another woman at the law firm where he worked in Washington. He told "Jane" that he was separated, that Gayla had left him, that they were getting a divorce, that he was falling in love with Jane, that he wanted to date her. He told each woman the same story about his background. At one point, he even had false separation papers drawn up to prove his story to one of them. The law firm wrote to say that he had used a fake résumé to get the job, with somebody else's name on it. The lawyer, a senior partner in a reputable law firm, talked about how charismatic Marc was, how Marc could get anyone to do anything. The owner of an athletic club in Washington called to say that he had once hired Marc and was ready to fly a couple of dozen employees to my trial to testify that when Marc worked there, he went after anything in a skirt.

Meanwhile, as the letters and phone calls were coming in, my parents had started a letter-writing campaign of their own. They contacted all the major women's organizations. They put together lists of friends from baseball, soccer, softball teams, and from our old neighborhoods in Atlanta and St. Louis. We asked our friends to contact their senators and representatives: as a result, thousands of letters went out to House Speaker Newt Gingrich and Senators Paul Coverdell and Max Cleland. Coverdell responded to people with an official letter from the Air Force explaining the charges. Gingrich wrote back saying that he had written to Widnall and was in contact with my family. In actuality, though my mother went to his local office every day, she never directly spoke with him. And during those daily visits, she learned that his staff was taking the pulse of the nation on the issue by listening to Rush Limbaugh.

The story was everywhere. It was no longer about a conflict between the Air Force and me; it was a lightning rod dividing the nation. In Congress, it galvanized arguments between supporters and foes of women in the military. It set liberals against conservatives, men against women, women against me. I received hundreds of letters of support, many from retired members of the Air Force, including the president of the 8th Air Force Historical Society. Senator Slade Gorton of Washington, a former active-duty Air Force lawyer, called the charges a "mistake" that was bringing the Air Force into "disrepute." "It's a case of the punishment being greatly disproportionate to the crime," he said. Senator Trent Lott of Mississippi told the Air Force to "get real" and grant me an honorable discharge. Senator Gorton later claimed that Lieutenant General Ford was more of a threat to national security than I was. Representatives Nita Lowey and Carolyn Maloney, of New York, were rallying congresswomen behind me and demanding the Air Force grant me an honorable discharge.

All this swirled around me like a dream. The more intimately the outside world got to know me, the less real I seemed to myself. I sat numbly, day after day, with the vague awareness that outside, a whole world was passing me by. In that world, people were on the news talking about a person named Kelly Flinn who—it would seem—was a robot with no feelings. Meanwhile, the real Kelly Flinn was using her million-dollar Air Force education to write up achievement medals. "These are the best medals I have ever seen come out of your squadron," wrote the 5th Operations Group's second in command. Writing them consisted of changing a word or two on a standard computer file and hitting "Print." Then I'd get out a ruler and make sure that the paper had printed out perfectly straight and centered. On the medal itself, I wrote a paragraph explaining why it had been awarded. This had to be accurate but not too full of jargon—"so Mom can understand," as the colonel who supervised me put it. Each medal then had to go up and down the approval chain. Usually, it took five or ten edits before the medal would be accepted by Colonel Miller. Some medals were lost as they moved through the bureaucracy. When I started the job, we were 130 medals behind schedule. Working on this eight hours a day, I was caught up within two weeks. After that, I had nothing to do but read novels. I read one a day. I tried to buy books in series, because there were so many more of them. I escaped into the fantasy world of dragons, knights, and damsels in distress. A science fiction series by David Eddings particularly appealed to me. Its theme was that you have to live the events of your life over and over again until you get them right. Then you can move on.

At first, I'd kept going out for drinks with two guys in my squadron. (I stuck to water because I did not need any more depressants in my body.) But whenever I went out I was aware of a security police officer watching me. Soon a wall went up between me and most of my old friends. I couldn't tell them anything about my case, because they might be called upon to testify against me (as some were). And some of them I simply came to resent. One night I went out with an officer friend and the wife of another officer. They had lied to investigators about their relationship. As we said good night and I watched them go off together, I thought, "I'm going to jail for what they're about to go off and do."

I had never been a depressed person in my life. Now I went to bed every night praying to God that I wouldn't wake up in the morning. I woke up in the morning cursing God because I was still alive. I never actually attempted suicide. But I thought about it, hard. I imagined what my suicide note would say and to whom I'd send it. I knew where a gun was hidden in a friend's house; I imagined myself driving by and getting it. Shooting myself would have been too messy, though. I didn't want my parents to have to clean up a mess. So I'd go to the drugstore and look at all the sleeping pill racks and think about which pills would work best. I searched the Internet for the most lethal combination of barbiturates. I went on this way for weeks and weeks.

It's a strange thing to be logical and sane when you're thinking of committing suicide. You have a sense of knowing what you're doing. Suicide doesn't seem a "crazy" choice; you know what the consequences are. And you know that it's a permanent end to your difficulties. But the difference, I think, between me and those who really do kill themselves is this: I knew, even in those darkest days, that there was a light at the end of the tunnel. I just did not want to go through the tunnel to get to the light. People who really kill themselves, I think, don't see that light at all. Also, there's no stopping people who really want to commit suicide. I learned from this experience that when someone really wants to die, they will do it. They won't tell you what's going through their mind. They'll smile and say everything's all right and then kill themselves during the night.

What stopped my suicidal attempts was a message on the Internet: "If you're thinking about killing yourself, just wait twenty-four hours." I waited. I still had not discovered a non-messy solution. So I waited another twenty-four. And another. Eventually, if you wait, the thoughts of suicide subside. However, the wounds left by climbing back up from such a low are deep and take a long time to heal.

AS THE COURT-MARTIAL DATE approached, the media storm intensified. Every day as I walked in and out of the building where the court-martial was to take place, I passed a whole squadron of press. The base was filled with news trucks. Was everyone in the country waiting to hear what the decision would be? I'd gotten one clear benefit from all the attention: after Tamara Jones of *The Washington Post* had remarked on the blank spot on my flight suit, I'd been given back my patch. And judging from all the letters I was receiving, and the tone of editorials and call-in shows, we were winning the war for public opinion. But the barrage of unfavorable coverage was doing nothing to change the minds of the commanders— Lieutenant General Ford all the way down to Lieutenant Colonel La Plante—who were set on court-martialing me. The government continued to deny our motions to delay the trial; they barred our evidence and disqualified our witnesses. The government would not even let us interview Marc's parents, although if anyone knew his true character, they did. Early on, investigators had refused to let Melody Brown retract her statement, as she'd wanted to do once she figured out that Marc had been lying to me. ("If he told me that the sky was

blue, I'd have to go outside to check before I believed him"
was how she later put it in a letter to Secretary Widnall.) Now,
the government moved to exclude any evidence of my good
character. They refused to hear any mention of Colin Thompson's prior disciplinary actions, which happened to include
being given a no-contact order with respect to a married
woman and a charge of reckless driving. Yet he had claimed
during his Article 32 hearing that he had never been in any
trouble or received any type of punishment for any actions.
We couldn't mention Marc Zigo's conviction for fourth-degree
assault against his wife.

At the same time, *everything* was being used as evidence
against me: An e-mail I'd sent Jackie Bieker saying that I understood it was her job to tell me what items I had to bring to
Leavenworth, the maximum-security prison, and was ready to
hear about it whenever she pleased. An e-mail I'd sent to the
new squadron commander saying that my office was cleaned
up and that I supposed I'd be leaving in a few weeks. Lieutenant Bieker for some reason felt it was necessary to forward
these to La Plante, who in turn forwarded them to the prosecutor. They were taken as admissions of guilt. So was a "Days
of Freedom" countdown that I'd put up on the wall of my office as a black joke. Academy graduates were used to count-
downs from the beginning: days left till the end of basic
training, till the end of freshman year, till graduation. I was
trying to make light of things. I even joked with a radar navigator, Rob Bortree, that soon I might be trading in my green
flight suit for an orange one—orange being the color of choice
at Leavenworth, of course. Bortree felt some need to disclose
this information to the prosecutor and now was bragging to
the squadron about how he had to testify at my trial.

I learned that the investigators had set up surveillance at
my parents' home in Georgia during my Christmas vacation.
The security police even followed me off base after work—

something they were not allowed to do unless I was in the act of fleeing after committing a felony on base. They also set up illegal surveillance at my downtown house, and recorded my daily comings and goings. They seized my credit records. They found out that I'd gone shopping at Victoria's Secret and wanted to find out what items I'd purchased. The prosecutor, Major Wade Pittman, must have felt that buying underwear was an admission of a criminal act. He showed no human feelings whatsoever. After Lieutenant Colonel Karen Tew had killed herself after being found guilty of fraternization because of Pittman, and his prosecution team's excellent casework, he rushed down to Mississippi to convict a female nurse of fraternization. He rushed from that case up to mine, ignoring some of his bigger cases, including those involving child abuse.

WHILE I WAS PREPARING my defense, my sister Patti was waging her own separate war with the Air Force. As I've mentioned, Patti is deaf. She wanted to participate fully in the trial process and for that she needed a sign language interpreter.

For three weeks my sister researched interpreters and requested funding support from the United States Air Force, according to Section 503 of the Rehabilitation Act of 1973, which set forth the court's responsibility and duty to provide interpreters. Instead of using the certified legal interpreter Patti found, the Air Force supplied its own. The wife of someone on base, this woman was not a certified legal interpreter and had not used sign language in over eleven years. Patti was completely left out and felt helpless not knowing what was happening during defense team discussions and in conversations with reporters.

My attorneys continued to ask the government for support and never received a response. After Patti returned home, when the case was over, she finally received official word that the Air Force had denied her request. "No way! We are not going to pay for that!" the Air Force replied.

A RAY OF HOPE came less than a week before the court-martial was scheduled to begin. Sources close to Sheila Widnall leaked to *The New York Times* that the secretary was willing to consider an honorable discharge. The *Times* made sure to hold the story until the Air Force would confirm it. Everyone was now rallying to try to convince me to submit a resignation package detailing the mitigating circumstances, my Air Force accomplishments, and awards, and saying that I would take any kind of discharge, including an other than honorable discharge. Resign, Captain Shestko said. Despite the leak, my defense team did not believe the secretary would actually grant me an honorable discharge. I felt that by dangling an honorable discharge in front of me, the Air Force was trying to trick me into submitting a resignation package with the standard letter attached saying I would accept any kind of discharge. Then "any kind of discharge" would be what I'd get: other than honorable. I adamantly refused. I had served honorably for eight years. I could not force my hand to sign that piece of paper.

All three lawyers ganged up on me one day in the legal defense room and pressed their argument. "What about our case?" I said. We now had so much more evidence on Marc. We would be able to go after him for lying during the Article 32 hearing. After I'd read the Report of Investigation, I had started recording my phone conversations with him. On tape, he'd admitted to having pushed me and to having lied to me and to the investigators.

But it was pointless to go to trial, my lawyers said. It was just too clear that the deck was stacked against me. All the cards were held by the convening authority, Lieutenant General Ford: he'd handpicked the jury, decided who the witnesses would be, and chosen the judge. And he'd already shown himself to be completely unsympathetic to my case. The badgering continued until I finally conceded. "Fine, I'll do it! I'll sign the damned paper!" I stormed out of the office to be alone.

Frank came to talk to me later. He said it would be unethical for the lawyers to put together the package and submit it for consideration when I did not want to resign. He feared a conviction, because we had no defense to the charge of making a false official statement.

I cried and screamed and yelled. I told him about all the assaults, the sexual harassment, and all the times I kept my mouth shut just so I could do my job. The charge of lying, I screamed, how hypocritical! In pilot training, it was cooperate and graduate. After watching the *60 Minutes* interview with Colonel Reed, the Air Force's chief of Military Justice, it seemed to me that if you were in a position of power, you could lie to the American public. Morley Safer asked Colonel Reed several times if he knew of any high-ranking officers who had ever fraternized, committed adultery, or had oral sex and gotten away with it. Reed was evasive and tried not answer. Finally, after Safer's fourth repetition of the question, Reed shifted in his seat, averted his gaze, looked down at the floor, and responded, "No, I don't know of any." I ranted and raved for hours. Frank finally left the room, he too in tears.

Later that evening, Captain Shestko called with an idea. She was worried that if I did not submit a resignation package, the Air Force might convict me, sentence me to jail, and then claim it had offered me an honorable discharge, but I wouldn't take it. So we decided to call the Air Force's bluff. If the *Times*'s sources said Secretary Widnall would consider an honorable discharge, then I would ask only for an honorable discharge. My two military attorneys worked all weekend long preparing my resignation package. Frank Spinner and my brother Don juggled the press. I sat patiently, refusing to hope. It hurt too much.

The package contained all my performance evaluations, with glowing comments from my commanders. My entire academic and military history. A psychological profile prepared by Dr. Duncan. Letters attesting to my good character and to Marc's pattern of lies. In my own letter, imploring the secretary to let me resign with honor, I poured my heart out: "It is extremely difficult, if not impossible, to put into words my love for the Air Force. This is the hardest decision I have made in my life and it feels like part of me has died."

We filed the resignation package the day before the court-martial was scheduled to begin.

All we could do now was sit and wait and prepare for trial. The next morning, May 20, 1997, my family piled into the courtroom at nine A.M. My whole family was now back on base. So was Marc. Don described the scene in the courtroom, since I was not there (I was waiting to walk in with my attorneys). My family perched tensely on the mauve chairs in the long rectangular room. The prosecutor walked in with stacks of books; he would not meet the eye of anyone in my family. At 9:30 Frank Spinner came in and explained that the judge had decided to postpone opening arguments until Secretary Widnall had had a chance to decide on the request for an honorable discharge.

That bought us a little time. Time enough for my lawyers to interview Marc Zigo—and for him to throw a temper fit once Frank left the room and he was left under the unforgiving gazes of Shestko and Hecker. Time enough, too, for the arrival of a piece of evidence that we'd long ago requested: Marc's application for a job on base. The form clearly stated that falsifying information is punishable by law: five years of confinement for each falsehood. Marc's application claimed he was a professional soccer player. Frank Spinner was more excited than any of us had ever seen him. Judging by his performance with the lawyers this morning, he said, and given the evidence we had against him, the prosecution's star witness was going to have to be granted immunity or self-incriminate on the stand. That was a nice thought.

But our enthusiasm didn't last long. After confirming the honorable-discharge story, the Air Force now denied it just as soon as the *Times* appeared. Now the military affairs pundits were saying that were Widnall to intervene in the course of my court-martial and grant me an honorable discharge, she'd be violating military rules against using a position of command to influence a court proceeding. She couldn't, the naysayers said, even suggest to my commanders that such an offer should be made. This was a convenient argument for the Air Force. And it was patently unfair. Unlawful command influence happens all the time. Later in the week, the Air Force chief of staff, General Ronald Fogelman, even made an attempt at it. I knew through various sources of a commander being court-martialed on charges of having physically and sexually abused a little boy. The prosecutor was sure that he was guilty. But the wife of Lieutenant General Swope—he was the court-martial convening authority—had testified in the defendant's favor. The commander was acquitted of all charges.

Things were rapidly falling apart. A letter ostensibly from Gayla Zigo surfaced at CNN. It read: "Less than a week after we arrived on base, Lieutenant Flinn was in bed with my husband having sex. . . . On several occasions, I came home from work and found her at my house with Marc. . . . She was always in her flight suit flaunting the fact that she was an Academy graduate and the first female bomber pilot. She told me once that she wanted to settle down with someone. I didn't know that somebody was my husband." The letter (which sounded nothing like Gayla Zigo) was perfectly timed to portray me as a husband-stealing shrew. It might have been shrugged off as just another skirmish in the PR wars, except that it was written on official 5th Bomb Wing letterhead (Gayla worked at the 91st Missile Wing) and had been released by the Air Force itself. It seemed to give a sense of the Air Force's official position. Then, despite his protestations that he could not comment on how to handle the case because to do so would constitute an exercise of unlawful command influence, General Fogelman weighed in. "In the end, this is not an issue of adultery," he told a congressional committee. "This is an issue about an officer entrusted to fly nuclear weapons who lied." He told the Congress and everyone in the entire nation who was listening that he expected the court-martial to find me guilty. Secretary Widnall sat next to him silently.

It was a very bad sign. I didn't see or hear of this comment, but my family did. After leaving the base on Wednesday to wait for Secretary Widnall's decision, we had dinner together downtown. I checked my answering machine and found a message from Frank Spinner. The Air Force had been sending a "fact sheet" around Congress that listed my crimes and detailed my alleged sexual exploits. The fact sheet neglected to mention that I had not yet been tried. Frank's source at the Pentagon reported that the secretary would not sign an honorable discharge, but might consider a general discharge, under honorable conditions. This status would bar me from flying in the National Guard or Air Force Reserves. At eleven o'clock that night, Frank Spinner called my family together for a meeting at the Holiday Inn in Minot, where my parents were staying. Dr. Duncan came with him. He reported the bad news: Widnall had decided not to grant the honorable discharge. "Take the general," Frank said. "You're looking at a very real possibility of prison time." The fact that Widnall had sat idly by while Fogelman called for my head now made him fear the worst.

I said I still wanted to go to trial. All the details of my personal life were already out in the public domain. Now I wanted to tell my side of the story. I wanted to tell about the surveillance and the snooping, about how the Air Force had given me an order that it knew very well I couldn't possibly obey. I wanted the public to see that despite the Air Force's claims of not looking in bedrooms, my house and my parents' house had been under surveillance. I wanted to see Marc Zigo crash and burn on the witness stand. Never, I said, would I take a general discharge.

"If you don't take it," my lawyers and family told me, "you're going to go to jail."

My family argued that I couldn't possibly get a fair trial, particularly not now that Fogelman had told the jury what to do. My proverbial day in court just wasn't going to happen. I was only digging my grave deeper. I was so sick of being threatened and reacting to threats, rather than sticking up for myself. I was tired of being pushed around. I had been living with Marc's threats for a year, and now the Air Force was threatening me. "Resign or go to jail!" I was angry at everyone in the room: my mom and dad, Frank, Don and his wife, and Tim—and Dr. Duncan. Especially Dr. Duncan. She had, I'd just found out, told my mother that I had chosen to fly a B-52 because it was the largest penis I could find. She also revealed to my mother the intimate details of my sex life with Marc and told her I had the social skills of a twelve-year-old. I felt betrayed. I had trusted her and asked for her help. She was even the one who'd pointed out that every time I asked for help, the request had backfired on me. Now she was trying to convince me that handing in my resignation wasn't the same thing as succumbing to threats. She was pretending to have some great insight into my feelings. I'd say what I thought, and she'd "translate" my feelings to the family. I was becoming more and more angry. Finally, I gave up. I pointed directly at her, said to the room at large, "*You* deal with that bitch!" and left.

I climbed into my Jeep and drove back to my house in a rage. Why were they doing this to me? I had done everything right, right up to the point when I became human, when I stopped being a performing machine and fell in love with the wrong guy. They—that gray, bureaucratic "they"—hadn't wanted to hear my excuses. "No excuse, sir!" was my freshman response. *They* hadn't wanted to help me find a way out of the mess. *They'd* set me up to fail to obey an order. *They'd* given me one shot at absolute, inhuman perfection, and when I'd screwed that up, when I'd fallen from grace, they'd refused to give me a second chance. I was shaking with rage. I kicked open the door of the house and marched into the living room. I stood with my hands on my hips, looking around. Over the couch, I had hung my "plaque and saber"—the sword that we carried at the Air Force Academy, and beside it an engraved plaque, all mounted in glass. On another wall I had a huge framed picture of a B-52. Next to that was a smaller picture of a B-52 signed by all the former B-52 pilots who were now student pilot instructors at Columbus. I took the plaque and saber off the wall and threw it on the ground. It broke in half. Glass shattered everywhere. The sound of glass shattering did not break my rage. I went over to the big framed B-52 and threw it to the ground. It didn't break enough, so I picked it back up and with all my might threw it across the room. It landed with a satisfying crash. I smashed the smaller B-52 too. Then I overturned my big blue chair. I walked down the hallway toward my office. On its wall was a present Gail had made for me when I graduated from pilot training. It was my "gold album." A B-52s vinyl record, on a blue background, framed in gold. The gold plaque that accompanied the record said, "First Female B-52 Bomber Pilot." There were framed pictures of a

T-37 and a T-38, other pictures from pilot training, my framed diploma from the Air Force Academy, some awards I'd received. I pulled each and every one of them off the walls. Everything I had earned and worked toward was for nothing. It meant nothing to anyone. *I* meant nothing to anyone, once I stopped performing like a robot. So one by one I went through every single award I'd ever won, every plaque, every certificate, and added them to the pile of glass that was building all around the house.

Finally, when I'd broken everything I could, I crawled into bed and called my uncle John Sullivan in New York. I still wanted to fight and wanted his opinion. Uncle John had seen trouble before. As principal of Eastchester High School in New York, he'd stepped on too many toes and as a result had been charged with insubordination, misappropriation of funds, and the inappropriate use of district employees. Unwilling to be cowed, he'd taken on the Eastchester School Board of Education, sued them for defamation, and won.

"They're all ganging up on me," I said. "Nobody listens to me. I still want to fight."

We spoke a few times during the night. Uncle John had always been the strongest supporter of my decision to stand up to the Air Force and fight. Now he ran interference between the rest of the family and me. They begged him to talk me into agreeing to meet with them again. Finally, at about three or four in the morning, I agreed. But I set my own terms: *One* person could come over and present the family's case. I would sit and listen, and I would make a decision, and then that person would have to leave.

They agreed. I crawled out of bed and walked into the living room to wait. Don and Tim arrived. Apparently, my request for one person hadn't been clear enough. I was so angry that I turned my back on them and stalked into the living room, where I sank into a chair and curled up in a ball. They came in and stood staring silently, at a loss for words. There was broken glass everywhere. My face was swollen with crying. I had blood on my hands from breaking everything, and I'd smeared some blood on my face. I was sitting curled up in a fetal position. I was holding a stuffed elephant that my elementary school soccer coach, Mr. Belatti, had given me when my family moved from St. Louis. Across its chest was printed the word "Remember."

Tim and Don cleared away some glass and sat down. Tim's voice shook when he started talking to me. I didn't hear a word he said. I was so angry—so mad and frustrated at the whole world—that I wasn't interested in talking or even thinking. I only wanted to fight. I knew I couldn't win; I just wanted to prove my point. I was willing to go to jail just to stand my ground and make sure that my voice would be heard.

Now Don spoke. They kept talking and hounding me. I tried to go into my room and go to sleep, but they wouldn't leave me alone. Don and Tim just kept talking and talking and trying to convince me and refusing to listen to what I had to say. I tried to listen, tried to talk, but I just couldn't make them understand what I was feeling. And as the night ran into morning all I wanted, desperately wanted, was to go to sleep. So finally, when I realized that no one would ever understand my feelings, my pain, my frustrations, I screamed at the top of my lungs: "*I resign!* Just get out of my fucking house!"

In the long run, it was probably the right decision, but I did not make it thinking about the long run. I felt I was being forced to resign by my family, by my attorneys, by the Air Force. Although I knew everyone would stand behind me if I decided to fight, I believed I had lost some of their support. I also knew that no matter what was said inside the courtroom, I would go to jail. They were after me. I kept remembering a passage from the Air Force Code of Conduct: "I will never surrender of my own free will. If in command, I will never surrender the members of my command while they still have the means to resist." I caved in. I could no longer resist everyone's demands. I had no energy left to fight. A part of me will always feel I shouldn't have surrendered.

That didn't satisfy Don and Tim, though. They kept following me around. "Get out," I finally said calmly. "I've made the decision. Now go." They stayed. I begged them to leave me alone. "Please just leave me to my own hell," I cried. I slammed the door to my bedroom and through it I heard them rustling around, trying to pick up the broken glass. I called my uncle and cried, "I told them what they wanted to hear and they still won't leave! I can't get them out of my house!" They stayed until the sun came up. Then Don had to drive Tim to the airport to catch a plane. I went to bed and immediately fell asleep.

During the night and morning, Frank bargained with Secretary Widnall's office. This was also completely nonstandard and not allowed by the military judicial system. I suppose, however, that once you're at the top of the pyramid, as Widnall was, you can pick and choose your rules.

Sometime Thursday morning Frank and Karen and Barbara came by with the resignation sheet. I hadn't changed my clothes. The house was still full of glass, and I was still holding my elephant when I opened the door. My eyes were swollen and my face splotched from all the crying. The glass cracked under the lawyers' feet as they walked in. Captain Shestko put a hand on my shoulder. "Don't touch me," I hissed. I didn't read the paper. I could not read through my clouded-over eyes. I didn't know what it said. I just signed it, threw the pen down, and headed back to my room.

We told the press that I'd come to my decision after sitting down with my family and having a nice serious discussion. They did not need to hear the real details, the reasons why I didn't show up for any of the press conferences in the last few days before the TV crews pulled out of Minot. My mother and

Don took over. It was tough for my mom. She was afraid she'd break down while speaking. She and Don decided that the way to make it through was to focus on someone she really hated and despised. They started quietly chanting, "Limbaugh, Limbaugh, Limbaugh," because Rush Limbaugh had done some particularly unfactual reporting on my case. My parents had once been ardent fans. That made them dislike him all the more.

IT NORMALLY TAKES a minimum of two weeks to a month to process a resignation. There's paperwork to shuttle from agency to agency, equipment to return, signatures to gather. I made the decision Wednesday night; I signed the paperwork early Thursday morning. Later that same morning, while my family was sitting around the defense office preparing for the press conference, an instructor radar navigator from my squadron walked in and said, "I need to get the key to Kelly's life support locker. We need her helmet back." Less than two hours after they'd received the news, the Air Force was already outprocessing me. The paperwork was all ready; in less than five hours they would rid themselves of every trace of me. I was asked to come in that very day to complete all my resignation forms. Because of the state that I was in, I put them off until the following Tuesday, buying an extra day thanks to Memorial Day weekend.

I had requested a few extra days in the Air Force to complete my postsurgery gynecological exams. Colonel Elder denied this request, thus preventing an Air Force medical exam that would verify whether the cryosurgery had killed all the precancerous cells. In fact, the surgery had not worked, and I will have to go through it again.

I spent my last Memorial Day weekend as an officer in the Armed Forces packing my bags. I also did some shopping at the local mall, buying several "Kelly Flinn Got Screwed" T-shirts. How true, I thought to myself, both literally and figuratively speaking. Tuesday morning, I walked down the halls of my squadron for the last time. The one or two people who had stood by me greeted me warmly. Otherwise, wherever I looked, I was greeted with a sea of backs. People would run out of a room so as not to have to talk to me. The feeling was that I had torn the squadron apart—even though my troubles had had no effect on it until the Air Force released the news. My sex life had been no one's business. It was the way my commanders and the rest of the Air Force handled my case that tore the squadron apart and damaged my unit's morale. Would my commanders face criminal charges because of that?

The final resignation meeting was set for Wednesday, May 28, at noon. I went alone. Most of my family had left Minot on Memorial Day weekend. My parents left early Wednesday morning, finally heeding my pleas to be left alone, though they were terrified that someone in the Air Force would try to physically harm me.

The meeting took place in a conference room at the Air Force hospital. This was a tactical maneuver. The hospital was not situated inside base gates, so as soon as I turned in my ID card I couldn't get back on the base. There were about two hours of housing and finance briefings: all the paperwork and generic military forms that I should have spent weeks finding and filling out on my own. I signed my name and wrote the date. And that was that. I was outprocessed and out of the military. At the stroke of midnight, just like Cinderella, I would turn from a princess into a plain, unemployed civilian.

Lieutenant Colonel Hayner, La Plante's replacement, watched me outprocess. He had orders to make sure I was gone. Just as I was signing my last bit of paperwork—the DD214, the official separation document—he spoke. "I just got off the phone with Colonel Elder. He has a message for you: The Fifth Bomb Wing wishes you well." I gazed at him in disbelief from my seat at the ugly military-issue table. I looked at the clock. It was 1337 hours, 1:37 in the afternoon. I wrote the time down on a piece of paper. I looked at Hayner again. I don't know how long the silence lasted. I finally said, "I have nothing to say to that." Then I added, "Ask me in twelve hours and I'll tell you what I'm thinking." After midnight, I would be officially out of the military. He nodded. "I know," he said.

I could have jumped out of my chair and strangled him. I thought: You have no fucking clue! But I kept my mouth shut. Then Hayner shook my hand and wished me good luck. I got in my Jeep. Once on the road south, I turned up the radio loud and let the tears start to fall. I went to town and drank my first beer in almost six months. It made me sick to my stomach.

CHAPTER 9

Friendly Fire: Is the Air Force Killing Its Own?

The one who makes mistakes and recovers, wins.

THE AIR FORCE HAS COME OUT OF THE PAST YEAR LOOKING profoundly and unapologetically hostile to women. I'm not convinced that this is altogether true. True, I've suffered the indignities of tokenism and been singled out for shame in the media spotlight because I am a woman. True, women do pose a problem for the Air Force brass. But that problem isn't rooted in the fact that we are women per se. Rather, we're a problem because, in the Air Force's collective imagination, we're identified with sex. And while the Air Force, like all the American armed services, has made some good-faith efforts to integrate women into its ranks, it is absolutely dumbfounded about what to do about sex.

The Air Force has lumbered on for decades with a kind of 1950s-era morality: sanctioning sex within the confines of marriage or within the walls of brothels. The compartmentalization of sex was undoubtedly intended to create good warriors: men who could go into battle leaving their affective selves behind. But when the objects of their affections started accompanying them into battle, the whole system seemed to fall apart. The Air Force was confronted with a problem that all the flight manuals and checklists in the world couldn't solve: how to write rules to control the ungovernable rules of attraction. In desperation, the commanders have turned to punishment and harsh policing, to excision and erasure. But they can't rein in the irrational power of sex. And they know it. That's brought a crisis not just of "values," as the pundits like to say, but of identity. For if the men of the Air Force are no longer traditional macho warriors, upholding God and country by day and whoring at night, who are they? Sentimental soldiers who risk *falling in love* with their crew? Family men who want to fly fewer missions and spend more time at home taking care of their kids? The fear, I think, isn't just of women distracting men in the Air Force from their work. It's of women feminizing men *altogether.*

This is only one aspect of a larger identity crisis that is shaking the Air Force to its core. Part of the crisis has political causes. The reduction in force of the early 1990s took an emasculating swipe at the armed services and left many of our country's finest warriors jobless. In the Air Force, commanders who had come up through the ranks thinking in lofty terms of military readiness found themselves forced to think and behave like accountants. There were mass firings, handled with an utter lack of loyalty to the people who had once defended the nation. Fewer people were deployed to more places, and sent to perform more complicated missions. We were sent to Saudi Arabia to enforce the no-fly zone over Iraq. We were dropping supplies in Bosnia. We were also continuing to train for future war. Squadrons were deployed to Canada for Maple Flag, to Las Vegas for Red Flag and Green Flag, to South Carolina for Hornet's Nest. Plus, we were exercising at our home bases, preparing for the inspections that meant so much to our colonels. We spent hours packing our flight bags and then un-packing them for inspection, counting our socks, showing our underwear, proving we knew how to use our oxygen masks. We were treated like children. There was more stress, less fam-ily time, more family disintegration, fewer "family values." More corner-cutting and less motivation, despite talk from Secretary Widnall and General Fogelman emphasizing "core values." And there was an ever-greater chance that one day something would go seriously wrong. When I was in Minot, the feeling spread that it was just a matter of time before there was a run of disasters in the sky. This September that time came: six airplane crashes in one week and sixteen Air Force personnel dead.

My active-duty friends now tell me that the environment is growing worse. Troops do not trust their commanders. Troops do not trust one another. Work, they say, is getting done in an increasingly slipshod manner. The Air Force's response to date has not been encouraging. There has been talk about "ac-countability." In the name of "accountability," General Fogel-man stepped down this summer as Air Force chief of staff. Sheila Widnall has resigned, too. That, as far as I am con-cerned, is the upside of the Air Force's current need to point fingers and assign blame. The downside, though, takes place far from the bright light of press conferences. There, in the rel-ative obscurity of the bases, the Air Force has managed to avoid looking closely into why it is that personnel are careless and demoralized. It has avoided examining the working con-ditions that led more than one hundred pilots this year to ask that their names be removed from promotions lists. It isn't asking itself profound questions about why, after all its careful bean-counting and talks of surplus, the Air Force now has a shortage of pilots. Instead, for most of the service's officers and enlisted, "accountability" has led to a witch hunt. "Check six" used to be a term for pilots dog-fighting in the air and watching their tails. Now, it describes the tenor of daily life in the Air Force. "I have to force myself to put on my uniform every day," one officer told me recently. "I'm always watching my back."

The Air Force must maintain discipline. I respect that. Anyone who takes an expensive flying machine into the air knows that discipline is crucial and must be enforced. But "accountability" has created something different: an atmosphere in which investigators go looking for private infractions—particularly "moral infractions"—and then selectively punish them to the greatest extent possible. This has led to an atmosphere in which the Air Force spies on its personnel, intercepting e-mail and setting up home surveillance. The Air Force uses taxpayer money to compile reports on birth-control use, preferred sexual positions, fantasies, and gynecological exams. And it then metes out punishment almost blindly, as though severe retribution could make long-term problems go away.

"When there is a visible enemy to fight in open combat," President John F. Kennedy said to the graduating class of the U.S. Naval Academy in June 1961, "many serve, all applaud, and the tide of patriotism runs high. But when there is a long, slow struggle with no immediate, visible foe, your choice will seem hard indeed." With no visible enemy, it seems that the Air Force has begun turning its massive fire power on itself.

In August 1997, Chief Master Sergeant Deborah MacDonald, one of the highest-ranking enlisted personnel at Minot, shot herself through the heart after she was told to resign or face criminal charges for an adulterous affair she was allegedly having with a married enlisted man. She was divorced, her children no longer lived with her, and to avoid working with the man she was said to be seeing, she had put in for a unit reassignment, even though she'd dedicated years of her life to working with the B-52. Friends said that she had simply loved the Air Force so much that she could not face leaving it.

When her life fell apart, none of the other chiefs on base had rallied to support her. They'd just left her alone to die. "The only way to get the attention of the chain of command is to kill yourself," a friend of mine at Minot commented after MacDonald's death. "She obviously understood that."

In March, Lieutenant Colonel Karen Tew, a nineteen-year Air Force veteran stationed at Scott Air Force Base in Belleville, Illinois, put a bullet between her eyes. She had just been court-martialed for having an affair with an enlisted man. She had wept in the courtroom, expressing aloud her worries about her two teenage daughters and her elderly parents. One of her daughters was being treated for a brain tumor. Colonel Tew had just found a lump in her own breast. Air Force prosecutor Captain Kirk Obear asked the jury to show no mercy. "Lieutenant Colonel Tew traded the integrity of the military profession for sexual desire," he said. "She traded the honor of wearing the military uniform for lust and she traded her ability to act as an effective leader in a position of authority for sexual intercourse." The jury voted to dismiss her. Just one year short of retirement, she lost her pension, her benefits, and her livelihood. In her suicide note, she wrote: "Now the healing process can begin." She had found a way to preserve her Air Force benefits for her family: dying before her dismissal could be processed.

Technical Sergeant Thomas Mueller, a mechanic stationed in Germany, killed himself after he was charged with negligent homicide and dereliction of duty when an F-15 he had worked on crashed and killed the pilot flying it. Despite the fact that the crash had been caused by a long chain of events, despite the fact that the pilot himself had missed the malfunction in his preflight checks, the Air Force, in its drive for "accountability," had come down with all its force on Sergeant Mueller and his colleague, Technical Sergeant William Campbell. Sergeant Mueller shot himself in the head. "I am not going to make excuses," he wrote in a note to the pilot's widow. "If I

made a mistake, it was unknowingly and most of all uninten-
tional." All charges were eventually dropped against Sergeant
Campbell, who was nonetheless forced to resign with a general discharge. Accountability, he commented, seems in the
Air Force to have become "a life for a life."

Shelly (Scotty) Rogers was an Air Force lieutenant colonel
stationed in Italy when he was brought up on adultery charges.
He was a married man and a true advocate for women who
had requested to have women pilots assigned to his unit. The
female intelligence officer with whom he allegedly had an affair was granted immunity upon agreeing to tell all about
him—and she swore, under oath, that nothing had happened.
The jury dismissed the adultery charge for lack of evidence,
but the court instead found Lieutenant Colonel Rogers guilty
of having an unprofessional relationship: he had been seen
going to the gym with the intelligence officer. For this, he was
stripped of his command and became a convicted felon. He
will never be able to vote again.

The identity of the real culprit became clear as the dust
cleared from Scotty Rogers's case. His supposed lover, Lieutenant Julie Clemm, had recently filed a sexual harassment
complaint against Colonel Rogers's second in command, Major
Michael Cloutier. Cloutier counteracted by filing the adultery
complaint against Clemm. Cloutier was a "Barstooler": a member of a secret society committed to making sure that boys remain boys and women don't get too much respect in the Air
Force. Was his complaint also directed at Colonel Rogers's obvious commitment to promoting women? Colonel Rogers will
never know. Nor will I ever know for sure if the Barstoolers
played a role in my fall from grace at Minot. I've been told that
they did, and that their members, who have been referred to as
an "alternative chain of command" within the Air Force, have
weighed in on other judicial cases, most notably winning a not-
guilty verdict for an accused child molester in 1995.

I have no nostalgia for the "good old days" of gentlemen's rules that allowed base personnel to get away with drunk driving and sexual assault—all in the name of man-to-man understanding. That's Barstooler stuff. So is, according to the Command Barstool Association newsletter, *Drink Booze News*, exclaiming "If you ain't flying, drinking, or screwing, you're wasting your time." So is praising a fellow officer who "is renowned for charming the pants off any bimbo wandering into the bar, and making amorous charges at any female in an Air Force nurses' uniform." So is finding another officer with "his cranium between his knees, hands grasped firmly upon each cheek, spreading his gluteus maximi to a cavernous expanse, and revealing the biological functions of his prostate gland." This has no place in a modern fighting force.

But there is something missing these days in the new, putatively puritanical Air Force. The human element has been lost—that suppleness that allows rules to be bent sometimes, when extenuating circumstances compel it. People, after all, can't be handled like missiles and airplanes. They have to be treated like individuals, listened to, talked to. If that's a dangerous form of "feminization," then so be it. I'm all for it. The fact is, the Air Force is a human machine. And without proper care, its parts will wear down.

I CONSIDER MYSELF LUCKY. I was not destroyed by the Air Force. I am twenty-six years old. My entire life lies ahead of me. I am a highly educated, skilled pilot. And, through experience, I've gained some of the insight into love and real life that was lacking from my education in the skies. The Air Force, after some growing pains, now seems poised to move on, too. It has had its own casualties along the way: most famously, General Joseph W. Ralston, who was forced to withdraw his candidacy for chairman of the Joint Chiefs of Staff because he had an affair with a civilian woman more than ten years ago. It was, I think, an absurd penalty. Having swung so far into the self-immolation of "accountability," the Air Force may now come back to its senses and be ready to ask some serious and worthwhile questions about the peaceful coexistence of men and women in its ranks. There are questions that need answers: How do you regulate behavior for the good of a fighting force without treating people like machines? How do you respect order and discipline without trampling all over the anarchy of the human heart?

The armed services have every right to be concerned about sexual relationships between men and women that threaten to interfere with the performance of their duties. You can't have an aircraft commander and a copilot get into a lovers' quarrel at six hundred feet and crash their plane into the side of a building. But things are rarely as drastic as that. And there's rarely any real justification for drastic measures, because most aviators are professional when on duty and wearing a uniform. Rather than hunting down and prosecuting cases of fraternization by noncoworkers and out-of-wedlock sex, wouldn't it be a better use of Air Force resources to try to come up with some meaningful and realistic new rules? Rules, for example, that would bar people with romantic attachments from flying together. Or even from serving in the same chain of command. Rules that would distinguish between harmful and harmless relationships. And that would be applied evenly to men and women, regardless of rank. A new, clearly defined, fairly applied set of rules could put an end to the witch-hunt atmosphere that currently prevails in the Air Force. It could turn the force's sclerotic old-boy culture into something strong and resilient enough to assimilate *all* the members of the Air Force of tomorrow.

There are some signs of hope. There seems to be a solid feeling now, both in Congress and in the country at large, that what happened to me should not happen to anyone ever again. Members of Congress have started calling upon the Pentagon to review the Uniform Code of Military Justice. A legal code that punishes oral sex even between married couples but does not recognize marital rape as a crime has no place in the modern world, they say. Members of Congress are also fighting for protection of whistle-blowers. Even the Air Force seems to be waking up to the need for change. Prosecutors are now being told to proceed with reason, not with zeal. And, in the wake of my case, at least one career has been saved.

Christa Davis was a classmate of mine at the Air Force Academy. She was single and became pregnant by a married man while she was stationed at Barksdale Air Force Base. Because Christa had written the man's wife a letter detailing the affair, because she'd left base in a hurry and without leave (to have her baby), because of language she used and because she'd committed adultery (according to military law), the Air Force threw the book at her. It preferred charges against her that could have led to more than fifty years in jail. But after all the public outcry about my case, no one wanted to create another martyr. When the time came for Christa to go to court-martial, the Air Force reversed itself and decided to spare her. Christa received an Article 15 and had to pay a fine. She is still fighting for her future in the Air Force, but whatever happens, she won't have to face criminal prosecution.

*In life, what sometimes appears to be the end
is really a new beginning.*

LAST JULY, I made a sentimental journey back to the Air Force Academy. I wanted to return to the scene of the crime, so to speak: to revisit the place where I became who I am, and where I sowed the seeds of the life that I would lose. A friend from the

Academy came with me. We started our visit with a pilgrimage to one of our old favorite restaurants. The Pub-n-Grub is a tiny restaurant hidden in Green Mountain Falls, Colorado, about forty-five minutes from the Academy. My friend and I used to love to go there because (a) there were virtually no other cadets from the Academy, and (b) because they served great chicken wings. You could order wings by the tens, twenties, thirties, or fifties; plain or spicy; hot, hotter, or hottest. On this visit, we were shocked to find that the menu listed no wings. We called the waitress. "Don't you have chicken wings?"

"Sure," she said.

"Any flavors, any special spices?"

Nope. The restaurant had changed hands. The chicken wings came as a platter of twelve. They were generic and bland. My friend and I looked each other in the eye.

"The wings of Pub-n-Grub are not the same," I said.

AS WE DROVE through the gate, I felt the familiar tightening in my stomach at the sight of the glass-and-marble buildings of the Academy. But things had changed. The upperclassmen no longer had the right to scream outlandishly at the basics. There were footprints painted on the pavement at the base of the Bring Me Men ramp, marking how to stand in the position of attention. The cadets no longer had the right to kick basics' feet into place. The Bring Me Men ramp had changed, too. Now the three famous words that had stood so starkly alone were credited to the poet who had penned them. That was the work of some women professors in the English department. Uncredited, they said, "Bring Me Men" just sounded like an exclusionary school creed. Political correctness had made it into the temple of the incorrect. I was shocked, and not entirely displeased.

Inside the Visitors' Center, there was another surprise too: a display case dedicated to "Women in Motion"—female Academy graduates who had gone on to shine in their Air Force careers. I recognized the astronaut Susan Helmes and Captain Deborah Dubee, who was the first female Academy graduate to become an air officer commanding a squadron of cadets. I realized with a pang that I might one day have had my own place on that wall: "First Female Bomber Pilot." Then I realized, just one second later, that I would always have my place in history. I had earned it—nothing could take that away. I didn't need to be there, pinned to the wall in the Air Force Academy. I didn't belong there. I had graduated into the real world. I had grown up and now could proudly be myself—whatever kind of woman I wanted to be.

"Let's get out of here," I said to my friend.

"Not a moment too soon," she answered.

And so we took off, just two tourists out for a ride, carefree and laughing in the Colorado sunshine.

"SO, HOW DO I TELL my daughter now to go after her dreams?" my sister-in-law Laura asked me when I returned home for the first time as a civilian, stripped of my rank and silver wings.

"She should go after them with all her heart," I replied. "But tell her to watch her back."

I hope that she will soar. I hope that every child in America who has great dreams—boy or girl—will be allowed to soar.

I HAVE turned my back on Minot, North Dakota, with its cold loneliness. I have driven my Jeep to warmer climes, and they agree with me. I can see my life's promise again. I can dream about my future. I may work as a commercial pilot. I may go back to school and earn an advanced degree, perhaps reviving an old dream of becoming a doctor (if I can get past organic chemistry). I've been asked to run for Congress—and, in the short term, have been asked to assist a congressional commission to review military policies on sex and justice. I plan to petition Congress to grant me an honorable discharge through legislation. This would permit me to fly again for the Air Force in the National Guard or a reserve unit. And in the meantime, I am starting the Foundation for a Second Chance, to provide funds to get people back on their feet and help them get a second chance in life (www.KellyFlinnFoundation.org). People can learn from their mistakes, I know—if you let them.

I FLEW AGAIN, after months on the ground, on a cool, crisp day in September. It felt like a turning point as I woke up that morning and drank my preflight coffee. The ghosts of the past terrible year—my annus horribilis—were passing. I was starting to feel like myself once again.

Of course, as I approached the Westchester County airport in New York, feeling like myself brought back to the fore all my old fears about flying. Would I perform like a pro? Would I be able to land? Or would I—flying as a civilian—have to hand the aircraft over to the instructor accompanying me and bow my head in defeat?

The feelings were like family, both irritatingly and comfortingly familiar. And they dissipated the minute I walked out onto the runway and saw the Cessna that awaited me. It was a small, single-engine propeller plane—the same kind of plane that I'd first learned to fly during T-41 training. It all came back in a rush of recognition: the checks, the instruments, the feel of the airplane in the air.

"Are you ready?" my instructor asked. I grinned at him through my sunglasses. It may have been his airfield, but this was my turf. I walked out to the plane with my old Air Force swagger.

"Let's go," I called behind me. "Let's get up into the air."

I hadn't forgotten how to perform preflight checks. I hadn't forgotten how to read my instruments. As I reached for the controls, I felt I was shaking hands with an old friend. I smiled to myself as the engine started to turn, and a familiar thrill crept up from the base of my spine.

I locked eyes with my instructor, took a deep breath, and said, "I have the aircraft."

APPENDIX

19 May 1997

MEMORANDUM FOR SECRETARY OF THE AIR FORCE
FROM: First Lieutenant Kelly J. Flinn

SUBJECT: Request to Resign from the United States Air Force

Secretary Widnall, it is extremely difficult, if not impossible, to put into words my love for the Air Force and my devotion to the Air Force. It is with heartfelt agony and the deepest sadness I have ever experienced that I submit my resignation from the Air Force.

I truly love the United States Air Force, and would like the opportunity to continue to serve my country. I realize that I have made mistakes and errors in judgment. I have learned so much from these mistakes, and through this entire experience. It is a huge personal loss for me, to be asking to resign from the United States Air Force. This is the hardest decision I have made in my life and it feels like part of me has died. If given a choice, I would prefer to receive some form of non-judicial punishment, return to flight status, and continue to use all of the training I have received to benefit the Air Force and my country. I am not asking to be absolved of my mistakes. I am not asking to escape punishment. Leaving the Air Force is the worst punishment I can imagine. I would never intentionally do anything to bring discredit upon the Air Force. I truly fell deeply in love with a man who led me down this path of self-destruction and career destruction.

I have so much passion for the Air Force. I am an excellent officer, who has devoted my entire adult life to the Air Force. I entered the United States Air Force Academy at the age of 18, with the hope and dream of making the Air Force a career, and then possibly becoming a member of the astronaut corps. I still hold all of these hopes and dreams. I still hope, deep down inside, that there may be some better solution to my case, for both myself and the Air Force. It is difficult to put into words the passion I feel in my heart for this institution. It has encompassed me. I only want to serve my country and to be forgiven for my human faults. I don't think this is too much to ask. I only wish that someone in my chain of command would have asked what was happening in my life. Then they would have learned of the fear and darkness in which I was living. I did not turn to anyone for help when I should have. Instead, I decided to handle the threats of a detestable man, and live in fear of him and his possible actions. That is where I showed my greatest weakness, and did not stand up for myself as a human being. That will never happen again. I have learned how to handle my personal decisions and to be more careful with my feelings.

I have dedicated my life to becoming an Air Force pilot. I have endured comments, videos ridiculing my arrival at Minot AFB, sexual molestation, and harassing comments, just to fly. I never wanted to be treated as something special, I just wanted the chance, as my counterparts have, to fly for the Air Force as a trained combat pilot. If there was anyway to undo all the wrongs, I would. Unfortunately, at this point, I can only learn from my mistakes and move forward with my life.

I would never wish my ordeal upon my worst enemy. Deep in my heart, I believe that no punishment the Air Force renders will ever compare to the public humiliation I have suffered, the loss of my trust, and the loss of my innocence. Before this happened, I never dreamed that people like Marc Zigo existed. Perhaps that was my first mistake. Secondly, I, myself, should have researched the legalities of the situation, instead of trusting his word. However, hind sight is 20/20. Looking back, I should have done many things differently. Lying was the worst possible action, yet I did not have the courage then to admit my faults and shortcomings. I now recognize them. I just want the chance to reconcile this situation and perhaps have the opportunity to redeem myself in the eyes of the Air Force.

I do have integrity. I now have the courage to admit my mistakes, in the public forum, move forward, and take the lessons I have learned to heart. I have so much to offer this Air Force. I am an intelligent and dedicated worker. I have excelled in all of my activities since earning my Air Force wings. Perhaps I am feeling such a loss because I am an excellent B-52H pilot. I did not excel with the T-37 and T-38 programs. I made many mistakes during those training programs, but was able to learn from them and earn my wings. I took those lessons and applied them to the B-52 and excelled. I was exceptionally qualified to fly the B-52, a rating few pilots ever earn. I was the distinguished graduate from my B-52 training class. More than anything, I wish that you would accept my apology and give me a second chance.

Madam, the thought of leaving the Air Force, never to set foot upon another base, never to stand at attention as the Colors pass by, never to wear the wings of an Air Force pilot is the cause of my relentless tears, a punishment that I will live with the rest of my life.

KELLY J. FLINN, 1ST LT, USAF

ACKNOWLEDGMENTS

First and foremost, I would like to thank my family for helping me complete this book and tell the true story. Without their help and fact gathering, I would never have been able to present a clear picture. My brother Don spent endless hours documenting the entire story, all the way down to the meals I ordered. He also worked with my uncle John Sullivan to organize our media strategy. My brother Tim researched many of the supporting documents for claims made in this story. My sister Gail, as always, provided an ear for my grief when times grew rough and helped me respond to thousands of letters of support. My sister Patti researched all the Americans with Disabilities Act information and provided it to me. My mother and father continue to correspond with senators and congressmen. And to my cousin F.X., who created the website members.aol.com/KJFdefense; to my aunt Nina and cousin Anne, for their continual encouragement; to Sister Gloria for her prayers and masses; and to John Sullivan, who provided me a home after I left the Air Force and helped me get back on my feet: thank you for everything. To my nieces Erin, Melissa, and Meghan, and nephews Patrick, Danny, and Ian, thanks for the smiles and stories that took my mind off the tough times. May your dreams come true one day.

I want to thank Judy Warner, whose expertise helped me complete this book. Judy and I spent hours together, working chapter by chapter. She turned my anecdotes into a story, and my story into a book. She put so much time, effort, and energy into this work and did a magnificent job.

At Random House, I am grateful to Harold Evans, Ann Godoff, Jonathan Karp, Benjamin Dreyer, Jolanta Benal, Carole Lowenstein, Joanne Barracca, Robbin Schiff, Andy Carpenter, Carol Schneider, Thomas Perry, Liz Fogarty, Michele Martin, and Bridget Marmion.

To my attorneys, Paul Montclare and Lauren Wachtler, who helped negotiate this deal and gave me the forum to tell my story.

My defense attorneys during the Minot trial period ensured that I would not be writing this from jail. Captain Karen Hecker, Captain Barbara Shestko, and Mr. Frank Spinner were an integral part of my life for months when it was turned upside down. They have also helped me gather a great deal of information about the nature of Air Force investigations.

I want to thank Tamara Jones (*The Washington Post*), Harry Moses (*60 Minutes*), and Elaine Scialino (*The New York Times*), who did a fantastic job of investigating my story and bringing it to the attention of the American public.

Thanks to Mr. David Clemm, to his wife and daughter, and to Lieutenant Colonel Shelly S. Rogers, who provided me with information about the Command Barstool Organization. Thank you, Lieutenant Christa Davis and Lieutenant Bill Kite: you had the strength to fight.

To all those who opened their homes to this vagabond and let me find peace and seclusion while I completed this book—thank you.

To my dear friend Jessica, who supported me so generously throughout this ordeal and during my transition to the civilian world: Without you, I might not have made it. Thank you.

To Theresa, who helped me convert my military wardrobe to that of a civilian woman; and to Scott, who helped me find an elusive quote for an epigraph—thank you.

To all those who taught me the meaning of true friendship and sent me encouraging words—thank you, and the best of luck with your military careers: Krissy, Mo, Christopher L., Dan B., Cheryl Q., Kegger, Neal, and Giant Voice. "Do one more roll for me!"

Thank you to Jen, who supported me throughout the Academy and flying programs.

Thanks to the few at Minot who stood beside me, especially Amy and Justin. I wish you the best of everything!

Thank you, everyone who sent letters of encouragement and wrote to your senators and representatives.

And thanks to all those in Congress who supported me: Senator Slade Gorton, Senator Trent Lott, Senator Olympia Snowe, Senator Barbara Boxer, Senator Thomas Daschle, Senator John McCain, Representative Nita Lowey, Representative Carolyn Maloney, Representative James Traficant, Representative Louise Slaughter, Representative Rosa DeLauro, and so many others I may have missed.

Thanks to the Malloy airfield folks for the photo shoot, and for all the time Sal spent guiding us around the airfield.

Thanks to Joe Cowell, who has helped me establish the Foundation for a Second Chance (www.KellyFlinnFoundation.org).

To all of my silent supporters, whose thoughts and prayers give me strength: Thank you.

ABOUT THE AUTHOR

KELLY J. FLINN was born on December 23, 1970, in St. Louis, Missouri. At the age of twelve, she moved to Atlanta, Georgia. She graduated from Lassiter High School in 1989. On June 29, 1989, she entered the United States Air Force Academy and began her active-duty career in the U.S. Air Force. She graduated from the Academy on June 2, 1993, and from Undergraduate Pilot Training, Columbus Air Force Base, Mississippi, on January 28, 1995. In September 1995 she was the Distinguished Graduate in her B-52 Formal Training Unit, Barksdale Air Force Base, Louisiana. She then moved to Minot Air Force Base, North Dakota.

On May 28, 1997, Kelly J. Flinn resigned from active duty in the United States Air Force. Five days later, the Air Force mailed her a letter congratulating her on her promotion to captain, along with ten books on military leadership from General Ronald Fogelman.

ABOUT THE TYPE

The text of this book was set in Aster, designed by Francesco Simoncini in 1958. Aster is a round, legible face of even weight, and was planned by the designer for the text setting of newspapers and books.